LEGISLATIVE INSTITUTIONS AND LAWMAKING IN LATIN AMERICA

OXFORD STUDIES IN DEMOCRATIZATION

Series editor: Laurence Whitehead

Oxford Studies in Democratization is a series for scholars and students of comparative politics and related disciplines. Volumes concentrate on the comparative study of the democratization processes that accompanied the decline and termination of the cold war. The geographical focus of the series is primarily Latin America, the Caribbean, Southern and Eastern Europe, and relevant experiences in Africa and Asia.

OTHER BOOKS IN THE SERIES

Rethinking Arab Democratization:
Elections without Democracy
Larbi Sadiki

Accountability Politics:
Power and Voice in Rural Mexico
Jonathan A. Fox

Regimes and Democracy in Latin America:
Theories and Methods
Edited by Gerardo L. Munck

Democracy and Diversity:
Political Engineering in the Asia-Pacific
Benjamin Reilly

Democratic Accountability in Latin America
Edited by Scott Mainwaring and Christopher Welna

Democratization:
Theory and Experience
Laurence Whitehead

The Politics of Uncertainty:
Sustaining and Subverting Electoral Authoritarianism
Andreas Schedler

The Politics of Accountability in Southeast Asia:
The Dominance of Moral Ideologies
Garry Rodan and Caroline Hughes

Segmented Representation:
Political Party Strategies in Unequal Democracies
Juan Pablo Luna

Europe in the New Middle East:
Opportunity or Exclusion?
Richard Youngs

Turkey's Difficult Journey to Democracy:
Two Steps Forward, One Step Back
İlter Turan

Foreign Pressure and the Politics of Autocractic Survival
Abel Escribà-Folch and Joseph Wright

Legislative Institutions and Lawmaking in Latin America

....

Edited by

EDUARDO ALEMÁN AND
GEORGE TSEBELIS

OXFORD
UNIVERSITY PRESS

OXFORD
UNIVERSITY PRESS

Great Clarendon Street, Oxford, OX2 6DP,
United Kingdom

Oxford University Press is a department of the University of Oxford. It furthers the University's objective of excellence in research, scholarship, and education by publishing worldwide. Oxford is a registered trade mark of Oxford University Press in the UK and in certain other countries

First Edition published in 2016

Impression: 1

Published in the United States of America by Oxford University Press
198 Madison Avenue, New York, NY 10016, United States of America

British Library Cataloguing in Publication Data
Data available

Library of Congress Control Number: 2015956091

ISBN 978-0-19-877786-1

Printed in Great Britain by
Clays Ltd, St Ives plc

To my love, Sofía, who has been my
companion throughout.
To the memory of my loving aunt, María
Eugenia, who left us too soon.

Eduardo Alemán

I would like to thank Barbara and Selene
for their indispensable support.

George Tsebelis

Acknowledgments

The chapters of this book were presented at a conference held at the University of Michigan, and we would like to express our gratitude to the participants for their recommendations and encouragement. We are also grateful to Kristin A. Romelhardt for helping us put together the conference, and to the University of Michigan Center for Latin American and Caribbean Studies (LACS) for financially supporting and sponsoring the event. We also want to thank the anonymous reviewers of our manuscript for their comments and suggestions, as well as Jean Clipperton and Margarita María Ramírez for their excellent research assistance. A special thanks to Sebastián M. Saiegh, Jon Slapin, Pablo Pinto, and the contributors to this volume who offered us feedback and encouragement throughout this process.

George Tsebelis would also like to thank the Department of Political Science at the University of Michigan for financial support.

Contents

List of Figures

List of Tables

List of Contributors

Eduardo Alemán (PhD, University of California, Los Angeles 2003) is an Associate Professor in the Department of Political Science at the University of Houston. He specializes in the comparative analysis of political institutions and Latin American politics. His research focuses on executive–legislative relations, legislative politics, and political parties. He has published articles in such journals as *World Politics*, *Comparative Politics*, *Comparative Political Studies*, *Legislative Studies Quarterly*, and *Latin American Research Review*.

Ernesto Calvo (PhD, Northwestern University 2001) is an Associate Professor and Associate Chair of the Department of Government and Politics, University of Maryland–College Park. His research examines political representation, elections, and legislatures. He is the author of *Legislator Success in Fragmented Congresses in Argentina* (Cambridge University Press, 2014) and *La Nueva Política de Partidos* (Buenos Aires: Prometeo 2005). His work has been published in journals such as the *American Journal of Political Science*, *Journal of Politics*, *World Politics*, *British Journal of Political Science*, and *Comparative Political Studies*.

Royce Carroll (PhD, University of California, San Diego 2007) is an Associate Professor of Political Science at Rice University. His research focuses on the comparative study of democratic institutions, particularly legislatures and coalition politics. His current work includes the spatial analysis of legislative voting and other choice data. He has published articles in such journals as *American Journal of Political Science*, *Comparative Political Studies*, *Comparative Politics*, *Legislative Studies Quarterly*, and *Political Analysis*.

Ma. Amparo Casar (PhD, Cambridge University 1997) is a Professor and researcher at the Department of Public Administration of the Centro de Investigación y Docencia Económicas (CIDE) in Mexico City. She specializes in the study of the Mexican Congress and executive–legislative relations. Her research also includes the comparative analysis of elections and presidential systems. Her latest book is *The Mexican Political System* (Mexico City: Oxford University Press, 2010). She is also a contributing editor of *Reforma* newspaper and her opinion pages appear regularly in major newspapers and other media.

Daniel Chasquetti (PhD, Universidad de la República 2009) is a Professor at the Political Science Institute of the Universidad de la República, Montevideo,

Uruguay. His research interests include comparative political institutions, party politics, executive–legislative relations, and coalition governments. He has published on Latin American electoral and legislative politics in journals and book chapters, including *Legislative Studies Quarterly*, *Journal of Legislative Studies*, and *Journal of Politics in Latin America*.

Taeko Hiroi (PhD, University of Pittsburgh 2005) is an Associate Professor of Political Science at The University of Texas at El Paso. Her research areas include legislative politics, electoral systems, corruption, democratization, political instability, and comparative and international political economy. Hiroi is currently working on legislative coalitions and obstructionism, fairness in elections and electoral accountability, and autocratic backsliding and coups d'état. Some of her recent publications have appeared in *Comparative Political Studies*, *Journal of Legislative Studies*, *Studies in Comparative International Development*, and *Democratization*.

Patricio Navia (PhD, New York University 2003) is a full Professor of Political Science at Universidad Diego Portales in Chile and a master teacher in Liberal Studies and adjunct Assistant Professor in the Center for Latin American and Caribbean Studies at New York University. He has published scholarly articles and book chapters on democratization, electoral rules, and democratic institutions in Latin America. He has written four books that have been best sellers in Chile, including *El discolo. Conversaciones con Marco Enríquez-Ominami* (Santiago: Editorial Debate, 2009), and *Las grandes alamedas: El Chile post Pinochet* (Santiago: La Tercera-Mondadori, 2004).

Mónica Pachón (PhD, University of California, San Diego 2008) is an Associate Professor in the Department of Political Science at the Universidad de los Andes in Bogotá, Colombia. Her research focuses mostly on legislative behavior, executive–legislative relations in Latin America, and Colombian politics. Her articles have appeared in such journals as *Legislative Studies Quarterly*, *Electoral Studies*, and *Revista de Ciencia Política*.

Aldo F. Ponce (PhD, University of Houston 2012) is an Assistant Professor in the Department of Political Studies at the Centro de Investigación y Docencia Económicas (CIDE), Mexico City. His research focuses on legislative politics and political parties. His work has appeared in such journals as *Studies in Comparative International Development*, *Latin American Politics and Society*, *Journal of Politics in Latin America*, and *West European Politics*.

Lucio R. Rennó (PhD, University of Pittsburgh 2004) is an Associate (Adjunto) Professor in the Political Science Institute of the University of Brasilia. His publications on legislative politics, voting behavior, and public opinion have appeared in such journals as *Comparative Political Studies, American Journal of Political Science, Legislative Studies Quarterly, Latin American Politics and Society*, and *Journal of Politics*. His most recent co-edited book is *Reforma Politica: Lições da História Recente* (Rio de Janeiro: Fundação Getúlio Vargas, 2006). He is co-author of *Legitimidade e Qualidade da Democracia: Uma Visão da Cidadania* (São Paulo: Intermeios, 2011).

Iñaki Sagarzazu (PhD, University of Houston 2010) is a Lecturer in Comparative Politics at the University of Glasgow. He was a postdoctoral researcher at Nuffield College in the University of Oxford. His research focuses on political parties, legislatures, and political communication. His work has been published in journals such as the *American Journal of Political Science, Latin American Politics and Society, Electoral Studies*, and *European Union Politics*.

George Tsebelis (PhD, Washington University in St. Louis 1985) is Anatol Rapoport Collegiate Professor of Political Science at the University of Michigan. He is a comparativist who specializes in political institutions. His works covers Western European countries and the European Union. His more recent work studies political institutions in Latin America and Eastern Europe. He is the author of four books: *Nested Games* (University of California Press, 1991), *Bicameralism* (co-authored; Cambridge University Press, 1997), *Veto Players* (Princeton University Press, 2002), and *Reforming the European Union: Realizing the Impossible* (co-authored; Princeton University Press, 2012). His work has appeared in numerous academic journals and has been reprinted and translated in several languages.

1

Introduction

Legislative Institutions and Agenda Setting

Eduardo Alemán and George Tsebelis

In democratic regimes the proposals introduced in the legislature, and the rules that structure their debate, shape legislative outcomes. The ability to influence the legislative agenda is a valuable resource to affect the direction and scope of policy change, as well as to prevent past policy gains from being altered. Legislative and constitutional rules allocate formal prerogatives over the agenda to various offices that political actors struggle to win. But the advantages entailed in controlling such offices can be checked by the need to reach out to other legislative actors. Presidents with extensive legislative powers can be constrained by the policy positions of their legislative allies, and weak presidents may be well positioned vis-à-vis other players to build successful coalitions to legislate. The analytical basis of this book rests on the idea that in order to understand legislative outcomes one has to study not only the prerogatives of some privileged actors, like presidents or congressional leaders, but also the interaction between the institutional setting and the policy positions of the actors involved in lawmaking.

This volume presents a framework to understand agenda setting and its policy implications. We argue that there are three dimensions of agenda setting: *the partisan*, *the institutional*, and *the positional*. The *partisan* dimension examines if there is a stable and cohesive majority in the institutions responsible for policy-making. The *institutional* dimension studies the specific provisions regulating who makes the initial proposal, and who can amend it under what conditions and by how much. In other words, it includes all the rules of legislative interaction either inside the legislature or among the institutional actors involved in the legislative process (legislatures, committees, political parties, and presidents). The *positional* dimension examines the relative ideological positions of all the actors involved, because their positions along with their institutional prerogatives can increase or decrease the ability to promote their policy goals.

The way these dimensions of agenda setting are organized is (almost) lexicographic: in the case of cohesive partisan majorities, the institutional dimension will not be very influential. But in their absence (or if such majorities are weak, undisciplined, or not cohesive), one must focus on the institutions regulating the prerogatives of each actor. These rules, along with the relative positions of the actors, will shape policy-making outcomes. In the (counterfactual) case that agenda setting institutions did not exist, outcomes would be determined only by the actors' positions.

Consider the case of Mexico. In the heyday of the Partido Revolucionario Institucional (PRI) few paid attention to the specific institutional provisions inside the Mexican constitution. The will of the PRI was the rule. Yet, the same rules became highly consequential after the transition to competitive politics. For example, in December 2004, President Vicente Fox made use of the executive veto to introduce amendatory observations to a budget bill recently passed by Congress.[1] The president sought to modify changes introduced by Congress with which he disagreed. Congress responded by rejecting the validity of the president's move, and arguing that he could not exercise this institutional prerogative to amend the budget bill. President Fox responded by taking the case to the Supreme Court. Eventually, the Supreme Court resolved that the president had the right to exercise his veto prerogatives with regard to the budget bill, and that Congress could insist on its original version of the bill only with the vote of a two-thirds majority. So, the institutional provisions of agenda setting became important (and contestable) only after the partisan dimension, PRI's solid single-party majority, changed.

Now consider the case of Argentina, where presidents moved from having a single-party majority to having a plurality comprising less than 50 percent of seats. In congresses where the largest party has only a plurality of seats, executive bills are more likely to be reported from committee and receive final passage when they are initiated by presidents who are closer to the median voter of the chamber (e.g., President Carlos Menem in 1990–1) than when they are initiated by those that are further away (e.g., President Fernando De La Rúa in 2000–1).[2] In general, proximity to the median voter of the chamber is particularly important for major bills. So in this case, the same institutions produced different results depending on the positions of the key political actors, which underlines why we cannot study institutions in a void; we need to supplement them with the policy positions of the different actors.

This book explains the interactions between the three dimensions of agenda setting. The chapters analyze the constitutional and congressional rules that allocate powers to propose and veto legislation, and discuss who the relevant political actors having these advantages are and how their policy positions and relative strengths influence legislative decision-making. The volume covers seven Latin American presidential countries: Argentina, Brazil, Chile, Colombia, Mexico, Peru, and Uruguay. They are all major Latin American countries that offer wide variance in terms of legislative institutions and the ideological position of relevant actors. In terms of partisan majorities, some of the countries we study, like Argentina and Mexico, had single-party governments; others, like Brazil and Colombia, had majority coalitions; and still others, like Chile and Peru, had government coalitions that fell short of controlling a majority of congressional seats. Some, like Chile, Uruguay, and Brazil, give presidents substantial agenda setting powers, while others, like Mexico and Argentina, give their presidents more limited authority. We study the positions of the different actors and relate them to legislative outcomes.

The volume extends the range of comparative legislative studies to cover recently democratized countries in Latin America. The legislatures considered here are not new. They already had lengthy histories which included highly elaborated institutional traditions that preceded the establishment (or re-establishment) of solid and full-scale competitive electoral systems over the past few decades. But democratization enhanced the autonomy of these congresses and placed them in a much more pivotal position at the heart of the political process. Previously marginal questions of legislative procedure became of keen public interest, and began to play a much more determinate role in decision-making and resource allocation. In consequence, both professional politicians and informed opinion came to pay more attention to the intricacies of the institutional rules and their policy consequences. This has created new demands for precise analysis of how laws are proposed, debated, amended, and approved, all questions that are of central importance for the evaluation of democratic outcomes. On the one hand, these newly democratized legislatures have come to display many of the features already in evidence in longstanding presidential democracies (notably the United States). On the other hand, the range of variation uncovered by our multi-country analysis generalizes from and adds extra elements to established findings in the legislative studies literature.

While there has been an increase in research focused on Latin American legislative politics during the last two decades, the study of congressional rules and lawmaking remains scant. The chapters of this volume discuss the implications of institutional and positional variables for lawmaking outcomes. We illustrate some of these effects with legislative data on the initiation and passage of ordinary and major legislation, the issuance of vetoes, and recorded roll call votes.[3]

Understanding the institutions that regulate the congressional agenda is important because these institutions allocate power to affect political outcomes. Consider the case of a president elected with a popular mandate to reform legislation along some policy dimension. If agenda setters in congress have the power to prevent bills from reaching a plenary vote and want to preserve the status quo on this particular policy matter, then no change would take place despite the president's efforts.[4] However, if the president has the authority to force items into the congressional schedule, then she can pry open the gates and force the plenary to choose between the bill and the status quo.

The rest of this introductory chapter is divided into seven parts. The first provides a brief review of the literature on agenda setting in presidential countries. The second elaborates on our argument that analyses should be based not only on institutional rules, but also on the policy positions of the actors involved. The third, fourth, and fifth parts discuss the institutional dimension of agenda setting power in Latin American presidential countries. The sixth part addresses the positional one, while the seventh part presents our expectations and introduces the individual country chapters of the book.

LEGISLATIVE RULES AND AGENDA SETTING

Legislative agenda setting involves proposal, amendment, and veto power, as well as influence over the timing of bills. Positive agenda setting refers to the right to make proposals or bring amendments to consideration, while negative agenda setting or veto power refers to the ability to prevent bills or amendments from being introduced or from moving forward in the legislative process (McCubbins 2001). Agenda setting rules may be entrenched in the constitution or may be part of the congressional rules of procedure and subject to majority change. As Cox (2001: 187) has argued, "legislative rules have effects because they distribute real resources whose effects cannot be undone without incurring real costs in time and effort, because they confer benefits that parties find worth preserving through extra-legislative means, and because they are sometimes entrenched legally."

We discuss agenda setting on the basis of the three dimensions we introduced in the first part. The partisan dimension of agenda setting stresses the differences between a unified majority and other types of governments. The literature on parliamentary governments has remarked on the cohesive character of single-party majority governments, which can pass their legislative programs without the need to resort to the institutional tools of agenda setting. Different authors have debated whether the disciplined character of single-party and coalition governments in parliamentary systems stems mainly from the vote of confidence (e.g., Diermeier and Feddersen 1998), or the prevalent electoral incentives (e.g., Cheibub 2007). The literature on presidential countries, however, rarely considers government majorities as unitary cohesive actors.

Studies of the legislative consequences of unified and divided government in the United States inform us about the impact of positional differences between Congress and the president. Authors have analyzed the implications of divided government on the number of major laws passed (Howell et al. 2000), the share of bills approved (Binder 2003; Edwards et al. 2007), the number of presidential vetoes (Cameron 2000), and fiscal (McCubbins 1991) and trade policy (Lohmann and O'Halloran 1994). Their findings suggest divided government lowers legislative success and (less evidently) productivity, increases the incidence of presidential vetoes, and may be associated with greater budget deficits and more protectionist policies. But even under unified government, the lack of party cohesion leads to substantial presidential defeats in the legislative arena, and congress amends a significant part of the president's legislative program that becomes law (Rudalevige 2002; Peterson 1990). These presidents do not govern without constraints or conditions. Comparative analyses of presidential countries have underlined the greater legislative success of executives in single-party governments vis-à-vis others, but even in this favorable scenario around 30 percent of executive proposals fail to become law (Cheibub et al. 2004; Saiegh 2015), and as the chapters in this volume will show, most major bills that pass are amended by congress. Moreover, cross-national studies have also shown that majority coalitions in presidential countries are not more successful than minority governments at enacting the executive's legislative program (Saiegh 2015). This is why agenda setting institutions are highly consequential for legislative outcomes in presidential countries, and why we need to study the policy positions of the different actors involved in lawmaking.

In terms of the institutional dimension, the analysis of how legislative institutions allocate power over the agenda began with studies of the US Congress. There is an empirically rooted literature that examined legislative offices with authority over the agenda long before the 1970s. These works analyzed how facets of permanent and conference committees (e.g., the scheduling power of the Rules Committee and the influence exerted by congressional leaders) influence the agenda (Steiner 1951; Robinson 1963; Patterson 1963; Hinckley 1970; Vogler 1970; Fox and Clapp 1970). These authors had already recognized that controlling key legislative offices influenced political outcomes. However, it was the finding that majority rule in multi-dimensional choice settings most often led to unstable results (Plott 1967; Kramer 1973; McKelvey 1976; Schofield 1978) that spurred the modern wave of studies on legislative agenda setting. This powerful argument from formal theory not only implied that legislative outcomes were potentially unstable and easily susceptible to change, but also that an agenda setter with sole authority over what is voted could effectively control the direction of policy change (Plott and Levine 1978).

Several works within what became known as the new institutionalism addressed these implications. Regarding the more general notions of instability, Shepsle (1979) argued that a jurisdictional arrangement and germaneness rules—both typical of most legislatures—can make most issues one-dimensional, in which case the predictable outcome under majority rule (and open rules for amendments) would be the median position (Black 1948). The influence of agenda setters in legislatures was underscored by an emerging body of institutionalist works. Numerous studies examined the gatekeeping and proposal powers of committees under so-called open and closed rules (Denzau and Mackay 1983; Sinclair 1986; Shepsle and Weingast 1987; Weingast 1989; Crombez et al. 2006), the strategic use of scheduling power (Webb Yackee 2003), and the veto power of majority parties (Cox and McCubbins 2002, 2005; Gailmard and Jenkins 2007; Stiglitz and Weingast 2010) and the president (Cameron 2000; McCarty 2000). Cox and McCubbins (1993) look at the membership of "privileged" committees (i.e., those that can circumvent the Rules Committee more easily) and find that the majority party stacks these committees with loyalists.[5]

The consequences of agenda power have also been evaluated by analyzing roll call votes. For instance, Cox and McCubbins (2002, 2005) examine the veto power of the majority party by looking at partisan rolls (i.e., votes where most members of the majority party vote Nay on a successful final passage vote), while Carson et al. (2011) examine individual roll rates. Evidence that majority parties are seldom rolled (less than 5 percent of the time) and that legislators from the majority party are significantly less likely to be rolled tends to support partisan theories of agenda setting.[6]

The work on the positional dimension is sparse. The literature on "conditional party government" explicitly recognizes variation in preferences within parties as the most important consideration affecting whether or not legislative party leaders will be given strong powers and supported when those prerogatives are actually exercised (Aldrich and Rohde 1998, 2001). The party controlling agenda setting offices is expected to use the prerogatives at its disposal more often when levels of intra-party cohesion are relatively high and party preferences are relatively far apart. Finocchiaro and Rohde (2008) use roll call data on procedural matters and find that the majority's ability to control the special amendment rules process and use it to the disadvantage of the minority depends on the homogeneity of the majority party. Dion and Huber (1996) also consider the ideological positions of key actors and argue that when the Rules Committee in the US House of Representatives and the permanent committee reporting the bill are on the same side of the floor median, bills are more likely to be voted under restrictive rules than if they are on opposite sides. They find that when the Rules Committee and the floor median have divergent preferences, the allocation of special rules followed their expectations. Closer to the approach of this book is the notion of "conditional agenda setting" introduced by Tsebelis (1994) in his study of the European Union, and Tsebelis and Alemán (2005) in their study of Latin American constitutions. These approaches trace bills as they are moved from one institution to the other, and focus on both agenda setting rules and the positions of the different actors.

While several analyses of agenda setting institutions and their consequences have focused on parliamentary countries (Doering 1995; Huber 1996; Strøm 1998; Tsebelis 1999; Rasch 2000; Cox et al. 2000; Heller 2001; Cox et al. 2008; Rasch and Tsebelis 2011) and the European Union (Tsebelis 1995; Crombez 1997; Tsebelis et al. 2001; Hix 2002; Konig and Slapin 2006; Proksch and Slapin 2011; Tsebelis and Ha 2014), there are comparatively few works examining legislative agenda control and its implications in Latin American presidential democracies. A central goal of this book is to contribute to fill this gap.

So far, most works on Latin American legislative institutions have focused on the powers of the president, including executive decrees, budgetary authority, and various types of vetoes (Shugart and Carey 1992; Metcalf 2000; Negretto 2009). The distribution of agenda setting power inside congress has been less studied than presidential prerogative, but there is an emerging literature focused on congressional institutions, including works on congressional committees, gatekeeping, and agenda control by congressional majorities.

Works focused on Latin American countries have shown how vetoes, amendments, decrees, and urgency motions facilitate presidents achieving their lawmaking goals, while constraining the actions of congressional actors in various ways (Carey and Shugart 1998; Reich 2002; Negretto 2004; Tsebelis and Alemán 2005; Pereira et al. 2005, 2008; Alemán and Navia 2009; Palanza and Sin 2013). For example, the extensive budgetary powers of the Chilean president have worked to favor the spending preferences of the executive over the legislature (Baldez and Carey 1999), while those of the Brazilian president have helped when the government negotiates the support of individual legislators (Pereira and Mueller 2004a). Overall, there is evidence that the economic powers of executives tend to reduce budget deficits, at least when combined with legislative electoral rules that emphasize the personal vote (Hallerberg and Marier 2004). Fewer studies have concentrated on committees. Finocchiaro and Johnson (2010), in their study of bill assignment and reporting in Colombia and Costa Rica, show that Speakers can kill a bill by assigning it to the "wrong" committee and cast doubt on the effect of partisan characteristics on the type of bills killed/reported by committees. Pereira and Mueller (2004b) present evidence from Brazil that suggests bills coming from outlying committees (vis-à-vis the median legislator) are more likely to have been brought to the plenary floor under urgency requests. Alemán and Pachón (2008) describe the significant advantages given to conference committees, and show how in Colombia the chamber's directorate stacks conference committees, while in Chile permanent committees benefit from less discretionary assignment rules.

Other works have examined partisan roll rates, searching for the implications of agenda setting power by majority parties or coalitions. So far the evidence suggests that leaders of the governing majority party in Argentina and the governing coalition in Chile use their authority over the legislative agenda to effectively prevent changes that would have the effect of making a majority of party (or coalition) colleagues worse off (Alemán 2006; Jones and Hwang 2005). In Brazil, it is not evident that presidents who form majority coalitions necessarily form "agenda cartels" with their coalition partners (Amorim Neto et al. 2003).

To sum up, the literature on agenda setting and legislative institutions that began in the late 1970s has had a tremendous impact in moving legislative research forward. Most analyses, however, have focused on the particular institutional and partisan make-up of the US Congress, which, according to Gamm and Huber (2003), has weakened our understanding of other types of legislatures. Latin American countries provide needed variation along the institutional and partisan dimension. The literature on legislative politics in Latin America has begun to address in more detail some of the institutions peculiar to non-US presidentialism. However, this body of work is still thin. This book contributes to the literature in two ways. First, it systematically addresses the rules that influence the legislative agenda and expands the theoretical approach by underscoring the interaction between institutions and policy positions. Second, the chapters in the book derive and test particular implications using extensive legislative records.

THE INTERACTION BETWEEN POLICY POSITIONS AND AGENDA SETTING

In the models that follow, we will examine the rules of agenda setting and the positions of the different actors. If there is a partisan majority, then the corresponding actors will have identical positions and all the results are going to be corroborated in a trivial way. However, as we said, even in the case of a single-party government, the absence of party cohesion makes this majority nominal only, so the detailed study of institutions and positions is necessary. The institutional dimension is determined on the basis of which actors have the authority to shape (or prevent the shaping of) legislative proposals. This relates to both presidential agenda setting and the distribution of agenda setting power among legislative offices. The positional dimension of agenda setting power is defined by how much discretion agenda setters have to exercise their authority given the relative policy position of other relevant legislative actors. The following two figures will make this point clear.

Figures 1.1 and 1.2 present an idealized legislature composed of five legislators or parties (A, B, C, D, and E) in a two-dimensional space. Let us assume (in the case of parties) that they have approximately the same strength, so that three out of the five actors are required to form a majority. The positions of the actors are identical in the two figures. One of the parties is centrally located (E) and the other four are in the periphery of the policy-making space. We will also assume that each one of the players prefers outcomes closer to his own policy position over outcomes further away (has circular indifference curves). In Figure 1.1, A can make a proposal to the whole legislature, while in Figure 1.2 proposal power is given to the centrally located E. In order to

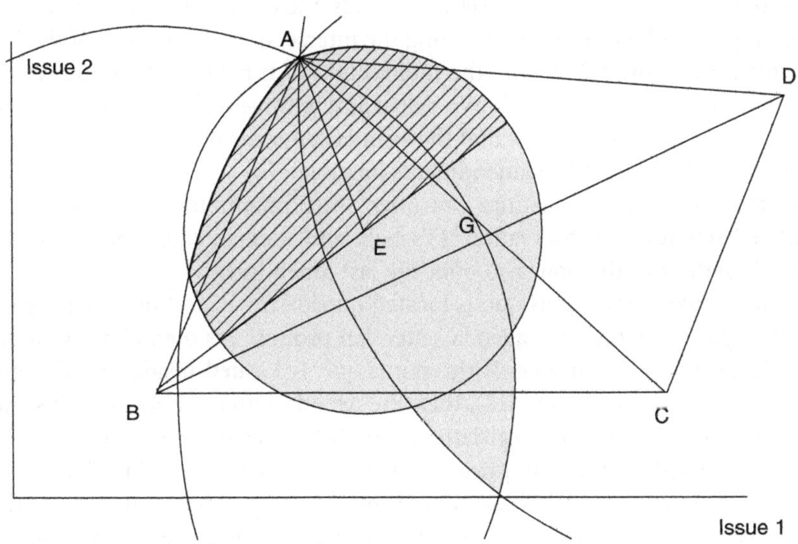

Figure 1.1 Five legislators in a two-dimensional policy space: agenda setter A

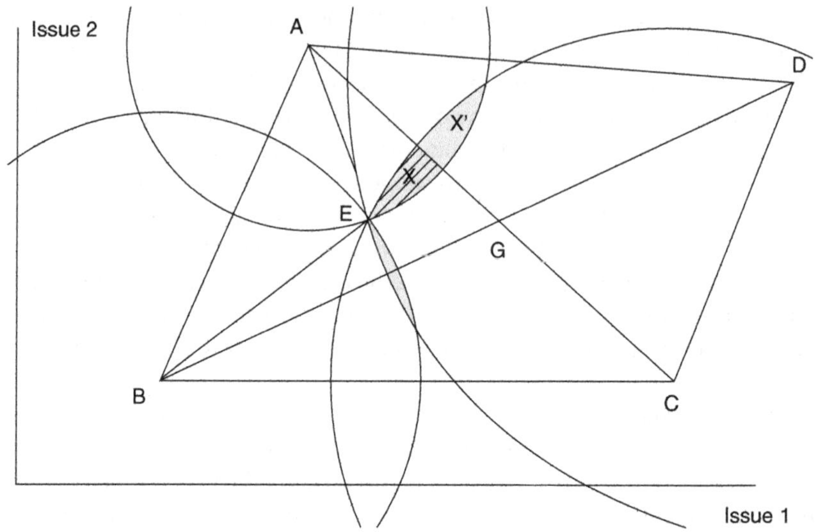

Figure 1.2 Five legislators in a two-dimensional policy space: agenda setter E

start the discussion, let us assume that in each case the agenda setter is proposing to the floor his own ideal point for consideration.

Both figures present the set of points that a majority would prefer over the agenda setter's proposal (the winset of A in 1.1 and the winset of E in 1.2). In Figure 1.1 we identify this winset by drawing the circles with centers B, C, D, E going through point A, and locating the intersection of three out of the four of them. In Figure 1.2 we find the intersection of three out of the four circles around points A, B, C, and D. We will examine three different agenda setting rules: (i) a closed rule means that the agenda setter makes a take-it-or-leave-it offer to the legislature (no amendments possible); (ii) an open rule means that any member of the legislature can offer amendments to the proposal; and (iii) an "amendatory observation" (Tsebelis and Alemán 2005) means that the agenda setter has the power to offer the last amendment.

Closed rule: If the status quo is located outside the winset of A (Figure 1.1) or E (Figure 1.2), then the agenda setter can propose his own ideal point and win in an up or down vote. If the status quo is located inside the winset of A (Figure 1.1) or E (Figure 1.2), then the agenda setter cannot have his own ideal point adopted by the legislature. This latter scenario does not mean that the agenda setter cannot improve the situation at all. He could calculate the winset of the status quo, W(SQ), and propose among all its points the one that is closest to his own ideal point. And here is the first consequential comparison of the two figures that we can make: the winset of point A (Figure 1.1) is much larger than the winset of point E (Figure 1.2). This is because E is centrally located inside the legislature, while A is in the periphery. Consequently, under closed rules, the centrally located agenda setter E is more likely to win acceptance for proposals that move policy closer to his ideal point than the more peripheral agenda setter A.

Open rule: When all actors can offer amendments, anything inside W(SQ) can be adopted (in Figure 1.2 this is the two shaded lenses in the center of the figure, while in Figure 1.1 it is the more complicated area which we shaded). This includes outcomes that the agenda setter prefers the least. Consequently, under open rule, E should be more likely to end up with an outcome closer to his own preferences than A.

Amendatory observation: The ability to introduce "amendatory observations" (i.e., amendments) to legislative proposals at the final stage gives the agenda setter a last line of defense. If he sees a particular unwanted amendment prevailing, he can still make a last counter-proposal, and he will prevail as long as it is inside the winset of this amendment.

For example, if, in the case of Figure 1.2, the legislature is about to adopt the point X′, the agenda setter E can propose X and have it accepted. As long as X is symmetric to X′ with respect to a line connecting two of the parties and having two parties on one side of it and one party on the other, X will be preferred by a majority over X′.[7] Such lines are AC and BD in Figure 1.2 (and BE in Figure 1.1). The hatched part inside the shaded areas shows where the agenda setter could move the final outcome given his ability to respond with a final "amendatory observation." Again, a comparison between the hatched parts inside the shaded areas in Figures 1.1 and 1.2 indicates that with "amendatory observations"—or any other similar procedure that allows agenda setters to "fight fire with fire" (Weingast 1992) by introducing a last proposal—the centrally located agenda setter E is better positioned to move the final outcome closer to his ideal point than the more peripheral agenda setter A. The advantage of E increases even more if his policy position moves closer to the intersection G of the lines connecting legislators (A and C) and (B and D). Indeed, as E moves closer to G, the two lenses composing the winset of E (Figure 1.2) shrink until they become empty (actually the winset of G is empty). In other words, if the agenda setter happens to be located at point G, his proposal will be able to prevail no matter what agenda setting rule is in place.

To conclude, for all three models (closed rule, open rule, and conditional agenda setting), an agenda setter located close to the center of the policy space is more likely to get a point close to his own ideal point adopted than an agenda setter located in the periphery. We considered two absolute extremes in the agenda setting scale (the closed rule where the agenda setter has absolute proposal power, and the open rule where anything the agenda setter proposes can be altered) as well as one presidential prerogative with a wide range of variations (as we will see in what follows). We have not proven that our argument is true regardless of the institutional provisions. However, the underlying argument revolves around the size of the winset of the agenda setter's ideal point: the larger this winset, the more likely it is that some point far from the agenda setter's ideal point will be adopted. Points closer to the center of policy space have smaller winsets. So, the distance between the final outcome and the ideal point of the agenda setter depends not only on the institutions prevailing, but also on the position of the agenda setter. A corollary to this view is that the weaker the formal prerogatives over the agenda the more important locational advantage becomes.

The country chapters that follow will address not only the institutional rules under which policy-making is performed, but also the relative policy positions of the actors involved in lawmaking. The chapters use one-dimensional models instead of the two-dimensional one we present here. There is a reason for this simplification in the empirical chapters: they use aggregate data, and therefore all the variation is in the dominant left–right dimension. There is also a reason for a presentation of a two-dimensional model in this introductory chapter: we make a point that holds, regardless of the number of dimensions, and consequently we want to enable researchers who wish to study specific (multi-dimensional) bills to know that they can apply the arguments and conclusions of this introduction in their own research. In other words, what we say here holds regardless of the number of relevant policy dimensions, and the subsequent chapters apply it to one-dimensional settings.

THE POWER TO OBSTRUCT

The main goal of veto (or negative agenda setting) power is to preserve past gains.[8] Once political actors achieve policies close to their own ideal ideological positions, holding veto power becomes particularly important. It is helpful when threatened with unwanted policy change since it allows an agenda setter to protect the status quo (or the reversionary outcome). Prerogatives, such as gatekeeping and the executive veto, epitomize this power. The former prevents bills from moving forward in the legislative process or from being introduced in the first place, while the latter implies a wholesale rejection of a bill.

Gatekeeping

In several Latin American countries, only the president can initiate legislation in certain policy areas. Monopoly to initiate certain policies implies authority to preserve the status quo.[9] Exclusive initiation rights make presidents gatekeepers of the status quo in those particular areas of policy determined by the constitution. The scope of the president's exclusive power of initiation varies by country, but it is usually circumscribed to economic legislation and proposals to alter the government bureaucracy.

For example, in Brazil only the president can initiate bills related to tax and budgetary matters, the public administration (appointments, raises, structure, and scope of authority), the executive cabinet (establishing new ministries, cabinet structure, and jurisdictional powers), the organization of the judiciary, the Public Ministry, and the Public Defender. In Chile, only the president can introduce bills related to the political and administrative division of the country, retirement and pension benefits (establishing, modifying, or increasing benefits), the minimum wage, collective bargaining, social security, and most tax (establishing, reducing, or condoning taxes, establishing or modifying tax exemptions) and spending matters (modifications to the budget bill). In Colombia, the president has exclusive initiation powers over bills related to the Central Bank, foreign trade, public administration (including salaries), and the executive cabinet (establishing, eliminating, or merging ministries), as well as those that establish public expenditures and the multi-year National Development Plan. In Uruguay, only the president can initiate bills that set the minimum wage, establish price controls, allocate or increase pension or retirement benefits, create employment in the public sector or raise public employees' wages, and give tax exemptions. In contrast, countries such as Argentina and Mexico do not give their presidents exclusive initiation powers over significant areas of policy aside from the right to introduce the budget bill.

Agenda setters inside congress, such as the chamber's directorate (*Mesa*), can also have gatekeeping power. They may, for instance, have the power to prevent a bill from being scheduled for a plenary vote. Avenues to override such decisions usually exist, such as a force discharge, but are typically costly and occasionally require high thresholds. It is more common for bills to die in committee. In some countries committees have pre-established deadlines to issue bill reports, but these are not usually enforced. Presidents may also open the committee gates when they have the authority to declare a bill urgent.

President's Block Veto

In the US literature, the veto is the quintessential presidential power. An absolute or block veto allows the president to reject the entire bill, thereby preserving the status quo. The power to veto significantly restricts the outcomes of the policy-making process, as Figure 1.3 demonstrates (Tsebelis and Alemán 2005).

The figure shows the status quo and an oval representing the set of points that defeats it (the winset of the status quo). In this simple model, it does not matter whether Congress is unicameral or bicameral. The legislature can select any point within the winset of the status quo (W(SQ)) as the final outcome of legislation. If the presidential veto requires a qualified majority to be overruled, this qualified majority *may* prefer some set of outcomes over the status quo. We call this set Q(SQ), which we also draw in Figure 1.3. Of course, this set may be empty (this is why we used the word "may" in the previous sentence). The presidential veto restricts the final outcome to the set Q(SQ) instead of permitting any outcome inside W(SQ) to prevail. If Congress proposes an outcome inside Q(SQ), such as X in Figure 1.3, the president's

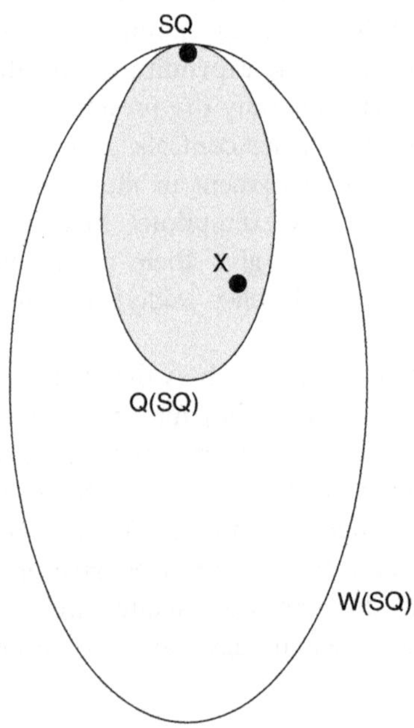

Figure 1.3 The president's block veto

veto (if exercised) would be overridden. If Q(SQ) is empty (because there is a sufficiently large minority in Congress that agrees with the president), then the presidential veto becomes final. As long as Congress cannot muster a majority large enough to override the president, a new bill cannot be enacted into law.

Thus, presidential veto power forces congress to consider the president's position vis-à-vis the status quo and the bill likely to be enacted. Veto threats, which make legislative goals deemed unacceptable to the president public, should persuade congressional actors to modify their course of action and re-evaluate the content of legislative proposals.

Qualified-majority thresholds necessary to override a veto increase the president's power over simple or absolute-majority thresholds. Constitutions in countries such as Argentina, Chile, Mexico, and Uruguay require qualified majorities to override a presidential veto. In Brazil, Colombia, and Peru, for example, constitutions require an absolute majority for overriding the president's veto.

President's Partial Veto

Partial vetoes can be conceptualized in two ways. One is to consider just the vetoed (i.e., deleted) part of the bill. Then, the mechanism is similar to the block veto, where congressional outcomes are restricted to the Q(SQ) area of the part of the bill that the president partially vetoed. This conceptualization may fit well with the rules regulating the Argentine and Brazilian partial veto, which include the partial enactment of the bill (i.e., the non-deleted parts). In these countries, congress deals only with the objected part. The default outcome if congress does not override the veto is the bill without the sections deleted by the president.[10]

A second way to conceptualize the partial veto is to consider the entire partially vetoed bill as an alternative proposal to the bill without deletions. Then, the mechanism becomes a restricted version of the amendatory observation procedure, which is described in the following section. It is restricted because the president can only amend the bill sent by congress through deletions (additions or modifications are not permitted). This conceptualization fits well with the legislative rules in place in Colombia, where Congress has to choose between the partially vetoed bill and the bill without such deletions, or else the status quo prevails.

THE POWER TO PROPOSE

Positive agenda setting power has to do with the ability to make offers under a favorable institutional context. The ability to impose limits on the amendments that can be offered to bills is particularly important for agenda setters. An example of restrictions regarding the extent to which legislative proposals can be changed is the germaneness rules that forbid amendments that touch on policy areas not addressed by the bill being debated. At least as relevant, but less common, are mechanisms that permit agenda setters to make take-it-or-leave-it offers to the full membership. Other relevant prerogatives have to do with the advantages agenda setters may have to respond to amendments they dislike when operating under "open" rules (i.e., rules that allow legislators to offer amendments to bills).

Amendatory Observations

Many Latin American presidents have the power to offer one more round of amendments after congress passes a bill. Constitutions incorporate this prerogative as part of the president's veto power. These amendments—*observations* to a vetoed bill—are returned to congress for an up or down vote. Presidents in Chile, Mexico, Peru, and Uruguay, among others, have the power to introduce these "amendatory observations." The right to introduce germane amendments to vetoed bills gives the president the opportunity to make a last counter-proposal, and given that the set of possible responses is usually wide, a strategic president can take the initiative and respond with a modified bill that is better for congress to accept than to reject.

Table 1.1 presents the rules for the countries studied in this volume. The first column lists the countries and the second the type of executive veto. In seven countries presidents can partially veto a bill, and in four countries they can also introduce amendments. The third column of the table indicates the required majority to overrule the president and insist on enacting the bill congress first sent to the president (let's call this Bill B). In some cases it is simple majority, in others it is a majority of members, while in others it is a qualified majority of votes or members. The more stringent the majority requirement to overrule the president is, the more difficult it is to override the president. The fourth column refers to a rule that is even more significant for the president's influence: it determines the default solution if congress fails to either approve the president's amendatory observations or override. In

Table 1.1 Amendatory observations and partial vetoes

Country	Type	Override requirement	Default	Feasible set and outcome
Colombia	partial veto	> 1/2 of members	SQ	$X \in W(B) \cap W(SQ) = X$
Brazil	partial veto	> 1/2 of members	X	$X \in W(B) = X$
Argentina	partial veto	≥ 2/3 of votes	X	$X \in NQ(B) = X$
Peru	partial + amendatory	> 1/2 of members	SQ	$Y \in W(B) \cap W(SQ) = Y$
Mexico	partial + amendatory	≥ 2/3 of votes	SQ	$Y \in NQ(B) \cap W(SQ) = Y$
Chile	partial + amendatory	≥ 2/3 of members	X	$Y \in NQ(B) \cap W(X) = Y$
Uruguay	partial + amendatory	≥ 3/5 of votes	Y	$Y \in NQ(B) = Y$

some cases the situation reverts to the status quo (SQ), in others it is the parts of the bill not modified by the president's amendments that become law (let's call this Bill X), while in others it is the bill as amended by the president that becomes law unless there is a qualified majority against it (let's call this Bill Y).[11] The last column of the table indicates the choice set for the president, and the expected outcome. For example, in Colombia, if the partially vetoed version of the bill (Bill X) is the intersection of the winset of the status quo (W(SQ)) *and* the winset of the bill (W(B)), then it will stand. In the rest, it is a more convoluted configuration, such as the set of outcomes that do *not* command a qualified majority against the bill (NQ(B)) (Tsebelis and Alemán 2005).

"Closed" Rules for Committee Proposals

The substantial advantages given to actors that can present take-it-or-leave-it proposals are well studied by the institutional literature. Unlike in the US House of Representatives, where "closed rules" are widely used to protect committee proposals from floor amendments, Latin American congresses usually allow individual legislators to offer amendments to most bills that come up for a plenary vote. The openness of the amendment procedure, however, varies across legislatures.

One instance where the norm is a "closed" rule (i.e., no amendments) is when conference committee proposals are brought to the plenary for a final vote. While permanent committees most often lack such power when first reporting ordinary legislation, conference committees make take-it-or-leave-it proposals to the full chamber. The influence of conference committees as agenda setters is particularly relevant since it comes towards the end of the legislative process. In Latin America, only Colombia and Chile use conference committees to resolve inter-chamber disputes.

Sequencing Prerogatives

When operating under open rules, agenda setters (e.g., committees or a committee manager) can still make use of some mechanisms to mitigate unwanted outcomes from rival amendments. These involve giving the agenda setter opportunities to respond to the amendments seeking to modify the reported bill in the plenary floor. It is not uncommon that an agenda setter, typically a committee manager, is given the opportunity to make the last counter-proposal. When agenda setters can offer the last amendment, they can evaluate what would potentially pass in the plenary floor and anticipate a threatening amendment by responding with another potentially successful one that moves the final outcome closer to their position (if such proposal exists). This mechanism shares fundamental properties with the presidential amendatory observations discussed earlier. The identity of the agenda setter, however, changes: it is the committee instead of the president.

One sequencing mechanism typically employed in Latin American congresses involves establishing a strict pre-filing requirement for amendments. By prohibiting new amendments during the bill's debate and requiring amendments to be revealed before a plenary vote, agenda setters (e.g., committees or bill managers) have the opportunity to evaluate their impact and when necessary respond with their own counter-proposal.[12] Pre-filing requirements, for example, are in place in the internal rules of congresses in Brazil, Chile, Mexico, and Argentina's lower chamber.

Executive Decrees

Some Latin American constitutions, under special circumstances, provide the president with the opportunity to legislate through decrees. These tend to go further into the legislative arena than the typical executive order in the US case. Constitutional scholars disagree about the extent to which decree power can be used to unilaterally legislate on matters that ordinarily would require congressional involvement. While constitutions usually include some form of executive authority to issue orders in case of national emergencies, few countries have constitutions that provide the executive wide decree power.

One type of decree power is provisional. It demands congressional ratification or the reversionary outcome is, eventually, the status quo *ex ante*. For example, in Brazil, decrees take effect immediately and lapse after a certain period of time unless Congress ratifies them. They are provisional measures that must be approved by Congress in order to acquire the final status of law. The Brazilian Congress can amend the provisional decree before approving it. This type of decree, which moves bills to the top of the congressional agenda and require congressional action (approval and the possibility of amendments) before becoming law, is an agenda setting tool.

Another type of executive decree—much more constraining for members of congress—gives the decree the status of a permanent law unless congress votes to reject it (or passes a law that nullifies it). In Peru and Argentina, decrees become law right away and Congress is limited to passing a resolution voiding it.[13] Inaction on the part of Congress equals acceptance. Given the unilateral authority conveyed in this type of decree, and the absence of mechanisms for congressional involvement (prior approval or opportunity for amendments), it is less obvious that it should be considered an agenda setting tool.

THE SCHEDULING POWER OF AGENDA SETTERS

Influence over the timetable is a coveted agenda setting prerogative. Numerous bills, resolutions, and other types of proposals struggle to reach the plenary floor. Agenda setters with authority over the scheduling of bills (e.g., chamber authorities, and sometimes the president) can use their privileged position to try to delay or prevent bills they dislike from reaching the plenary. They can also bring forward those bills they want to promote, sometimes through procedures that speed up their discussion.

Urgent Bills

Some constitutions have provisions that give the president the power to declare a bill urgent. This compels congress to attend to the particular proposal before a specified deadline. Congress can meet and then proceed to reject (or amend) the proposal made urgent by the president, but nonetheless, it is a way for presidents to force congressional action in the face of delay or inaction. When presidents can force bills to the plenary, it means they have de jure authority to overcome congressional gatekeeping.

In Latin America, Brazil, Chile, Colombia, Ecuador, Mexico, Paraguay, and Uruguay include this provision in their constitutions.[14] Mexico added this provision in a constitutional reform in 2012.[15] How soon the bill must be reported to the plenary floor varies by country—sometimes it is within a few days, other times a few months. Urgency motions provide even greater discretion to the agenda setter when the rules state that congressional inaction results in the automatic passage of the bill. Under this scenario, the president wins by default. This is the case in Uruguay where, according to the constitution, the lack of congressional action within the stipulated time is sufficient to get the president's urgent bill enacted into law.[16]

Authority over the Schedule (the Order of the Day)

Power over the timetable allows actors to prioritize certain proposals and delay or obstruct others. Typically, majority-elected chamber authorities craft the day-to-day scheduling of legislative proposals. In many chambers, a steering committee composed of the leaders of the legislative party blocs is also involved in this activity.

Agenda setters with authority over the timetable sometimes have at their discretion specific procedures for fast-tracking bills. This is usually applied to consensual proposals. This may involve avoiding committee reports or reporting bills as part of a package with other proposals without objections. In some chambers (e.g., Brazil and Costa Rica), committees may approve some ordinary bills without reporting them for a plenary vote by the full membership. While fast-tracked bills are unlikely to address controversial (or national issues), they are usually important to individual legislators.

Presidents have an additional mechanism to influence the congressional schedule: extraordinary sessions. Most Latin American constitutions allow presidents to call special sessions of congress in which the agenda is determined solely by the president. Many congresses have extraordinary sessions every year, and in some, this special period lasts as long as the regular sessions. Again, congress may reject or re-commit bills, try to deny quorum, or only attend a sub-sample of scheduled bills. Nevertheless, special sessions are another useful presidential agenda setting mechanism to try to move proposals forward. The Chilean Congress eliminated this longstanding provision from the country's constitution in 2005, and in Mexico, only Congress may call for extraordinary sessions.

To conclude, we have summarized legislative prerogatives inside congress in Table 1.2. The first column lists the countries, the second the chamber, the third the office in charge of the legislative calendar, the fourth notes whether the executive can compel congress to attend bills by forcing them into the calendar, the fifth specifies the majority needed to force a bill out of committee, the sixth identifies when conference committees are used to resolve bicameral disagreements, and the seventh column notes whether legislators need to pre-file amendments to legislation before debate.

POSITIONAL ADVANTAGE

The extent to which agenda setters can take advantage of their power most often depends on their ideological position with respect to other relevant players. Whether an agenda setter can steer policy change in her direction, and how close, hinges on the preferences of those who must agree for that change to occur.

Separation of powers involves not only the creation of legally distinct institutions, but also the development of rules to ensure that different interests are represented in different institutions (Cox and McCubbins 2001; Shugart and Haggard 2001). This is also conducive to different policy positions between branches of government and between chambers in bicameral congresses. Tsebelis (2002) used the concept of veto players (actors whose agreement is necessary to change the status quo) to argue that the more distant veto players are, the more they restrict the winset of the status quo, and consequently limit the discretion of agenda setters. This implies that more extreme veto players become more influential. As shown in the second section of this chapter, the opposite is true for agenda setters. Being more centrally located in the policy space increases their influence over outcomes (keeping the institutional details constant). The same can be said of opposition parties in a minority government.

But policy positions do not affect policy-making alone. Because the effects on policy can be anticipated, policy positions also affect the coalition-making stage. When elected presidents lack a congressional majority, they have to consider whether forming a government coalition or relying on ad hoc alliances would be better for achieving policy-making goals.[17] More often than not, minority presidents form multi-party coalitions by bringing non-presidential parties into government. In general, presidents tend to have greater leeway to change policy when they make government coalitions with

Table 1.2 Agenda setting institutions in thirteen Latin American chambers

				Committees		
Country	Chamber	Scheduling body[a]	Executive power to force bills into the schedule	Force bill out of committee	Conference committees	Legislators pre-file amendments before debate
Argentina	deputies	CA + PLC	*no*	*qualified majority vote*	*no*	*yes*[g]
	senate	CA + PLC	*no*	*qualified majority vote*	*no*	*no*
Brazil	deputies	CP + PLC	*yes*	*majority vote*	*no*	*yes*[h]
	senate	CP	*yes*	*majority vote*	*no*	no[i]
Chile	deputies	CA + PLC	*yes*	*majority vote*	*yes*	*yes*[g]
	senate	CP	*yes*	*majority vote*	*yes*	*yes*[g]
Colombia	deputies	CA	*yes*	*not stipulated*	*yes*	*no*
	senate	CA	*yes*	*not stipulated*	*yes*	*no*
Peru	unicameral	CA + PLC	*yes*[c]	*majority vote*[e]	~	*no*
Mexico	deputies	CA + PLC	*yes*[d]	*qualified majority vote*[f]	*no*	*yes*[j]
	senate	CA + PLC	*yes*[d]	*qualified majority vote*[f]	*no*	*yes*[j]
Uruguay	deputies	CP	*yes*	*majority vote*	*no*	*no*
	senate	CP + PLC[b]	*yes*	*majority vote*	*no*	*no*

a. CA: Chamber's Authorities; PLC: Party Leadership Committee; CP: Chamber's President.

b. The internal rules of the Senate establish a standing party committee to decide on the schedule, but the norm is that the president of the Senate consults with the party leadership.

c. It makes a bill a priority in the committee's agenda, but there is no deadline.

d. Since 2012.

e. It is a parliamentary norm.

f. A two-thirds majority vote can declare a bill urgent to avoid the committee stage. Otherwise committees work under short deadlines and the chamber's authorities can deny extra time and force a bill to the plenary for debate.

g. Amendments must be presented during a seven working day period after the committee report is made public.

h. Amendments must be sent to the committee.

i. Floor amendments must be sponsored by 1/3 of the chamber's membership.

j. Amendments must be presented at least one day before the committee report begins to be debated.

parties that are positioned ideologically close to them rather than further away. By doing this, presidents minimize the deadlock region between coalition partners. Evidence shows that in Latin America, when a president decides to incorporate other parties in government, parties positioned ideologically close to the president are more likely to be incorporated into government than those positioned further away (Alemán and Tsebelis 2011).

When parties act in a rather disciplined manner, it makes sense to focus on parties and their relative position vis-à-vis others. But on occasions parties do not act in a unified way. If this is the result of different unified factions taking different stances, then their relative positions should be taken into consideration. If instead it is the result of widespread lack of cohesion, then the analysis must pay greater attention to the positions of individuals within the party. While most parties in the Latin American countries studied in this volume act in a rather unified way, the researcher must evaluate to what extent looking at the aggregate positions of parties is an effective strategy.

IMPLICATIONS AND PLAN OF THE BOOK

We have underlined the importance of a series of rules that allocate rights over legislation and the congressional agenda. In addition, we have said that the policy positions of key legislative players impact the extent to which those holding agenda setting offices can influence the lawmaking process. We expect the legislative record to reflect these effects.

At the more general level we expect that the constellation of formal powers regarding proposal and scheduling prerogatives previously described should lead to different styles of presidentialism. On the basis of the institutional powers discussed in the prior sections (including Tables 1.1 and 1.2), we can differentiate between presidents who have various tools to shape the congressional agenda, such as those in Chile, Uruguay, and Brazil, and presidents who have few powers at their disposal, such as those in Argentina.[18] Mexican presidents also have few prerogatives to shape the congressional agenda before Congress passes a bill; afterwards they have the power to affect the bills through amendatory observations. We hypothesized that this difference in agenda setting power should be reflected in the involvement of executives in the bill-to-law process, and their ability to overcome the challenges of governing without a majority or with heterogeneous coalitions.

Second, we hypothesized that increasing the range of positions inside a government coalition hinders congressional action. Institutionally powerful presidents, however, are better equipped to prevail in this context. This implies, for instance, that Colombian presidents should be more constrained by increasing the range of preferences in their government coalitions than Brazilian presidents who can use their substantial agenda setting powers to move proposals forward.

Third, we have two different expectations regarding executive veto usage. We hypothesize that the shift from majority to minority government should increase the frequency of executive vetoes (in all its variations). In addition, we hypothesize that in those countries where presidents can respond with partial and amendatory vetoes, these should be used more frequently than the block veto. Losing a congressional majority should increase the number of bills that incorporate provisions and amendments disliked by the government. This is likely to create more opportunities where presidents consider that they can make successful improvements to bills thorough partial and amendatory vetoes. Within the sample of countries and time periods analyzed in the chapters of this volume, we find a change away from majority government in Argentina, Uruguay, and in Mexico and expect to find a corresponding increase in the usage of executive vetoes (and amendatory observations in Uruguay and Mexico).

Fourth, given that Latin American countries have multi-party systems, the lack of a majority government most often does not lead to a majority of an opposition party, as in the case of divided government in the United States. Instead, the positions of minority presidents and their parties vary. In some cases, the president and the party in government are positioned around the center with regard to the other legislative actors. As noted before, we expect centrally located actors, such as presidents or particular governing parties, to be well positioned to succeed in lawmaking. These situations are unlikely to significantly dampen the legislative achievements of a centrist president. This configuration is akin to those found in Peru under President Toledo (2001–6) or in Uruguay under President Battle (2002–5). In the case of Uruguay, institutional powers further strengthen the ability of minority presidents to push bills and amendments forward.

In other cases, a large plurality (almost majority) party may be able to seek out ad hoc alliances with very small parties or enough independent members of congress to legislate with mild consequences for executive bills. Such configuration is similar to that of Argentina under Menem (1993–5) or Néstor Kirchner (2005–7). Presidents can co-opt a few legislators or small parties and overcome the loss of the majority status. Yet, with or without a majority in Congress, Argentine presidents are comparatively weaker in terms of agenda setting prerogatives.

The situation is different if the minority government is away from the center. This configuration is closest to the political context in Mexico during the first two Partido Acción Nacional (PAN) governments (2000–14) and in Chile during the Concertación governments (1990–2010). In these cases, presidents should be constrained by their need to seek out allies among the opposition. We expect that the passage of legislation should either be hindered or should consistently incorporate (typically through amendments) the positions of those in the opposition, most likely those opposition parties positioned around the center.

Fifth, the cross-national literature has shown that presidents are rather successful at getting their bills passed by congress (Cheibub et al. 2004; Saiegh 2011). Yet, we lack information about whether those bills passed as crafted by the executive or with substantial amendments by congressional actors. The literature on the US Congress underlines that a large share of executive bills that pass are amended before becoming law (Rudalevige 2002; Peterson 1990). We expect this to be also the case with major bills introduced by presidents in Latin American countries. Major legislation is always difficult to categorize. For illustrative purposes, we have chosen bills mentioned on the front page of a national newspaper.[19] This follows prior works, such as those of Binder (1999), which use national newspapers to capture salient public policy issues that are part of the agenda of potential enactments.[20] While Binder focuses on *New York Times* editorials, we focus on all proposals that make it to the front page of one of the main national newspapers in the country. Our approach broadens the sample of potential enactments and makes it less susceptible to the ideological leanings of particular editorial boards. But we must also be aware that by focusing on the first year of a presidential term, it is possible that there is a bias in the sample inflating the number of executive-initiated bills over congressional-initiated bills.

Lastly, given the internal rules of procedure described in prior sections (including Table 1.2), congresses should tend to be organized in a rather centralized manner. We expect to see more consequential committees in those countries that give these offices significant agenda setting powers, such as in Chile, Colombia, and Argentina. Yet, since parties in these countries exert significant control over committee assignments and the composition of the chambers' leadership, they are unlikely to behave autonomously from the party and/or chamber leadership.

The following chapters have been written by country specialists and examine legislative institutions and lawmaking in seven Latin American countries. They describe the rules structuring decision-making inside each congress and underline the most consequential institutions. They also identify the offices and political actors with agenda setting power, and explain the extent to which they can influence lawmaking given the political context. This includes commenting on how these political actors are constrained by the positions of other actors they have to deal with in order to achieve legislative outcomes.

The chapters present empirical evidence to illustrate arguments about the influence of agenda setters, as well as to evaluate some particular implications specific to the country being examined. While cross-national differences underlie different allocations of agenda setting power, in most countries institutions have remained constant and the main changes are in regard to the ideological positions of key legislative actors. Some of the outcomes examined by the authors of the chapters are binary (e.g., bill passage or veto issuance) while others are duration outcomes (e.g., time until enactment). The rest of this book is divided into seven country chapters and a concluding one.

The chapter on Argentina, written by Ernesto Calvo and Iñaki Sagarzasu, investigates how the change from a majority-party-dominated chamber to a plurality-party-led chamber impacts committee gatekeeping and the legislative success of presidents. They advance the counterintuitive argument that the loss of majority party control should actually reduce the amendment instances associated with executive bills. They expect more extensive, yet friendly, amendments to executive bills when the government has a majority of seats, and cross-partisan committee bargains to be less vulnerable to amendments when the majority becomes a plurality. In addition to finding support for this hypothesis, the authors show that when the president has a majority, the number of proposed amendments to executive bills is lower when the president is closer to the median member of the majority. When the president has a plurality, the number of proposed amendments is reduced as the president approaches the median of the chamber.

Contrary to conventional depictions of the Argentine executive (Mainwaring and Shugart 1997) but consistent with our review of institutional power, the authors characterize the agenda setting prerogatives of the president as limited. The passage rate of executive bills is comparatively low, and moving from having a majority to a large plurality does not alter the passage rate of executive bills by much. Calvo and Sagarzasu's findings are also consistent with our view that after losing a majority, presidents are more likely to get outcomes closer to their position the more centrally located they are in the policy space.

The chapter on Brazil, written by Taeko Hiroi and Lucio R. Renno, underscores the challenges of governing with a large and heterogeneous coalition. Brazilian presidents (who have always lacked a party majority) build large multi-party coalitions and assign government allies to important congressional offices. Hiroi and Renno note that given the different position of parties in government, intra-coalition management becomes crucial. On roll call votes, the executive's position wins most of the time. Yet, on occasions the president's position loses. Furthermore, despite the president's majority status, many presidential bills fail to become law, and those that do tend to be amended by Congress. The analysis shows how a united opposition and greater use of obstructive measures slow down the passage of legislation while the use of urgencies speeds it up. In terms of coalition management, when presidents build "fair" coalitions bills appear to spend significantly less time in congress before enactment.

The chapter shows that Brazilian presidents, governing with large multi-party coalitions characterized by a wide range of ideological positions, have impediments to pass their legislative programs through ordinary channels despite their majority status. Presidents overcome some of these challenges by exercising their legislative powers, particularly urgencies and the temporary measures that are placed on top of the congressional agenda. Hiroi and Renno show that ordinary bills introduced by the Brazilian president have a rather modest approval rate and note that presidents regularly use temporary measures to pass a substantial part of their legislative programs.

The chapter on Chile, written by Eduardo Alemán and Patricio Navia, describes the significant agenda setting power in the hands of the president as well as the significant positional constraints with which presidents had to govern. The latter was caused mainly by the lack of unified government and super-majority requirements for changes on several substantive policy areas. The authors find that most major presidential bills that pass include amendments incorporated by legislators. Presidents regularly fight off unwanted changes to bills with proposed amendments of their own offered during the committee stage or via amendatory observations at the veto stage.

Despite lacking a congressional majority, Chilean presidents have had a comparatively high rate of bill approval and have initiated most laws, which is consistent with the view that having strong legislative powers contributes to overcoming some of the challenges that the lack of unified government entails for the enactment of executive bills. In addition, the chapter shows that who controls the offices with agenda setting power matters for the voting behavior of legislators. Majority control in the Chamber of Deputies leads to significant advantages to members of the governing coalition, while in a split Senate there are no significant differences between the two coalitions (leftist senators and appointed senators on the right-wing opposition do slightly worse). Consistent with our expectations, the authors portray committees as strong and find that conference committee proposals, always voted under closed rules, are highly successful.

The chapter on Colombia, written by Royce Carroll and Mónica Pachón, discusses the institutional rules and partisan contexts that affect the passage of bills. Permissive rules to amend bills and a highly fragmented Congress leave bills introduced by the Colombian president vulnerable to harm. Multi-party coalitions are nowadays common, but the authors show that such coalitions do not advantage the president because they fail to organize the legislative process. The most important institutions influencing the legislative process are legislative committees. The Constitutional Court is also an important institutional player that regularly reviews legislation, often decides on its content, and, on several occasions, vetoes passage.

The authors reveal an executive weaker than the one portrayed in conventional accounts of the Colombian presidency. Presidents have gatekeeping powers over a few areas of policy and can accelerate the analysis of bills deemed urgent, but have the weakest veto powers of the countries studied in this volume. They find that executive bills pass at a higher rate and in a shorter period of time than congressional bills. Executive bills, however, are routinely amended, and most laws actually originate with legislators. Major bills are passed sooner and at a higher rate than others, but they are also typically amended. In addition, the chapter underlines the importance of conference committees' ability to make proposals under closed rules, which we note in Table 1.2.

The chapter on Mexico, written by Ma. Amparo Casar, reveals a Mexican Congress far different from that of the old era of PRI dominance. Power has shifted away from the executive and given new relevance to Congress and political parties. Casar shows that the end of PRI dominance brought about a drastic reduction in the number of executive-initiated bills. Nowadays most laws are initiated by members of Congress. In this new context, political parties have played a relevant role building the consensus necessary to legislate under minority government and have done so despite increases in intra-party conflict.

In Congress, parties dominate the offices with agenda setting power and control committee appointments. The use of the executive veto increased, as we expected, and most major proposals that became law were previously amended in Congress. Despite facing new constraints, Mexican presidents have not been deadlocked by congressional actors. Instead they have built ad hoc coalitions with opposition parties. Consistent with our view, Casar shows that minority governments positioned on the right (PAN) most often formed alliances on the congressional floor with the centrist party (PRI).

The chapter on Peru, written by Aldo F. Ponce, discusses the institutional and partisan context that affects the enactment of the president's legislative program. He shows that Peruvian presidents have a first-move advantage on economic matters (via urgent law decrees) and the chance to make the last amendment (via amendatory vetoes). Inside Congress, formal rules centralize power in a steering committee composed of party leaders, but Peruvian parties tend to be weak and short-lived without strong and stable leadership structures. So in practice, members of Congress and committees are less beholden to the party leadership than the legislative rules would lead us to believe.

Despite their minority status, Peruvian presidents succeed at getting most of their bills enacted into law, which Ponce attributes to their centrist positions and institutional powers. Yet, he finds that the usage of presidential decrees is not the result of minority presidents being unable to pass their legislative proposals. In addition, and also consistent with our argument, he shows that the centrist party has a more favorable legislative record than others. The chapter also shows that members of Congress initiate a majority of laws, including some important ones, and amend most major presidential bills.

The chapter on Uruguay, written by Daniel Chasquetti, examines how legislative rules and changes in government status impact lawmaking. Uruguayan presidents have important agenda setting powers, but they must negotiate with congressional actors—faction leaders of the same party and often other parties. The president also has an ally in the vice president, who has a key role in assigning and scheduling bills in the Senate. Chasquetti notes that the status of government changes often in Uruguay, and that under minority governments power tends to shift away from congressional committees and towards the leaders of the parties' factions.

As we would expect, Chasquetti's findings reveal that the approval rate of executive bills is comparatively high and that there is not much of a slump following the loss of a majority. In the end, legislators manage to amend a large number of government bills. Presidents respond with vetoes, often followed by amendatory observations. The analysis shows that, consistent with our prior arguments, the use of presidential vetoes increases when legislative support decreases.

The last chapter reviews some of the important conclusions of the book. First, it discusses empirical findings that show that the lack of a majority government increases the complexity of bargaining, makes changing the status quo more difficult, and favors centrist parties. Second, it highlights how some Latin American presidents benefit from substantial institutional prerogatives over the congressional agenda, while others are more restricted by the rules in place. Third, it describes the cross-national variation found in terms of legislative productivity and approval rates of bills initiated by presidents and members of congress.

NOTES

1. The bill was the Presupuesto de Egresos de la Federación.
2. See the chapter by Calvo and Sagarzazu on Argentina for more details.
3. We operationalized major bills as those that became front-page news in major national newspapers. We focus on major bills mentioned in the press during the first year of the president's term in office. Sarah Binder (1999), for instance, examined legislative gridlock in the US Congress by focusing on major bills, which in her study are those that appear in the editorials of the *New York Times*.
4. Examples abound. For instance, US President Barack Obama's 2011 half a trillion dollar jobs bill did not make it to the floor of either chamber, despite the president's push. Another example was Argentine President Carlos Menem's proposal in the mid-1990s to give the right to vote to nationals living abroad, which was not enthusiastically received by congressional leaders and was never reported for a vote on the floor of Congress.
5. Along the same lines, Leighton and López (2002) find an association between legislators' party discipline and assignment to more valuable committees.
6. Lawrence et al. (2006) examine individual win rates based on roll call votes and also find an advantage for members of the majority party consistent with the view of a partisan control of the legislative agenda.
7. Strictly speaking the legislature will be indifferent between X and X′; X has to be slightly closer to the line than X′ in order to be preferred.
8. Some authors (Shepsle, Weingast, Tsebelis) call the ability to reject a bill "veto," while others (Cox, McCubbins) tend to call it "negative agenda setting." We will use these two terms in congruence with the relevant literature.
9. An exception is the budget bill, which all presidents are constitutionally required to initiate yearly.
10. In Argentina and Panama, a qualified majority of two-thirds is required to override the president's partial veto, while in Brazil, Colombia, and Paraguay it is a majority of the membership.
11. The latter case (Uruguay and Ecuador) allows for some decree-like presidential advantages.
12. This pre-filing mechanism is also frequently used in the US House of Representatives (Sinclair 1994).
13. Peru restricts such decrees to fiscal matters, and in Argentina, the executive cannot issue decrees on electoral, penal, and tax matters or regarding political parties.
14. In Ecuador, the president can only declare economic legislation to be urgent.
15. It limits the presidents to two initiatives per year. Congress has thirty days to address them, or they end up on top of the schedule. Failure to address it does not lead to automatic passage.
16. This provision is also in place in Ecuador and Paraguay. In Paraguay, a two-thirds majority can rescind a presidential urgency.

17. In parliamentary systems, parties in government are veto players (Tsebelis 2002): they need to agree in order for a significant policy change to take place; otherwise, either there will be no change or this change will be made by a different government (which will not include the parties that disagree). In presidential systems, however, the parties in government are not necessarily veto players; that is, they can vote against a bill and the bill may still be enacted.
18. While the Argentine president can issue decrees, they do not directly shape the congressional agenda. The partial veto, however, is more significant in this respect.
19. Most use data from the first year of a presidential term. See country chapters for specific information including the newspaper used.
20. For her, this choice rests on the assumption that the newspaper responds to issues under consideration in Congress and highlights public problems that deserve attention. It captures issues at the "much talked about stage," as well as issues that may be considered "the agenda of potential enactments."

2

Presidential Agenda Authority in Plurality-Led Congresses

Agenda Setting Prerogatives without Majority Support

Ernesto Calvo and Iñaki Sagarzazu

Presidents with plurality support in congress are among the most pervasive and less studied phenomena in Latin America. Often conflated with divided government, where an organized opposition controls a majority in congress, presidents whose allies control fewer than 50 percent of the seats still benefit from institutional resources to facilitate the consideration and approval of their preferred legislation. Indeed, when holding a bare plurality of seats, allies of the incumbent president may still control key authority positions and dominate the legislative process. Gatekeeping authority without majority support, consequently, forces the president's allies to take advantage of existing congressional rules in ways that differ significantly from contexts in which they have majority support on the plenary floor.

As this chapter will show, the strategic use of rules, and their effects, will differ when majorities or pluralities are in control of the legislative gates. In particular, we show that the loss of majority support affects (i) the use of motions during debate, (ii) the level of amendments of presidential initiatives, and (iii) the overall legislative success of the president. To this end, we conduct three distinct statistical analyses that provide support for the overall argument of the chapter.

Our findings also support the guiding thesis of this book, that legislative behavior is determined not only by formal rules but also by the distribution of preferences of legislators and the president (Alemán and Tsebelis, this volume). In this chapter, we show that partisan, institutional, and positional effects interact with each other so that, even if and when rules remain stable, lawmaking patterns will differ across partisan contexts in congress.

In the particular case of Argentina, the gatekeeping prerogatives of the president and her allies serve different purposes when in control of a majority of seats, when in control of a plurality of seats, and when facing an organized majority opposition. Presidents in plurality-led congresses, we will argue, are subject to distinct constraints and anticipate legislative outcomes that differ from those observed in majority-led congresses, irrespective of whether the government's allies or the opposition control a majority of seats. In this chapter we analyze in detail how the loss of majority support alters the gatekeeping behavior—and the legislative success—of the president and her allies in congress. We do so by analyzing twenty-five years of congressional activity in Argentina. The implications of our analysis, however, extend well beyond the particulars of the Argentine case.

PLURALITY-LED CONGRESSES IN LATIN AMERICA

As shown in Table 2.1, approximately 42 percent of congresses in Latin America are led by a party or coalition that fails to control a majority of seats.[1] Furthermore, cases in which allies of the president control the largest legislative delegation are three times more frequent than those in which the largest opposition party or coalition controls a plurality of seats. However, in most presidential regimes, congressional rules endow the largest party or

Table 2.1 Plurality-led, coalition majority, and single-party majority congresses: presidential democracies, Latin America, 1980–2008

	Is largest party in the government or government coalition?		
Type of legislative majority	Opposition-led congress	Government-led congress	Total
Plurality-led congress	41	98	139
	12%	30%	42%
Coalition majority	14	68	82
	4%	21%	25%
Single-party majority	18	90	108
	5%	27%	33%
Total	73	256	329
	22%	78%	100%

Note: Elaborated using data from Saiegh (2009, 2011).

coalition with extensive agenda setting prerogatives, even when plenary majorities are lacking. The authority to set the agenda, as said before, will be used differently as the partisan context in congress changes.

In this chapter we use the term *plurality cartels* (Calvo 2014) to define a legislative party or coalition that is endowed with the authority to restrict the menu of bills that can be considered in committee or reported to the plenary but lacks the votes to pass legislation with the sole support of its members.

Plurality cartels benefit from institutional resources that restrict the set of bills reported from committee and debated on the floor, granting senior party members the authority to prevent the consideration of policies whose current status quo is preferred to the likely outcome on the plenary floor. However, plurality cartels face greater perils than majority cartels (Cox and McCubbins 2005: 20–5) when reporting legislation to the plenary floor. Consequently, plurality cartels require considerably more information to successfully advance their legislative goals and to prevent the consideration of initiatives on the plenary floor.

The goals of simultaneously restricting unwanted amendments and attracting enough floor support, however, may be inconsistent with each other. As we will show, the sequential organization of the legislative process in Argentina provides party leaders with resources to "lock in" amendments that have been agreed upon with the leaders of other legislative blocs[2] and successfully advance their legislative goals. The loss of majority control, in consequence, leads to more extensive bargaining in committee, with fewer presidential initiatives being discharged from committee, fewer opportunities to deviate from the plenary schedule, and a lower capacity to propose amendments on the plenary floor.

The main findings presented in this chapter show that:

1. The loss of majority support in congress does not significantly affect the overall legislative success of the president. We will explain this as a function of both changes in the importance of the median voter of the Chamber of Deputies (preferences) and changes in the use of institutional rules by actors (institutions). As described in the introductory chapter to this volume, both preferences and rules matter when explaining legislative success.
2. *Preferences*: As we will show, the loss of majority support will increase the relative importance of the median voter of the chamber, both when amending and approving presidential initiatives. The increased importance of the median voter when majority control is lost, consequently, raises the issue of how close or how distant is the president from the median legislator. As discussed in the fourth hypothesis of the introductory chapter by Alemán and Tsebelis, in multi-party systems the

party of the president may be away from the center (as in Chile) or at the center (as in Mexico today). This has implications for explaining executive legislative success.

3. *Rules*: A more novel contribution of this chapter is that the loss of majority support significantly alters the gatekeeping strategies of the plurality party, forcing more extensive bargaining which then makes bills less vulnerable to modifications once they reach the plenary floor. That is, while formal rules may not change, the loss of plenary majorities oftentimes will make consideration through some legislative venues more likely to succeed. Indeed, most legislative rules provide for different venues to approve legislation, and success in each of those different venues will be affected by the partisan context.

The organization of this chapter is as follows: first, we detail the basic rules and procedures that govern the consideration and approval of law initiatives in the Argentine Congress. We describe how initiatives are referred to committee, reported from committee, scheduled by the chamber directorate, and approved on the plenary floor. We emphasize that each new instance of legislative consideration provides new opportunities to enter into binding agreements with other legislative blocs and/or to limit future consideration of the proposed bill. Second, we discuss the different types of motions that can be used to force consideration of law initiatives on the plenary floor. We show that quorum rules reduce moral hazard on the plenary floor, validate interparty agreements, and facilitate the approval of executive initiatives. Third, we provide statistical evidence that distinguishes the type of presidential initiatives that succeed in majority and plurality-led congresses. We find that the major and minor presidential bills are affected to a different extent by the partisan context and the institutional rules in Congress. We conclude by discussing the importance of plurality cartels in other Latin American contexts.

PRESIDENTIAL AUTHORITY AND THE ARGENTINE CONGRESS

Argentina is a federal country composed of twenty-three provinces and one autonomous district (Ciudad Autónoma de Buenos Aires). The executive is elected every four years by popular vote in competitive elections, with constitutional provisions that allow for a one-time consecutive re-election. To be elected in the first round, the leading presidential candidate needs to collect at least 45 percent of the vote or 40 percent of the vote and at least a ten-point difference over the runner-up. Otherwise, a run-off election is used to select the winner among the two most voted candidates of the first round. Congressional elections take place every two years in each of the twenty-four electoral districts, electing half of the 257 deputies under proportional representation rules and a third of the seventy-two senators under majority/minority rules.[3]

The legislative prerogatives of the Argentine president are less extensive than generally recognized by the public and the media, with fewer institutional resources to shape the consideration and approval of law initiatives than most other Latin American presidents (Alemán 2006; Alemán and Navia 2009; Alemán and Tsebelis 2005; Saiegh 2011; Bonvecchi and Zelaznik 2010). As in all other countries of Latin America, the Argentine president has the authority to propose legislation to Congress. However, the consideration of presidential initiatives is not conducted under guidelines or procedures that differ from those proposals sponsored by deputies or senators. The Argentine president cannot attach "urgency" motions to speed up consideration as in Brazil and Chile (Figueiredo and Limongi 2000; Alemán and Navia 2009); she cannot impose a different schedule, affect the selection of committees that read a project, or force plenary consideration (Aparicio and Langston 2009; Pereira and Mueller 2004b; Santos and Renno 2004); she is unable to propose modifications or amendments, or to alter the content of the initiatives once in committee or on the floor; she cannot participate in the deliberations, inform, or argue in favor of an initiative being debated unless she is requested to do so by the committee and chamber authorities. In sum, once a bill has been proposed to Congress, the Argentine president has no institutional resources to affect the content of the bill and/or its approval. Instead, the president needs to rely on the legislative clout of her co-partisans in Congress.

However, the Argentine president has two important legislative prerogatives at her disposal: first, the president has the capacity to veto legislation both in general and in particular (partial veto). As described by Alemán and Tsebelis in this volume, this power does not allow the Argentine president to amend bills, but both the veto threat and its use may significantly affect the final character of the enacted bill as some articles are eliminated. Recent research has shown that moving from a majority to a plurality increases the incidence of vetoes (Palanza and Sin 2013).[4] This is consistent with the third hypothesis laid out in the introduction, where the loss of majority support moves policy away from the preferences of the president, increasing the likelihood of a veto. In the case of Argentina, this results from more extensive amendment of presidential proposals in plurality-led congresses. Second, the president has the capacity to enact legislation through decrees of "necessity and urgency." The extent of such decree authority has varied over time, with more extensive discretion observed after the constitutional reform of 1994 and until a congressional law to regulate decree usage was enacted in 2006 (Carey and Shugart 1998; Negretto 2004; Ferreira Rubio and Goretti 1996; Calvo and Sagarzazu 2011). Since 2006, the institutional authority to enact legislation by decree is considerably more limited than in Brazil (Saiegh 2010) and the actual number of decrees[5] represents but a small fraction of the legislative agenda of the president.[6]

WHEN THE PRESIDENT CANNOT LEGISLATE ALONE

Because of the limited legislative role granted to the Argentine executive by the constitution—mostly to propose or to veto legislation—policy that cannot be enacted by decree is subject to a difficult approval process that requires the acquiescence and support of members of Congress (Ferreira Rubio and Goretti 1996; Mustapic 2002). Indeed, the legislative interests of the president in each chamber need to be furthered by the leaders of her party and, in consequence, the congressional rules and procedures that constrain the legislative behavior of the majority or plurality bloc are of critical importance. These include rules that refer legislation to the proper committees; rules to consider, amend, and discharge initiatives from committee; rules to schedule initiatives on the plenary floor; and rules to give plenary consideration and approval in each chamber. The sequential organization of the legislative process in the Argentine Congress, consequently, provides multiple opportunities not only to prevent legislation from being considered but also to reach binding agreements with different legislative blocs.

The Argentine Chamber of Deputies provides a fixed schedule for the treatment of all legislation proposed by the president that is identical to legislation sponsored by deputies and senators. All law initiatives need to be formally proposed to Congress in *mesa de entrada* and reported to the Secretaría Parlamentaria—a congressional agency similar to the Parliamentarian in the US Congress, charged with the responsibility of providing logistic and administrative support for the discussion of all initiatives. Presidential initiatives are frequently co-sponsored by the minister with jurisdiction on the initiative's subject matter (Economy, Public Works, Chief of Staff, etc.).

Once an initiative is formally proposed to Congress, a *reading* by nonpartisan personnel of the Secretaría Parlamentaria decides which committee or committees will be charged with the responsibility of discussing the bill. Committees have complete autonomy to decide whether the initiative will be given consideration in committee.

The authority of the Standing Committee chairmen in the Argentine Congress is very extensive. Committee chairmen are in sole control of the scheduling of bills in committee. Consequently, they can decide to *kill* a bill in committee without ever bringing it to the consideration of members. While it is uncommon that committee chairmen will withhold debate on very important or salient bills, the authority to dominate committee proceedings also induces other members to "play by the rules" if they want to see their own pet projects being considered and reported to the floor. Calvo and Tow (2009) provide evidence of significant proactive and reactive gatekeeping authority being exercised by committee chairs in the Argentine Chamber of Deputies explained solely by control of committee rules.

An important feature of the Argentine Congress is that committee chairs are assigned in proportion to the number of seats controlled by a party delegation. Consequently, changes in the partisan composition in Congress will result in a small change in the number of committee chairs for each party. However, because committee chairs are assigned in proportion to seats, small changes in seat shares will result in small changes in committee assignments even if majority control is lost. The result is that the allocation of authority to majority party members will not be all that different from the allocation of chairmanships to plurality party members.

While gatekeeping discretion is extensive and routinely used to kill bills in committee, until 1994, almost all presidential initiatives were given consideration, amended, and discharged from committee. However, congressional behavior has changed significantly since the late 1990s and close to a quarter of presidential initiatives fail to be reported from committee.

Discharging a law initiative from the committee to the floor requires a majority report signed by all intervening committees. Any individual committee member or group of members can also write minority reports. More importantly, any member of Congress—even if not a member of the committee—can write amendments, objections, comments, or corrections to the bill, and the majority and/or minority reports after the bill is reported from committee and before it is scheduled for plenary consideration. If a bill has not been reported from committee, special procedures can force plenary consideration with two-thirds majority support (when the floor votes the daily schedule) or with three-quarters majority support if the motion is requested after the schedule has been approved.[7] Before a bill is scheduled for plenary consideration, however, two critical institutions will intervene: the pre-floor party meetings and the chamber directorate—Comisión de Labor Parlamentaria.

As is also the case with the Rules Committee in the US Congress, the chamber directorate has immense power to decide which bills will be entered into the daily agenda of the plenary and how debate will be conducted. The chamber directorate in Argentina is composed of the leaders of each legislative bloc and chaired by the president of the chamber, who belongs to the legislative bloc with the most seats. In order to decide whether a bill is to be scheduled for further discussion on the plenary, pre-floor party meetings are conducted by each legislative bloc. In these meetings, senior party members can gauge the party's mood regarding those bills that are objected to by at least some of its members.[8]

Then, in the chamber directorate meeting, any member can request that a bill with a majority report be placed on the agenda for the incoming session or let the other parties know they object to approval. Once a bill has a signed majority report in committee and has been scheduled by the chamber directorate, plenary approval requires a simple majority vote. This vote is preceded by debate that, while heavily regulated, still consumes considerable time on the floor.

Amendments on the floor may be approved by simple majority. However, stringent quorum rules are always in effect requiring at least 50 percent of members to be present at all times during debates.[9] As shown in Calvo and Sagarzazu (2011), deviating from the agreed wording of bills will often result in a vanishing quorum that will halt floor proceedings.[10] The loss of majority support, consequently, will prevent the party from dominating floor proceedings. Vanishing quorums, as we will show, will force consensual strategies *ex ante* when majority control is lost.[11]

LEGISLATIVE SUCCESS IN MAJORITY- AND PLURALITY-LED CONGRESSES

When a party or coalition controls a majority of Chamber of Deputies seats, strictly partisan amendments can be proposed in committee, a majority report can be drafted to discharge the initiative from committee, the chamber directorate can schedule the project to be considered on the floor, and the bill can be approved by a simple majority of votes during the session. In consequence, when holding a majority of seats, presidential initiatives that are preferred by the median voter of the majority party can be scheduled and approved in each of the different legislative stages. As in the majority cartel model of Cox and McCubbins (2005), it is expected that bills that will not *roll* (divide and defeat) the majority party will be scheduled for plenary consideration.

However, the loss of majority support will prevent the plurality cartel from quickly advancing its legislative goals. Let us describe what happens in each stage of the legislative process: first, because committees replicate the partisan composition of the chamber, the loss of majority support in the Chamber of Deputies will be accompanied by the loss of majority support in most committees. This loss of majority support will also result in a larger number of committee chairs being assigned to the opposition. Given that a signed majority report is required to report initiatives to the floor, the loss of majority support will effectively prevent reporting of presidential initiatives unless agreements with other blocs muster the required support.

Second, because extensive agenda setting prerogatives are granted to committee chairs, minority parties will be unable to demand committee consideration or report legislation that is not supported by the leaders of the plurality bloc. The prime role granted to committee chairs by Chamber of Deputies rules, in consequence, will prevent consideration of legislation by opposition blocs that collectively hold more than 50 percent of seats but fail to control the legislative gates. Therefore, while the plurality party needs to accommodate the preferences of minority blocs to discharge legislation from committee, the opposition needs to accommodate the preferences of the plurality party to schedule initiatives for committee consideration.

Third, if the committee is unable to sign a majority report, the plenary can request discharging of a bill using a preference motion. However, preference motions for unreported bills require a two-thirds majority vote, making it very difficult to force open the committee gates.

Fourth, while amendments proposed before a bill is scheduled for debate can be approved by simple majority, quorum requirements make it very difficult to forfeit on existing agreements when majority control is lost. Indeed, attempts to default on existing agreements will expose the plurality party to a vanishing quorum and almost always result in the closing of plenary proceedings. In fact, the threat of a vanishing quorum, often announced by minority members during Directorate meetings, constitutes the most important safeguard to force compliance on agreements once on the plenary floor. As was argued by the first minority chairman, Oscar Camaño (Partido Justicialista, PJ), during arguments regarding the bankruptcy of Argentina's main airline, Aerolineas Argentinas in 2001:

> What I intend is that once we open debate, nobody attempts to modify the decision we reached in the chamber directorate meeting. If that were to happen, there would be no agreement to continue debate... It is not my intention to introduce amendments during the plenary debate that have not been previously agreed by the chamber directorate. (Oscar Camaño (PJ), Argentine Chamber of Deputies, 2nd Ordinary Plenary Session, March 22, 2001)

In sum, while a party in control of a majority of seats will be able to schedule initiatives for committee consideration, sign the required majority report, schedule the bill on the plenary floor, validate amendments proposed ahead of debate by simple majority, and approve the proposed bill by simple majority, the loss of majority support will demand considerable bargaining in the early stages and binding agreements to approve proposals without modifications once they reach the plenary floor.

Just as rules prevent discharge from committee without a majority report, amendments will only be approved by a simple majority vote if they are proposed prior to a bill being scheduled for plenary consideration. Amendments proposed during debate, by contrast, will require two-thirds majority support to be approved. Reporting and amendments rules, consequently, will force more consensual committee strategies and a slight ideological drift away from the median voter of the plurality party.

MOTIONS, AMENDMENTS, AND THE FORGING OF LEGISLATIVE AGREEMENTS

The description of the rules and procedures that govern the consideration and approval of legislative initiatives yields a number of different predictions in regard to the use of plenary motions, the introduction of amendments, and the president's legislative success. In this section we will begin describing the consequences that the loss of majority support has on the use of motions and the introduction of amendments. We will then, in the next section, analyze how the loss of majority support affects the legislative success of the president.

As described in the previous section and in Table 2.2, a legislative initiative may receive consideration of the floor if it has a majority report and is placed in the plenary schedule by the chamber directorate. If a bill has not been added to the plenary schedule, a *preference motion* can be raised at the beginning of a session demanding that the bill be considered by the plenary in the following session. A preference motion to schedule a law initiative with a signed majority report in a future session requires a simple majority of the vote to be approved. However, a preference motion requesting immediate consideration (in the current session), for a bill with a signed majority report, still needs to be approved by two-thirds of current members.

The loss of majority support, consequently, will prevent the plurality party from scheduling law initiatives using preference motions. That is, the loss of

Table 2.2 Special motion rules in the Argentine Chamber of Deputies: summary information

Motion	Description	Vote	Debate
Recess (*Cuarto intermedio*)	Motion to suspend debate (generally 15 min.)	Simple majority	No debate
Motion to recommit (*Envío a comisión*)	Motion to send the initiative back to committee (often with a "fast discharge" request)	Simple majority	30 min.
Defer consideration (*Moción de aplazamiento*)	Motion to postpone debate on a bill	Simple majority	30 min.
Suspend rules (*Apartamiento del reglamento*)	Motion to bypass rules during debate (lift time constraints)	3/4 majority	Justification
Preference motion (with signed majority report)	Request to schedule a bill for a future meeting (if discharged from committee with a majority report)	Simple majority	Justification (10 min.), rebuttal (5 min.)
Preference motion (without majority report)	Request to schedule a bill for a future meeting (if still under committee consideration)	2/3 majority	Justification (10 min.), rebuttal (5 min.)
*Moción sobre tablas** (with or without majority report)	Request to schedule a bill on the current session	2/3 majority	Justification (10 min.), rebuttal (5 min.)

* *Moción sobre tablas*, the request to schedule a bill in the current session, should not be confused with the US Congress' motion to table, which describes a request to kill debate on an issue.

majority support will demand a more active role for the chamber directorate, which will be charged with the responsibility of validating agreements reached in committee (and defending them on the plenary floor).

The descriptive information is already suggestive. As shown in Table 2.3, motions to bypass the schedule proposed by the chamber directorate decline significantly when majority control is lost. In effect, the number of preference motions declines from 10.2 percent to 3.1 percent when the largest party holds a plurality of seats. Similarly, the number of motions *sobre tablas* declines from 31.1 percent to 20.5 percent of initiatives.

As we will show next, there are changes in the use of scheduling motions and also in the number and type of amendments proposed in committee. Such procedural changes alter the overall legislative success of the president. In the next sections we take a systematic look at the amendment process, the debate on the plenary floor, and the overall success of the president in the Argentine Congress. We begin by estimating the determinants of the number of successful amendments proposed to the original presidential bill.

Table 2.3 Use of scheduling motions on the plenary floor, Argentine Chamber of Deputies, 1984–2007

		Partisan control of the house		
		Majority	Plurality	Total
Preference motion	Withdraw	3	0	3
		0.8%	0.0%	0.5%
	No motion	348	217	565
		88.8%	96.9%	91.7%
	Affirmative	40	7	47
		10.2%	3.1%	7.6%
	Negative	1	0	1
		0.3%	0.0%	0.2%
	Total	392	224	616
		Partisan control of the house		
		Majority	Plurality	Total
Moción sobre tablas	Withdraw	0	0	0
		0.0%	0.0%	0.0%
	No motion	267	178	445
		68.1%	79.5%	72.2%
	Affirmative	122	46	168
		31.1%	20.5%	27.3%
	Negative	3	0	3
		0.8%	0.0%	0.5%
	Total	392	224	616

EXPLAINING AMENDMENTS TO PRESIDENTIAL INITIATIVES

In order to evaluate the legislative performance of presidents in majority and plurality-led congresses, we begin by analyzing the number of instances in which each executive initiative was effectively amended.[12] Our dependent variable is ordinal, reporting counts (instances) of modifications reported by the Secretaría Parlamentaria at each of the different stages, with a range from a minimum of 0 to a maximum of 6. Out of 1,985 law initiatives proposed by the president, 814 were approved without modifications (41 percent), 344 were approved with modifications (17 percent), 684 failed and no modifications

Table 2.4 Legislative success and the amendment of presidential initiatives, Argentine Congress, 1984–2007

		Major bill was approved in Congress					Non-major bill was approved in Congress		
		No	Yes	Total			No	Yes	Total
Major bill was amended in Congress	No	20	15	35	Non-major bill was amended in Congress	No	664	799	1,463
		18%	14%	32%			35%	43%	78%
	Yes	15	60	75		Yes	128	284	412
		14%	55%	68%			7%	15%	22%
	Total	35	75	110		Total	792	1,083	1,875
		32%	68%	100%			42%	58%	100%
		Approval of bills initiated in house					Approval of bills initiated in the Senate		
		No	Yes	Total			No	Yes	Total
Bill was amended	No	455	189	644	Bill was amended	No	229	625	854
		46%	19%	65%			23%	63%	85%
	Yes	88	253	341		Yes	55	91	146
		9%	26%	35%			6%	9%	15%
	Total	543	442	985		Total	284	716	1,000
		55%	45%	100%			28%	72%	100%

Note: Elaborated using data from the *Secretaría Parlamentaria*.

were proposed (69 percent), and 143 were modified but still failed to be approved (7.2 percent). As shown in Table 2.4, legislative success was lower and the number of amendments was more extensive for bills initiated in the Chamber of Deputies. By contrast, the legislative success of the president in the Senate was much higher and the number of amendments introduced much lower. It is worth noting that the president's legislative success in the Senate is almost identical when the executive is controlled by the UCR (Unión Cívica Radical) or the PJ. In fact, legislative success by UCR presidents stands at 73 percent while that of their Peronist counterpart is 71 percent.

Independent Variables

To explain amending rates in plurality and majority-led congresses we include variables measuring the distance from the ideal point of the president to the median of the majority party and to the median of the chamber. While we cannot observe the ideal point of the president directly, we are able to observe the location of the leader of the president's legislative bloc, who in Argentina has always been selected by the president rather than by the members of her bloc.

The leader of the president's legislative bloc has always been charged with the responsibility of advancing the executive's policies in congress and provides our best estimate of the preferences of the president. In fact, the leader of the president's coalition in congress has often diverged significantly from the median voter of her party as he is bound to act in representation of the president's preferences.[13] We use two different independent variables measuring (i) the squared ideological distance between the president (e.g., the leader of the president's bloc) and the *median member in each chamber*; and (ii) the squared distance between the president (e.g., the leader of the president's bloc) and the *median member of the majority in each chamber*.[14]

As described in the previous section, we expect that the number of amendments will increase with ideological distance in majority-led congresses. That is, when the majority party has the numbers required for signing a majority report and approving legislation on the plenary floor, it will modify presidential initiatives to the liking of the median member of the majority party. However, the loss of majority support will force the plurality party to bargain for support by accommodating the preferences of other minority parties. Consequently, we expect that legislation that has a more partisan content will be more likely to be amended. By contrast, legislation proposed by presidents that are further away from the median of the majority party will be less likely to be amended but will also have a more difficult time being approved.

To explain the number of modifications to the presidential initiatives we also consider a number of other behavioral, institutional, and contextual variables. We include a dummy variable *plurality* that takes the value of 1 if the largest party in the chamber has fewer than 50 percent of the seats and the value of 0 otherwise. Furthermore, we interact the variable *plurality* with the ideological distance terms to describe the conditional effect of spatial distance on amendments. We also control for the *public's positive perception of the president* using monthly survey data collected by *Nueva Mayoría*. Each observation describes the positive image of the president by survey respondents on a 0 to 1 scale. The average positive image of the president among respondents since democratization was 0.36 (36 percent), with a minimum of 0.08 (8 percent) for President De La Rua in his last month in office and a maximum of 0.86 (86 percent) for President Raul R. Alfonsín in 1984. We expect that more popular presidents will be able to better defend the original wording (intent) of law initiatives.

We also control for major bills, which take the value of 1 if they were reported on the first page of the newspaper *La Nación* in the first year of each presidency. We also estimate the conditional effect of ideological distance on amendments for major and minor legislation.

Results

Table 2.5 presents six models estimating the number of amendment instances of the different bills. To better interpret the results of the estimated models, we plot the marginal effect of ideological distance on amendments, conditional on the level of control (majority or plurality). This is shown in Figure 2.1, which describes the marginal effect of the president's ideological location on amendments, with arbitrary locations for the median voter of the majority party (–0.5) and the median voter of the chamber (–0.3). Figure 2.1 shows that when in control of a majority of seats, fewer amendments are proposed to bills initiated by presidents who are close to the median voter of the majority party. More frequent amendments, by contrast, are introduced when presidents with a majority support are beyond the median voter of the chamber.

By contrast, the number of instances in which amendments are introduced sharply declines when majority support is lost, with a larger number of initiatives approved without modifications or withheld from the floor. Interestingly enough, consistent with our description in the previous section, initiatives proposed by presidents who are more distant from the median voter of the majority party are more likely to be amended when majority control is lost. As shown in Table 2.5, major bills are significantly more likely to be amended. Figure 2.2 plots the linear effect of the ideological position of the president as it moves away from the median chamber voter and the median voter of the majority party. Figure 2.2 shows not only that major bills are more likely to be amended but also that major bills are amended irrespective of the ideological location of the president. The fact that major bills are more likely to be amended, and that they are less sensitive to the ideological leaning of the president, is an important result that deserves to be highlighted.

Other results are worth describing in further detail. As described in Table 2.5, the number of amendments increases when each chamber is controlled by different political parties (divided congress). As expected, public support allows the president to defend the initial intent of the legislation, with higher levels of public approval resulting in lower number of amendments. Results, however, are only statistically significant in Models E and F. As

Table 2.5 Explaining the number of amendment instances in the Argentine Congress

	Amendments, Model A	Amendments, Model B	Amendments, Model C	Amendments, Model D	Amendments, Model E	Amendments, Model F
Distance to chamber median	**−0.35***	**−1.35*****	**−1.32*****	**−0.35***	−0.17	−0.15
	(0.20)	(0.28)	(0.27)	(0.20)	(0.21)	(0.21)
Distance to median of majority	−0.26	**0.64*****	**0.61*****	−0.26	**−0.53*****	**−0.52*****
party in chamber	(0.17)	(0.22)	(0.21)	(0.17)	(0.17)	(0.17)
Plurality	0.05	**−0.34*****	**−1.27*****	0.05	0.08	0.09
	(0.10)	(0.13)	(0.26)	(0.10)	(0.10)	(0.10)
Plurality × distance to chamber	–	**2.60*****	**2.67*****	–	–	–
median	–	(0.36)	(0.35)	–	–	–
Plurality × distance to median of	–	**−2.20*****	**−2.24*****	–	–	–
majority party in chamber	–	(0.30)	(0.30)	–	–	–
Major bill	**1.11*****	**1.15*****	**1.14*****	**1.11*****	**1.06*****	**1.54*****
	(0.08)	(0.08)	(0.07)	(0.08)	(0.11)	(0.26)
Major bill × distance to chamber	–	–	–	–	−0.19	−0.19
median	–	–	–	–	(0.43)	(0.42)
Major bill × distance to median	–	–	–	–	**0.70****	**0.71****
of majority party in chamber	–	–	–	–	(0.32)	(0.32)
Success in committee	–	**1.38*****	**1.02*****	–	**1.32*****	**1.41*****
	–	(0.11)	(0.13)	–	(0.11)	(0.12)
Major bill × success in committee	–	–	–	–	–	**−0.53****
	–	–	–	–	–	(0.26)
Plurality × success in committee	–	–	**0.97*****	–	–	–

(continued)

Table 2.5 Continued

	Amendments, Model A	Amendments, Model B	Amendments, Model C	Amendments, Model D	Amendments, Model E	Amendments, Model F
	–	–	(0.23)	–	–	–
Divided Congress	**0.21***	0.09	0.12	**0.21***	**0.25***	**0.25***
	(0.11)	(0.12)	(0.12)	(0.11)	(0.13)	(0.13)
Presidential approval	−0.07	−0.27	−0.33	−0.07	**−0.43***	**−0.45****
	(0.22)	(0.23)	(0.22)	(0.22)	(0.22)	(0.22)
Initiated in Senate	**−0.69*****	**−0.68*****	**−0.68*****	**−0.69*****	**−0.70*****	**−0.71*****
	(0.08)	(0.07)	(0.07)	(0.08)	(0.07)	(0.07)
Extraordinary sessions	**0.18*****	**0.21*****	**0.21*****	**0.18*****	**0.18*****	**0.18*****
	(0.06)	(0.06)	(0.06)	(0.06)	(0.06)	(0.06)
Special sessions	**0.41*****	**0.47*****	**0.45*****	**0.41*****	**0.47*****	**0.47*****
	(0.10)	(0.09)	(0.09)	(0.10)	(0.10)	(0.10)
Constant	**−0.80*****	**−1.90*****	**−1.53*****	**−0.80*****	**−1.88*****	**−1.97*****
	(0.12)	(0.16)	(0.17)	(0.12)	(0.16)	(0.17)
N	1682	1682	1682	1682	1682	1682
LL	−859.27	−816.19	−813.2	−859.27	−823.99	−823.36
AIC	1742.53	1662.37	1658.39	1742.53	1677.98	1678.72

Note: Negative binomial model explaining the number of instances each presidential initiative was amended in the Argentine Congress. Clustered errors by congressional period. Two tailed significance: *$p<0.1$, **$p<0.05$, ***$p<0.01$.

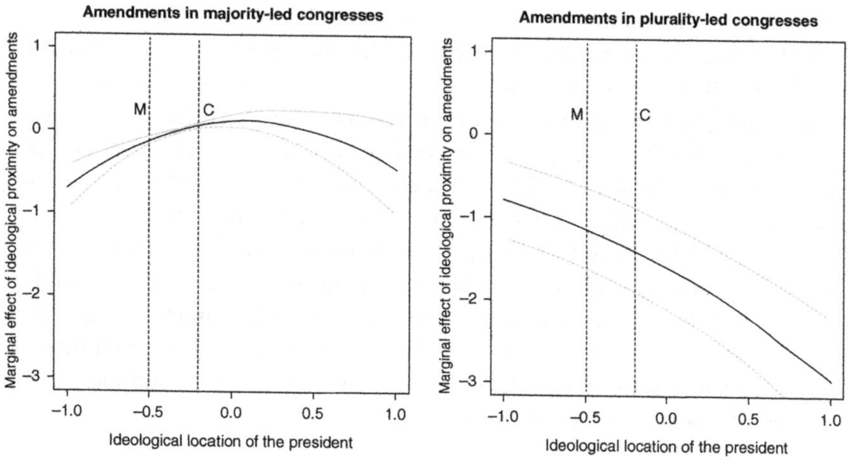

Figure 2.1 Linear estimate of amendment conditional on the ideological location of the president, majority- and plurality-led congresses, Argentina, 1984–2007

Note: Coefficients from Table 2.1, negative-binomial Model 3. Plots describe linear expected change in the log of the number of amendments, with locations for the median voter of the majority party (M) set at –0.5 and the median voter of the chamber (C) set at –0.2. Values larger than zero indicate a higher frequency of amendments and values smaller than zero indicate a decline in the number of amendments.

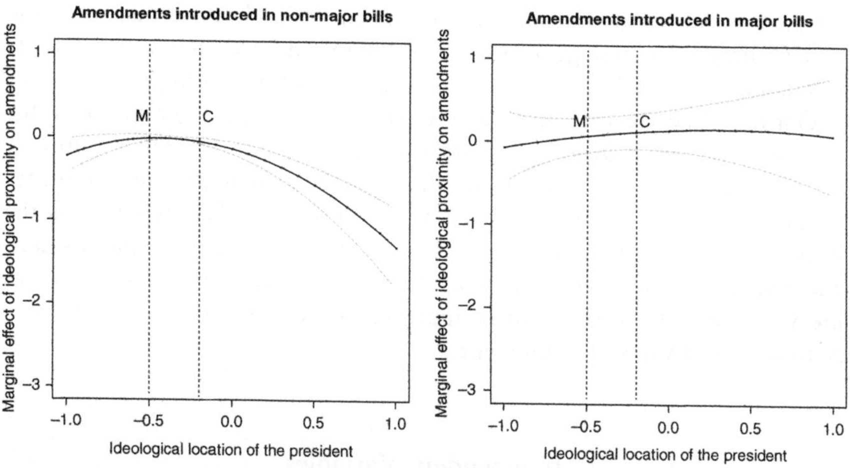

Figure 2.2 Linear estimate of amendment conditional on the ideological location of the president, major and non-major bills, Argentina, 1984–2007

Note: Coefficients from Table 2.1, negative-binomial Model 3. Plots describe linear expected change in the log of the number of amendments, with locations for the median voter of the majority party (M) set at –0.5 and the median voter of the Chamber (C) set at –0.2. Values larger than zero indicate a higher frequency of amendments and values smaller than zero indicate a decline in the number of amendments.

already noted, legislation initiated in the Senate is not amended to the same extent as legislation initiated in the Chamber of Deputies. This is both the result of differences in jurisdictions—i.e., initiatives on foreign affairs and nominations beginning in the Senate while most budget initiatives are initiated in the Chamber of Deputies—as well as procedural differences described earlier. Finally, results in Table 2.5 also show that initiatives that receive consideration in special sessions are more frequently amended.

Overall, results show that the majority party is more likely to amend the president's initiatives when in control of a majority of seats in the chamber and more likely to compromise with the opposition when majority support is lost. In the next section we describe the effect of ideological proximity on legislative success, conditional on the majority or plurality support of the president in each chamber of congress.

EXPLAINING THE PRESIDENT'S LEGISLATIVE SUCCESS

In the previous section we explored the degree to which the original legislative intent of the president was amended (or upheld) by deputies and senators. We now turn to analyze the determinants of legislative success in committee, on the plenary floor, and in the alternate chamber. We understand that success in each of these different stages provides relevant information on how the majority or plurality cartels take advantage of their agenda setting prerogatives.

Our first dependent variable, *success in committee*, takes the value of 1 if the proposal receives a majority report (dossier reporting the bill for further consideration by the chamber) or the value of 0 if it *dies* in committee (*cajoneada*).[15] Our second variable, *success in the initial chamber*, takes the value of 1 if the proposal is approved in the initial chamber (*media sanción*) and a value of 0 otherwise. Our final dependent variable, *final passage*, takes the value of 1 if the proposal is approved by the plenary of the alternate chamber and a value of 0 otherwise.

Independent Variables

As in the previous section, we include variables measuring the ideological distance from the president to the median voter of each chamber and to the median member of the majority/plurality party in each chamber. We also control whether the largest party has a plurality of seats, whether the proposal is a major bill (e.g., reported in the media during the first year), the type of legislative session, and whether the bill was initiated in the Chamber of Deputies or the Senate.

We also include a range of other variables that are relevant for explaining overall the president's legislative success (Alemán and Calvo 2010). To assess the effect of divided government on legislative success we add a dummy variable, *Divided Congress*, that indicates whether each chamber is led by a party of a different political color. Other variables that have been used in the models include the total *number of bills introduced by the executive branch* (ln) within that congressional period, the *number of presidential decrees* (ln) enacted within that congressional period, a variable indicating whether the bill was *amendments*, whether the bill was co-sponsored by the *Minister of Economy*, and the *chamber of initiation.* Finally, two other variables control for the percentage of *seats* controlled by the president's party or coalition.

Results

Results for the six models of legislative success are presented in Table 2.6 (full results are in the appendix). The first three models measure legislative success of law initiatives comparing the effect of ideological distances across plurality and majority congresses. The second group of three models measures legislative success of law initiatives comparing major bills versus all law initiatives.

As expected, Models 1, 2, and 3 show that when the president's party or coalition controls a majority of seats, presidential initiatives that are preferred by the median voter of the majority party are more likely to be reported from committee and are more likely to receive final passage. Furthermore, as shown in Figure 2.3, the positive effect of ideological proximity on reporting success is particularly important for major bills. In effect, major bills that are proposed by presidents who are further removed from the majority party are much less likely to be reported from committee. The positive effect of proximity to the median voter of the majority party is particularly large on the final passage of initiatives in majority-led congresses. By contrast, in plurality-led congresses higher legislative success is observed for presidents who are closer to the median voter of the chamber.

As depicted in Figure 2.4, Model 6 shows that proximity to the median voter of the chamber is particularly important for major bills. Taken together, models in Tables 2.5 and 2.6 show that major bills are more likely to be

Table 2.6 Logistic regression of success in committee, first chamber, and final passage: Argentine Congress, 1984–2007

	Model 1 Committee success	Model 2 First chamber	Model 3 Final passage	Model 4 Committee success	Model 5 First chamber	Model 6 Final passage
Distance to chamber median	−3.05	**3.98*****	**3.26*****	1.05	**2.01****	**2.34*****
	(1.92)	(0.75)	(0.68)	(1.24)	(0.78)	(0.71)
Distance to median of majority party in chamber	−2.81	**−3.31*****	**−2.85*****	−1.55	**−3.66*****	**−3.61*****
	(1.82)	(0.56)	(0.50)	(1.17)	(0.66)	(0.60)
Plurality	1.76	0.43	0.53	–	–	–
	(2.00)	(0.38)	(0.36)	–	–	–
Plurality × distance to chamber median	**−11.98*****	**−5.45*****	**−4.25*****	–	–	–
	(2.61)	(0.99)	(0.90)	–	–	–
Plurality × distance to median of majority party in chamber	26.00	**3.20*****	**2.30****	–	–	–
	(16.86)	(1.01)	(0.92)	–	–	–
Major bill	–	–	–	**−1.61****	−0.26	0.16
	–	–	–	(0.66)	(0.56)	(0.53)
Major bill × distance to chamber median	–	–	–	**3.29***	−1.05	**−5.20****
	–	–	–	(1.93)	(2.02)	(2.16)
Major bill × distance to median of majority party in chamber	–	–	–	−1.79	1.37	**4.92*****
	–	–	–	(1.57)	(1.50)	(1.59)
Constant	−11.54	−2.20	−1.45	**52.80*****	**21.25****	**23.03****
	(13.05)	(5.79)	(5.60)	(16.80)	(10.23)	(9.74)
N	1682	1682	1682	1682	1682	1682
LL	−525.37	−825.18	−971.67	−530.04	−833.16	−968.03
AIC	1086.74	1686.36	1979.33	1100.08	1706.33	1976.06

Standard errors in parenthesis.
Statistical significance at *p<0.1 **p<0.05 ***p<0.01.
Full model results can be found in the appendix.

amended and approved the closer the president is to the median voter of the chamber. By contrast, minor bills are less likely to be amended and more likely to be approved when they are proposed by presidents that are closer to the median voter of the majority party.

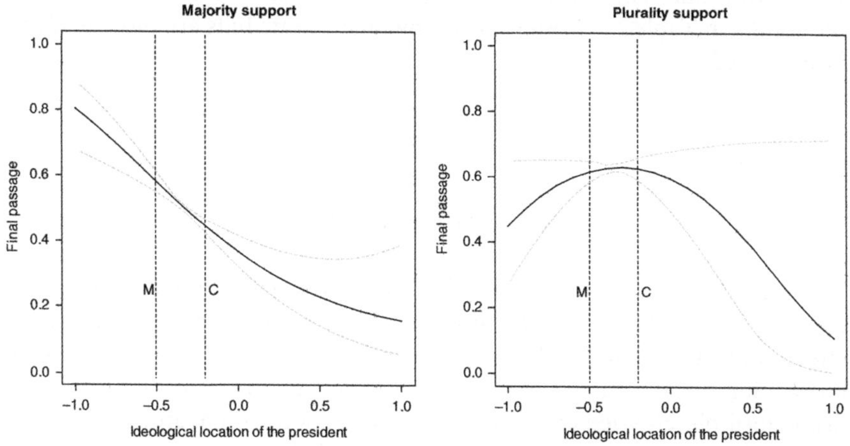

Figure 2.3 Estimated probability of final passage conditional on the ideological location of the president, majority- and plurality-led congresses

Note: Estimated probability of final passage from Table 2.6.

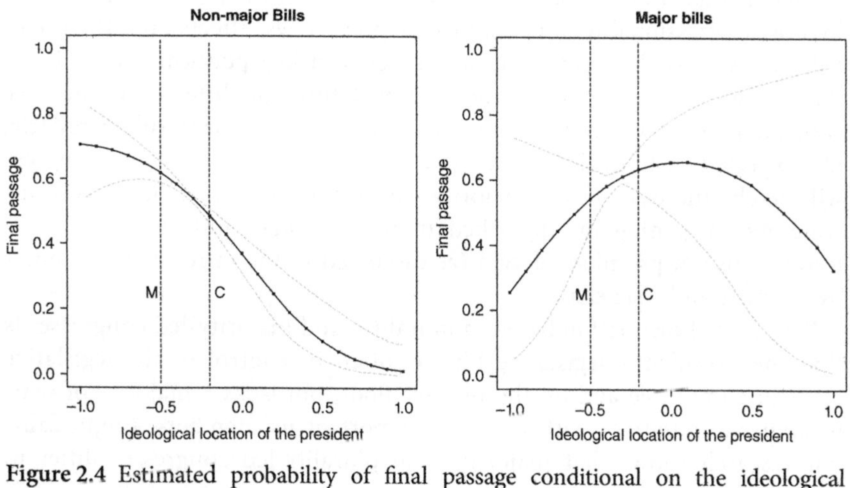

Figure 2.4 Estimated probability of final passage conditional on the ideological location of the president, major and non-major bills, Argentina, 1984–2007

Note: Estimated probability of final passage from Table 2.6.

Other results (shown in Table 2.A1 in the appendix) are worth mentioning. Consistent with Calvo (2007) and Alemán and Calvo (2010), high levels of presidential support among voters increase the legislative success of the president on the plenary floor but have no effect on committee success. Amended bills are considerably more likely to be approved, a result that is in line with our central argument in this chapter as well as consistent with the results in Table 2.6. Results also show that Senate bills are more likely to be approved.

CONCLUDING REMARKS

We began this chapter by noting that presidents with plurality support in congress have not received the level of scholarly attention they deserve. In effect, while a majority of elected presidents in Latin America today control but a plurality of seats, most existing comparative research has failed to distinguish plurality-led congresses from opposition-led congresses. The distinction between plurality-led and opposition-led congresses is not trivial, informing important features of presidential success in multi-party systems as described in the introductory chapter.

In the introductory chapter, Alemán and Tsebelis note that legislative success requires that we understand the effect of complex legislative rules as well as their interaction with the preferences of the political actors. The loss of congressional majorities, this chapter shows, affects both the use of rules as well as the relative distances between key political actors. Rules that allow for consideration and approval through different venues, we show, may be used differently under plurality and majority rule. Similarly, the expected distance in preferences between the president and congress will likely increase when majority control is lost, leading to within-congress bargaining (as described in this chapter) and also to a more frequent use of presidential veto (as discussed in the introductory chapter by Alemán and Tsebelis).

The crucial distinction between plurality- and majority-led congresses is that the president's legislative bloc is often in control of the legislative gates in committee and on the plenary floor, but lacks a majority of seats to approve initiatives with the sole support of its members. Empirically, our research shows that majority- and plurality-led congresses differ in important ways. Gatekeeping authority without plenary support prevents the president from rolling the opposition on the plenary floor but still ensures that legislation that is approved will be preferred to the current status quo by her legislative bloc. The loss of majority support, consequently, results in a change in the type of legislation amended in committee and in the type of legislation that is approved on the plenary floor. Our results also show an ideological drift away from the median voter of the majority party that benefits the median voter of the chamber. The result is an increase in the number of amendments in committee, a reduction in the overall number of amendments on the floor, and an ideological drift that favors the overall median voter in each chamber. Our results also show that the loss of majority control reduces the incentive to alter the plenary schedule agreed by the chamber directorate. Fewer incentives to amend the plenary schedule result in lower rates of introduction of preferential motions.

As in the other chapters of this volume, we analyze how congress deals with major law initiatives proposed by the president. Our results show that major bills are less likely to be reported from committee and more likely to be amended if reported. Major bills are also more likely to be approved when proposed by presidents who are closer to the median voter of the chamber. Furthermore, when major bills fail they are more likely to die at the committee stage. These important results are described in Figure 2.2, which shows that major and minor bills are affected to a different extent by the rules and the preferences of political actors. That is, major bills are more likely to be approved, more likely to be amended, and they are also less sensitive to the ideological leaning of the president.

Our research design seeks to understand how the sequential organization of the legislative process provides parties with multiple instances to reach binding agreements and advance their legislative goals. Our research on majority- and plurality-led congresses, however, also shows that there are significant benefits to measuring legislative success in different stages—committee, plenary, alternate chamber—and on different types of measures—motions, amendments, law initiatives. Our research shows that the loss of majority support does not affect all stages and measures to the same degree. In effect, the majority, plurality, and minority parties have different capacities to advance at least part of their legislative goals by maneuvering the rules and procedures that regulate the consideration and approval of law initiatives.

APPENDIX

Table 2.A1 Legislative success of the Argentine president

	Model 1 Committee success	Model 2 First chamber	Model 3 Final passage	Model 4 Committee success	Model 5 First chamber	Model 6 Final passage
Distance to chamber median	−3.05	**3.98*** **	**3.26*** **	1.05	**2.01** **	**2.34*** **
	(1.92)	(0.75)	(0.68)	(1.24)	(0.78)	(0.71)
Distance to median of majority party	−2.81	**−3.31*** **	**−2.85*** **	−1.55	**−3.66*** **	**−3.61*** **
in chamber	(1.82)	(0.56)	(0.50)	(1.17)	(0.66)	(0.60)
Plurality	1.76	0.43	0.53	–	–	–
	(2.00)	(0.38)	(0.36)	–	–	–
Plurality × distance to chamber	**−11.98*** **	**−5.45*** **	**−4.25*** **	–	–	–
median	(2.61)	(1.00)	(0.90)	–	–	–
Plurality × distance to median of majority party in chamber	26.00	**3.20*** **	**2.30** **	–	–	–
	(16.86)	(1.00)	(0.92)	–	–	–
Major bill	–	–	–	**−1.61** **	−0.26	0.16
	–	–	–	(0.66)	(0.56)	(0.53)
Major bill × distance to chamber	–	–	–	**3.29* **	−1.05	**−5.20** **
median	–	–	–	(1.93)	(2.02)	(2.16)
Major bill × distance to median of	–	–	–	−1.79	1.37	**4.92*** **
majority party in chamber	–	–	–	(1.57)	(1.50)	(1.59)

President of PJ	**−8.07*** **	−0.21	0.03	−1.24	−0.56	−0.73
	(1.92)	(0.98)	(0.90)	(0.80)	(0.67)	(0.62)
Presidential approval	0.73	**1.90*** **	**1.55** **	1.14	**1.73** **	**1.36** **
	(0.86)	(0.73)	(0.65)	(0.89)	(0.75)	(0.67)
% seats president's party	–	–	–	**−195.61*** **	**−45.36** **	**−50.64** **
	–	–	–	(34.40)	(22.73)	(20.11)
% seats president's party (sqrd)	–	–	–	**224.05*** **	39.49	**48.09** **
	–	–	–	(39.93)	(26.89)	(23.76)
Divided congress	−2.40	0.73	0.91	**−4.78** **	−1.03	−1.35
	(2.22)	(1.26)	(1.21)	(2.05)	(1.37)	(1.36)
Divided government	−1.70	0.30	0.00	**3.38* **	0.51	0.60
	(2.06)	(0.79)	(0.80)	(1.85)	(1.06)	(1.09)
Amendments	**1.62*** **	**2.22*** **	**1.36*** **	**1.69*** **	**2.25*** **	**1.40*** **
	(0.25)	(0.18)	(0.14)	(0.25)	(0.18)	(0.15)
Special sessions	**−0.79** **	−0.31	−0.17	**−0.66** **	−0.37	−0.27
	(0.32)	(0.30)	(0.27)	(0.32)	(0.30)	(0.27)
Extraordinary sessions	**0.39* **	0.22	**0.23* **	**0.38* **	0.26	**0.27* **
	(0.23)	(0.16)	(0.14)	(0.23)	(0.16)	(0.14)
Initiated in Senate	**0.48* **	**1.89*** **	**1.64*** **	**−2.08*** **	**2.69*** **	**2.01*** **
	(0.29)	(0.20)	(0.19)	(0.59)	(0.43)	(0.37)
# Executive decrees (ln)	**−0.75* **	0.32	0.11	**−2.15*** **	−0.33	**−0.45* **
	(0.43)	(0.19)	(0.19)	(0.42)	(0.25)	(0.25)
# Executive bills (ln)	**5.16** **	−0.22	−0.21	0.49	−1.56	−1.69
	(2.47)	(1.02)	(1.01)	(2.20)	(1.30)	(1.31)

(continued)

Table 2.A1 Continued

	Model 1 Committee success	Model 2 First chamber	Model 3 Final passage	Model 4 Committee success	Model 5 First chamber	Model 6 Final passage
Economy minister	−0.54	−0.20	−0.09	−0.41	−0.16	−0.07
	(0.39)	(0.20)	(0.18)	(0.38)	(0.20)	(0.18)
Constant	−11.54	−2.20	−1.45	**52.80*****	**21.25****	**23.03****
	(13.05)	(5.79)	(5.60)	(16.80)	(10.23)	(9.74)
N	1682	1682	1682	1682	1682	1682
LL	−525.37	−825.18	−971.67	−530.04	−833.16	−968.03
AIC	1086.74	1686.36	1979.33	1100.08	1706.33	1976.06

NOTES

1. The share of plurality-led congresses in Latin America is not very different from the world average. Approximately 39 percent of the congresses in presidential regimes fail to elect a majority bloc.
2. Rules in the Chamber of Deputies and the Senate recognize the legislative bloc—*bloque*—as the key partisan institution in the Argentine Congress. Each legislative *bloque* needs to be composed of at least three members to be recognized by the Chamber of Deputies. A representative in the chamber directorate, authority posts, and committee assignments are distributed to legislative blocs based on membership.
3. Two senators from the most voted party and one senator from the second most voted party are elected to Congress. A third of provinces elect senators every two years.
4. Interestingly, in those instances where the president's party is in the minority and lacks a plurality the incidence of vetoes is not higher.
5. It is important to note that in Argentina there are thousands of administrative decrees enacted every year that do not need Congress to act. Similar decrees are also routinely enacted in the United States to regulate the activity of state agencies, regulate contracts, set up administrative rules, regulate government purchases, etc.; often with significant budgetary implications. In Argentina, every single federal public sector employee has to be hired by an administrative decree signed by the proper minister or executive authority. We do not consider such decrees in our analysis, which is also the case with studies of decree authority in almost all existing research.
6. In fact, since being elected into office in 2007, Cristina Fernández de Kirchner has enacted approximately four decrees of necessity and urgency per congressional term, representing less than 7 percent of the total presidential initiatives approved by Congress. However, as in the United States, there are a large number of regular executive decrees that are enacted every year to administer the public sector (appointments, regulatory decisions, etc.). Those decrees do not enact new laws and are not considered in this chapter.
7. This second alternative requires three-quarters support because a special motion needs to be approved to "move away from the plenary schedule" previously approved at the beginning of the plenary meeting.
8. All proposals reported from committee with no dissents or objections are added to an omnibus package to be approved with a single vote at the beginning of the plenary session. Article 133 of the rules of the Chamber of Deputies indicates that proposals reported "without dissent or objections" should not be discussed in the plenary and will be subject to an expedited vote. From December 1983 to April 1988, each of these projects was voted separately—with no debate—at the beginning of the session. Since 1988, at the request of the then president of the Argentine Chamber of Deputies, all projects were bundled in a single vote at the beginning of

the session, a practice that remains in effect. Different from an omnibus bill in the US Congress, all sessions in the Argentine Congress include a vote on unanimous initiatives that, by Article 152 of the rules of the Chamber of Deputies, need to be included in the omnibus package solely because they satisfy the requirement of no dissent, rather than being the result of log-rolling among legislators and explicit bargaining. Moreover, the rules of the Chamber of Deputies preclude plenary debate on bills with no dissent or minority reports, clearing plenary time for bills where consensus is lacking and amendments are needed. However, it is uncommon for presidential initiatives to be approved under the provisions of Article 133.

9. Otherwise, the debate can only continue "in minority" and the plenary can reach no binding decisions of any type.
10. In this chapter we do not discuss in detail how minor parties can extract benefits from the plurality party by not granting quorum. This is a critical tactic by minority parties in plurality-led congresses, as the largest parties control the legislative gates but cannot ensure that the plenary will survive a quorum count. A detailed discussion of the vanishing quorum strategy is in Calvo (2014).
11. New agreements can be forged during debate. Oftentimes this will be preceded by a call to suspend debate for a short period of time, allowing party leaders to compromise on the wording of a particular bill outside of the floor. During debate, for example, chairmen of each caucus may introduce motions requesting suspension of debate for 15 minutes or more—*cuarto intermedio*—allowing party leaders to forge acceptable compromises when majority support is lacking. If an acceptable agreement is reached, upon reinitiating the session the proposed changes will be submitted to a vote requiring two-thirds support by the plenary members. Otherwise, proposals are sent back to committee, referred to a future plenary session, or, in a few cases, abandoned to expire at the end of the next legislative cycle.
12. This is not the same as the number of total changes introduced to the bill, as we do not have information to control the extent (or importance) of the amendments. In-depth analysis of the extent of the modifications was carried out in a sample of presidential bills by Bonvecchi and Zelaznik (2010). They show that the extent of the reforms proposed to presidential initiatives tends to be significant.
13. In fact, presidents have often selected feisty and sometimes younger leaders that aggressively manage their affairs. By contrast, chamber presidents tend to be more seasoned and accommodating.
14. The ideal point estimates of legislator preferences were retrieved using principal component analysis on the agreement matrix of co-sponsored legislation (Alemán et al. 2009). This procedure is a family relative of Keith Poole's Optimal Classification design (Poole 2005), retrieving ideal points estimates from co-sponsorship data. Alemán et al. (2009) find that in Argentina there is a primary dimension separating government from opposition that explains the largest variance in co-sponsoring decisions. We consider this first dimension when conducting our analyses, but models with two dimensions may be requested from the authors.
15. It is worth noting that the majority report is a joint report by all intervening committees.

3

Agenda Setting and Gridlock in a Multi-Party Coalitional Presidential System

The Case of Brazil

Taeko Hiroi and Lucio R. Rennó

Presidents in Latin America commonly have several agenda setting powers and are important lawmakers in the land. Yet, many of these presidents regularly face situations of minority governments or majority coalitions, with difficult intra-coalition bargaining and a significant potential for gridlock (Cheibub 2007; Shugart and Carey 1992; Tsebelis and Alemán 2005; Ames 2001). Although party systems in Latin America vary dramatically in their levels of institutionalization and fragmentation (Mainwaring and Scully 1995), overall the number of parties in the region surpasses the two-party logic of the US case. The dynamics of legislative conflict in such environments is quite distinct from that of divided government. Consequently, mapping agenda powers and the processes of negotiation within and between coalitions composed of heterogeneous parties is fundamental to understand lawmaking in the region.

Consider, for instance, that Brazilian presidents typically put together governing coalitions comprising various parties. With some twenty parties in the legislature, the president's party alone never holds more than 20 percent of the seats in the Chamber of Deputies, generating the need and incentive for coalition government. The low level of Brazilian party institutionalization and high party fragmentation add to the governability problem (Mainwaring 1999). For these reasons, since 1994 successive presidents—Fernando Henrique Cardoso, Luiz Inácio Lula da Silva, especially during his second term in office, and Dilma Rousseff—have held numerically large coalitional majorities in the Chamber of Deputies and variously sized coalitions in the Senate. Despite the large coalitional majorities that Brazilian presidents have amassed, they have not always been successful in getting their legislative initiatives approved by Congress. In the situations where Congress approves the government's proposals, the process is generally not swift or without major alterations to the proposal. Why is this? A part of the answer to this question requires us to look closely inside the coalitions. Coalitions in Brazil do not function like a single party. Consequently, we need to examine the cohesiveness of coalitions and their consistency over time to understand the dynamics of legislative conflict in Brazil. The political landscape of Brazil also reinforces the argument of Alemán and Tsebelis in the introduction to this volume that underlines why, in the absence of a cohesive government majority, studying the workings of legislative institutions and the positions of the main legislative actors becomes crucial to understand policy outcomes.

The Brazilian case is also a great example to study institutional incentives and constraints in legislative decision-making. There are several institutional factors, such as various tools of legislative obstruction, sequential examination by legislative committees, and bicameral deliberation, that impose hurdles for the lawmaking process. The layers of complexity are increased when we consider the three-fifths majority and two-round votes in both the Senate and Chamber of Deputies that are required to pass constitutional amendment proposals. Clearly, the obstacles are many for policy-making inside the Brazilian Congress.

Yet, presidents hold powerful prerogatives that centralize the agenda setting power in their hands. Presidents possess special legislative privileges, such as the power to present proposals for constitutional amendments, issue decree-like provisional measures, and request urgency for the consideration of their ordinary law proposals in Congress. In addition to their proposal powers, presidents can also veto legislation either partially or fully. Presidents also hold the power of the purse, being responsible for the formulation and presentation of annual budgetary laws and, later, the disbursement of discretionary transfers (Ames 2001). Finally, presidents have discretion in the nomination of many political appointees, with estimates of over 20,000 nominations, some of which carry with them power over significant budgetary funds. Amorim Neto (2006) points out that presidents allocate cabinet positions to manage their coalitions, and other authors have shown that such strategy also affects much lower levels of the bureaucracy (Praça et al. 2011).[1] Several studies have shown that the proportional distribution of cabinet positions among members of the coalition is an important factor to understand presidents' legislative success (Amorim Neto 2002) and choices of policy-making instrument (Pereira et al. 2005).

Rules inside the Chamber of Deputies and Senate strongly centralize agenda setting powers in the hands of the leaders of the largest parties and the majority coalition. The majority coalition usually controls key positions in the hierarchy of the two houses, such as the presiding officer of the steering committee (called Mesa) and chairs of key committees, including the Constitution Committee (Comissão de Constituição e Justiça e de Cidadania) which oversees the constitutionality of all legislative proposals.

Does the concentration of agenda setting powers in the president and the governing coalition in the legislature help overcome institutional and political hindrances to lawmaking? In this chapter, we address this question by examining various legislative data, including legislative proposals considered by the Brazilian Congress, roll call votes, obstructionist movements, and various configurations of the governing and opposition coalitions and their internal unity. We examine if Brazil is an example of how presidential agenda setting powers and a centralized decision-making process within Congress can offset the potential governability problems generated by complicated coalition building and management and the institutional complexity of the lawmaking process. In Chapter 1, Alemán and Tsebelis hypothesize that granting substantial agenda setting prerogatives to presidents should help overcome some of the problems generated by heterogeneous policy positions inside a governing coalition.

In the next section, we discuss the legislative processes stressing presidential prerogatives, actors, rules and procedures within Congress, and some current interpretations of lawmaking in Brazil. We then derive hypotheses from both the theoretical discussion and the implications of the Brazilian institutional and partisan framework. Finally, we test these hypotheses empirically using various legislative data.

LEGISLATIVE ACTORS, INSTITUTIONS, AND PROCESSES

This section discusses institutional prerogatives of the key legislative actors and formal legislative rules and procedures under Brazil's 1988 constitution. Brazil has a presidential system with a bicameral Congress. Several actors can propose bills, including the judiciary, private citizens, congressional committees, federal deputies, senators, and the executive branch. There are many types of bills with different majority requirements. The legislative process is one of sequential decision-making, prone to nested games (Tsebelis 1990) and various occasions for the blocking of legislation by veto players (Tsebelis 2002).

Presidential Prerogatives

Unlike the US president, the Brazilian president is endowed with substantial legislative prerogatives. In the Shugart and Carey (1992) classification assessing presidential legislative powers, the Brazilian president ranks among the most powerful presidents in the world. For example, the Brazilian president enjoys tremendous agenda setting power. The country's constitution grants the president the power to initiate any type of bill,[2] including exclusivity over the initiation of provisional measures, budgetary laws, and administrative changes. The president can also request urgency petitions and convoke extraordinary sessions. Executive proposals are automatically granted priority status for consideration in Congress, and with urgency motions (called *pedido de urgência*) the president can require Congress to expedite the examination of statutory bills. Should either house fail to conclude its deliberation of a bill under urgency regime within the deadline of forty-five days,[3] the deliberation of any other proposals is suspended in that house until the bill is voted on.

Presidents also have the prerogative to initiate budgetary laws and request additional budgetary credits during the year, tax collection permitting. The annual budget (called Annual Budgetary Law, or Lei Orçamentaria Anual) requires congressional approval to be effective, but its approval is not an automatic guarantee of its execution. In a given fiscal year, the Ministry of Finance monitors revenues and expenditures and exercises great discretion over the release of funds (Hiroi 2009). Known as the authorized budget (*orçamento autorizativo*) in Brazil, this prerogative grants presidents impressive leeway in deciding if and when budgetary funds will be transferred, especially the so-called voluntary (discretionary) transfers.[4]

Federal deputies and senators have the prerogative of presenting amendments to the budgetary law benefiting municipalities, states, and social organizations. Various studies have analyzed these transfers as forms of pork barrel politics (Ames 2001; Pereira and Renno 2003; Ames et al. 2011). After being approved as part of the annual budget law, the executive branch has the prerogative of deciding which and when budgetary amendments will be executed. Some authors argue that the execution of budgetary amendments is a bargaining tool of the executive branch, intermediated by party leaders, to increase support in floor votes (Ames 2001; Alston and Mueller 2005).

The most controversial among presidential prerogatives is probably the authority to issue executive decrees called provisional measures (*medida provisória* in Portuguese). Although the constitution allows the use of presidential decrees only in matters of "urgency and relevance" (Article 62), Brazilian presidents have used this prerogative in a wide range of areas—from purchasing an automobile for a vice president to outlawing bingo games, introducing new currencies, altering tax rates, and implementing economic stabilization plans. The range and frequency of policy changes enacted through presidential decrees have been such that many prominent members of Congress deplore that this constitutional authority is more authoritarian than the infamous institutional acts of the military regime.[5] Frustrated with the frequent use and coverage of presidential decrees, Congress attempted to regulate and restrict this powerful presidential power, which culminated in Constitutional Amendment No. 32 of 2001.

The 2001 constitutional amendment significantly curtailed the number of areas where decrees could be used. It also prohibits reissuing of decrees. Presidential decrees are now valid for sixty days, and are automatically renewed only once if Congress fails to vote on them expeditiously. The new rules also provide that the failure to vote on decrees within forty-five days triggers a suspension of deliberation of all other legislative activities in the respective house until final voting occurs. The modes of decree deliberation also changed. The constitutional amendment requires that a special joint committee of the National Congress (composed of senators and deputies) evaluate the urgency and need criteria before it could be voted on its merit. This joint committee, however, was never installed in practice until 2010, when deputies and senators reacted strongly against the abusive use of provisional measures (Renno 2010). Another major change introduced by the constitutional amendment is the sequential examination of decrees beginning in the Chamber of Deputies first, and then followed by the Senate, instead of requiring a joint session of the National Congress.

Some argue that the result of the 2001 reform was, ironically, an increase in the use of provisional measures (Pereira et al. 2008). The suspension of deliberation after forty-five days of the issuing of a provisional measure forces Congress to attend to the agenda of the executive branch. Therefore, presidents rely even more on provisional measures to further increase their control over the congressional agenda. In 2009, a new interpretation of the suspension clause emerged. Under the new interpretation, only ordinary law proposals would be blocked by a delay in a vote on a provisional measure, whereas complementary law proposals and constitutional amendments (along with all other types of legislative proposals) would not. Whether this change has had any effect in reducing presidential decrees is still being analyzed. Renno (2010) finds a reduction in decrees in the early aftermath of the reform, whereas Almeida (2011) has questioned these results with a slightly longer time frame.

The Brazilian president also has both partial and total veto powers. Although Congress can override the president's vetoes with the vote of an absolute majority of each chamber in a joint session, it has been very rare that Congress overrides presidential vetoes. Between 1988 and 2005, Congress overturned presidential vetoes only thirteen times (Hiroi 2005). Furthermore, Congress rarely votes on presidential vetoes in flagrant disrespect of the constitution. Only recently (in 2014) has Congress been forced to position itself in relation to prior vetoes that were not voted on, after a ruling by the

Federal Supreme Court. With the judicial ruling, Congress voted on hundreds of vetoes en masse, with almost all being sustained.

To sum up, the list of positive agenda setting powers held by presidents includes the prerogatives to issue provisional measures, originate any type of bill, and request urgency motions. Negative agenda setting powers used for gatekeeping include the exclusive power of initiation for administrative and budgetary bills, partial and total veto powers, and control over the disbursement of budgetary funds.

Congress

The Brazilian Congress consists of the Chamber of Deputies and the Federal Senate. Any member of Congress can propose a statutory bill. The most influential actors within each house are the presiding officer (Presidente) of the steering committee (Mesa), who retains agenda setting and gatekeeping powers, and party leaders, who appoint and discharge committee members and make recommendations for votes. The president of the Senate is also the president of Congress, presiding over joint meetings of the Chamber of Deputies and the Senate convened to analyze presidential vetoes.

In each house of Congress, the presiding officer is responsible for organizing the legislative agenda every month. In the Chamber of the Deputies, the presiding officer consults with the College of Leaders (Colégio de Líderes) composed of party leaders, minority and majority leaders, and a deputy representing the government. In the Senate, there is no equivalent leadership caucus, and therefore the presiding officer has even more leeway. In both houses, the presiding officer also arranges the order of the day (Ordem do Dia), indicating which legislative proposals will be moved to floor discussions that week. In the Chamber of Deputies, this occurs during the weekly meetings of the College of Leaders. This prerogative gives the presiding officer the ability not only to select the materials to be discussed but also to decide when they are voted on.

The presiding officers of the Chamber of Deputies and the Senate can also call for extraordinary daily sessions as needed, and jointly can convoke an extraordinary legislative session during seasons of congressional recess to deliberate on the materials of legislative priorities. They can also install ad hoc and special committees to consider issues of particular importance. Special committees are also automatically implemented when a bill is referred by the steering committee to more than three permanent committees to examine merit or, in the case of the Chamber of Deputies, to consider proposals for constitutional amendment.[6]

Party leadership also has significant control over the organization of legislative work in Congress. As discussed earlier, party leaders influence legislative priorities in the scheduling of the legislative agenda. Decisions in the College of Leaders are made by consensus whenever possible, and by an absolute majority of votes weighted by the size of each party when necessary. Party leaders also give vote recommendations to members of their parties and appoint (and discharge) their members to (or from) committees.

Party leaders and members of Congress also have many procedural prerogatives that may significantly affect the speed of decision-making within Congress. For instance, in the Chamber of Deputies, urgency motions (*regime de urgêngia*) may be presented (subject to approval by the plenary) by two-thirds of the members of the steering committee or one-third of the members of the house or party leaders representing this number. *Urgência urgentíssima*, a type of discharge petition requiring a bill to enter the order of the day immediately for discussion and votes, may be requested by an absolute majority of the chamber membership or party leaders representing this number and must be approved by an absolute majority in the plenary.

There are also procedures to delay discussion and votes. Party leaders, the rapporteur, and the author of a proposal may request postponing discussion and votes for up to ten days. A request for postponing the deliberation of materials examined under urgency regime and a request forcing a separate vote on distinct parts of a bill require a motion supported by one-tenth of the chamber members or party leaders representing this number.[7]

Committee membership in both houses is distributed to parties based on the proportionality principle. Party leaders appoint (and discharge) members to different committees. Each committee chooses its chairperson by a simple majority vote, and committee chairs designate rapporteurs for different proposals. Rapporteurs analyze bills and amendments submitted by committee members and make their recommendations about them. Each committee has forty legislative sessions to conclude its analysis, and rapporteurs must produce their reports within twenty days. It is up to the rapporteurs to decide, discretionarily, which amendments will be included in their reports. If rapporteurs fail to produce their reports within the deadline, they can ask for extensions. Committee chairs can accept the request or nominate another rapporteur, who will have five sessions to produce his or her report.[8]

The extent of changes on a bill proposed by rapporteurs varies. They can simply accept the initial bill without amendments, include amendments while maintaining the original text, or propose an altogether distinct bill, quite different from the original one, called a substitutive bill (*substitutivo do relator*). Rapporteurs and committee chairs who appoint them, therefore, are powerful actors in the legislative process. We can think of rapporteurs as agenda holders, as suggested by Silva and Araujo (2012), because of their control over the bill for a predefined period of time, with great influence on its content and destiny.

The committee then votes on the report that defines the amendments and any change proposed by the rapporteur. Committees make decisions by a simple majority vote. This vote is symbolic, by a raise of hands, or roll call, if there is a specific request for it. If the committee is unable to come to a decision, the bill may die a slow death at the committee stage without receiving a vote, unless a discharge petition is approved to bring the bill to the floor.

Bills classified as ordinary laws may be approved by the assigned committee and sent to the reviewer house dispensing with floor discussion and vote. This fast-track procedure, called conclusive power (in the Chamber of Deputies) or terminative power (in the Senate), allows for approval or rejection of this type of bills after being examined only by the relevant committees.[9] However, with the support of one-tenth of the members, deputies and senators can challenge the decisions made by the committees and bring the bill to a floor vote.

The most powerful committees in the Brazilian Congress are the Constitution, Justice, and Citizenship Committee (Comissão de Constituição e Justiça e de Cidadania), which verifies the legality of proposals in both houses, and Finance and Tax Committee (Comissão de Finanças e Tributação) in the Chamber of Deputies, which examines the financial viability of proposed projects. Both of these committees are gatekeepers, exercising negative agenda setting powers, with the prerogative to reject bills on the grounds of constitutionality and economic viability. After reforms in the early 1990s, the internal rules (Regimento Interno) of the Chamber of Deputies established that the evaluations of constitutionality and economic viability be issued after the debate on merit in the permanent committees with jurisdiction over a bill. This potentially weakened the gatekeeping capacity of the Constitution and Finance committees, as it may be more difficult to reject a bill that has already been approved by permanent committees.[10]

In a normal process (i.e., when the conclusive power does not apply), committees examine bills sequentially, and the ones approved by all committees then move to the plenary. If a committee rejects a bill, its examination by Congress typically ends. But committee decisions can be challenged with a request, supported by one-tenth of the house membership (or party leaders representing this number), to bring the bill to the plenary. In general, research on congressional committees is scarce in Brazil, and the actual powers of the committees are still relatively unknown.[11]

Referral of bills to multiple committees is common. For example, in the Chamber of Deputies,[12] all bills in principle must be referred to the Constitution Committee, which analyzes their constitutionality. All bills that have financial implications must also, in principle, be referred to the Finance and Tax Committee. In addition, bills are referred to other relevant committees to consider the merit of the proposals. As stated before, when the number of relevant committees to examine the merit of a proposal exceeds three, or when dealing with proposals for constitutional amendment, a special committee is formed to deliberate on the merit, rather than referring the bill to many standing committees. Committee deliberation is one area where many bills suffer a slow death, without ever reaching the plenary floor.

Decision Rules and Procedures

In Brazil there are three principal avenues of lawmaking through ordinary means: constitutional amendments and two types of statutory (ordinary and complementary) legislation. Complementary laws regulate provisions specifically referred to by the constitution. Ordinary laws are statutes that regulate areas not designated to complementary law. Article 60 of the constitution states that a constitutional amendment proposal may be submitted by: (1) at least one-third of the members of the Chamber of Deputies or of the Senate; (2) the President of the Republic; or (3) more than one-half of the Legislative Assemblies of the units of the Federation. In practice, all proposals for constitutional amendment have been submitted by the executive or Congress. The initial house of deliberation depends on the author of the proposal. The Chamber of Deputies is the first house to consider bills proposed by deputies and all executive proposals. The Senate is the initial house to consider bills proposed by senators. The initial house may approve the bill as it is, approve the bill with amendments, or reject the bill. An approval of a constitutional amendment proposal requires favorable votes by a three-fifths majority of its members taken by roll calls in two separate rounds. If the initial house approves the proposal, it moves to the second house for a review.

The reviewing house also has three options: approve the bill as it is, approve the bill with amendments, or reject the bill. If the reviewer house approves exactly the same text as the one approved by the first house, the steering committees of the Chamber of Deputies and the Senate promulgate the constitutional amendment. Constitutional amendments are not subject to presidential sanction or veto. If the reviewer house rejects the bill, it is sent to the archive. If the reviewer house approves the bill with amendments, the first house must consider the bill once again *as a new proposal.* It is worth re-emphasizing that the Brazilian constitution requires that an identical text of a constitutional amendment be approved by the two houses of Congress for enactment. Until an identical text is approved, the bill could shuttle between the two houses indefinitely until it is rejected or terminated. In addition, urgency may not be requested for an examination of constitutional amendments.

In both houses, committees review constitutional amendment proposals. As stated in the previous section, in the Chamber of Deputies, the Constitution Committee considers, in principle, all bills and produces reports on their admissibility. In the case of inadmissibility, the author of the proposal, with the support of at least one-third of deputies, may appeal to the floor to consider the reversal of the Constitution Committee's decision. If the Constitution Committee or the plenary floor votes in favor of admissibility, the presiding officer designates a special committee to examine the merit of the proposal. The special committee has forty sessions to produce its report. Amendments to the proposal must be submitted to the special committee with support by at least one-third of the chamber membership. After the examination by the special committee, the proposal moves to the plenary for discussion and vote.

In the Senate, the Committee on Constitution, Justice, and Citizenship analyzes the merit as well as the admissibility of constitutional amendment proposals. The Constitution Committee in the Senate has thirty days to submit a committee report. Following approval by the Constitution Committee, the plenary discusses the proposal for five sessions. Senators may submit amendments during these sessions with signatures of at least one-third of the members of the house. If no amendment is submitted, the bill is put for a vote at the fifth session. Should amendments be submitted, however, the bill returns to the Constitution Committee for their analysis. The proposal and amendments are voted on the floor after the Constitution Committee reports its analysis to the plenary.

Proposals for ordinary law and complementary law may be submitted by any of the following individuals or collectives within their competence: any member(s) or committee of the Chamber of Deputies, the Senate, or the National Congress; the President of the Republic; the Supreme Federal Court; the Superior Courts; the Prosecutor-General; and the citizens. An approval of a bill of ordinary law requires a simple majority whereas an approval of a bill of complementary law requires an absolute majority and roll call votes. Once a statutory bill is submitted, the presiding officer of the house distributes it to relevant committees, indicating whether the bill follows a normal or fast-tracking process. In the Chamber of Deputies, thematic committees and the Constitution Committee, in addition to the Finance and Tax Committee when it has financial or budgetary implications, examine statutory bills. In the Senate, only thematic committees examine these types of proposals. In the case of a fast-tracking process using conclusive or terminative power, members of the respective house submit amendments to the committees and the reporting officers prepare their analyses of the bill and amendments and make recommendations. The committees then vote on the bill and amendments. With committee approval, the proposal is forwarded to the second house for a review. In the case of rejection, it goes to the archive. As discussed in the previous section, deputies and senators who do not agree with the committee decision may appeal to the plenary if they have the support of at least one-tenth of their house membership.

Bills considered under the normal regime will move to the plenary for discussion and votes after committee examinations. The presiding officer of the house, in consultation with party leaders, determines when these bills enter the order of the day. Once included in the order of the day, deputies (or senators if the bill is initiated in the Senate) have five legislative sessions to present amendments, which are then sent to the relevant committees. Next, rapporteurs elaborate their reports on the floor amendments. The steering committee will then include the bill and accompanying reports again in the order of the day.

Inclusion in the order of the day is a very high hurdle, and it is at this point that the president of the steering committee very clearly exercises his agenda power. Inclusion in the order of the day then leads to debate on the floor and votes. Very few bills reach this stage of the process. Moreover, few bills that enter the order of the day are rejected; those bills are included precisely because they have the support of the party leaders for plenary deliberation. Hence, inclusion in the order of the day is a sign that there is enough agreement over content, at least among the majority, for the bill's approval. Conversely, the wait period may represent a slow death for the bill. Because of this, legislators and party leaders may request a discharge petition as a strategy to stop or slow down the processing of a bill. Discharge petitions remove ordinary bills subject to deliberation by conclusive power from committees and move them to plenary deliberation. Those bills then enter a long waiting list for inclusion in the order of the day. Thus, discharge petitions can paradoxically lead to delays in the final evaluation of a legislative proposal, even though they dispense with the committee stage of the legislative process.[13]

In both houses, if there is a substitutive bill prepared by the bill's rapporteur, the floor votes on it first. If it is approved, the floor subsequently votes on amendments and specific parts of the bill. If there is no substitutive bill or if it is rejected, then the original bill will be voted on, followed by votes on amendments and specific parts of the bill. Members of each house can contest the rapporteur's decision to reject amendments on the floor. Once bills are approved on the floor, they proceed to the reviewer house.

As with the case of constitutional amendment proposals, the reviewer house may approve statutory bills as they come from the initial house (i.e., without amendments), approve them with amendments, or reject them. Proposals received from the first house are examined by a committee or committees first, and, with favorable committee report, proceed to the plenary. If a bill is approved without amendments, the reviewer house sends the approved text to the president for enactment (or vetoing). If the reviewer house approves the bill but modifies the text, the bill is returned to the initial house for a review of the changes made by the second house. Unlike constitutional amendments, it is the prerogative of the initial house to accept or reject the modifications made by the reviewer house. In other words, the initial house may disregard all the amendments of the reviewer house and send its original text to the president. Hence, there is a substantial advantage to be the first house to consider statutory bills. Nevertheless, the reviewer house does have the power to veto bills sent by the other house.

Finally, Brazilian legislators have many instruments to obstruct or fast-track decisions. For example, legislators can ask for quorum and vote verifications, which change the votes from symbolic to roll call. They can also maneuver procedural rules by asking for votes on separate aspects of a bill, by requesting that discussion be postponed, or by requesting that a proposal be removed completely from the agenda. Such tactics may reconfigure the contexts of bargaining inside Congress. Indeed, the use of such instruments is on the rise in Brazil (Inácio 2009; Hiroi and Renno 2014).

Votes by which legislators can clearly delay legislative business include request for the removal of proposals from the order of the day, request to delay discussion and vote, and request to separately vote on different articles of a bill. Request for a removal of a proposal from the agenda may also be used as a defensive maneuver to avoid a defeat. In either case, it delays a final vote.

On the other hand, there are votes to expedite decision-making, such as urgency petitions or requests for termination of discussion, or agglutination of several amendments in a single one. A motion to invert the order in which a bill will be voted on can be used to delay a vote of interest in exchange for a less conflictual one, or to bring a more important vote to the top of the agenda.

There are also votes on substantive issues regarding the content of policy proposals. These can be in the form of a vote on an ordinary or complementary law proposal, constitutional amendment, or executive decree. However, some types of substantive votes may also result in prolonged debate. For instance, votes on a specific article that received a request for exclusive evaluation, a vote on an amendment, and votes on proposal reports (*pareceres*) all incur longer deliberation of single bills. Delays occur because they are split up and voted separately, generating a large number of votes on a single proposal.

In summary, the legislative process is long and arduous. Approving a bill in the committee or on the floor is not an easy task and transforming it into law is even harder given the requirement for bicameral approval and presidential ratification.

TAKING ACTORS' POSITIONS INTO ACCOUNT

In post-democratization Brazil, the ideological and policy positions of parties and their members have spanned from the left to the right. There are leftist parties, led by the Workers' Party (PT); centrist parties, represented mainly by the Brazilian Democratic Movement Party (PMDB) and Brazilian Social Democracy Party (PSDB); and right-wing parties, such as the Democrats Party (DEM, former PFL) and the Progressive Party (PP), which are diminishing in size in recent years.

Heterogeneous coalition members mean more distance between their preferred policy positions. If members of the coalition are veto players (Tsebelis 2002), heterogeneity implies a diminished winset size for policy change (see Chapter 1 of this book), thus making effective coalition management even more imperative. The governing coalitions of Presidents Cardoso, Lula (after the first year), and Rousseff have all been oversized, including diverse mixes of political parties. The coalitions of Lula and Rousseff were particularly heterogeneous, including parties that are positioned on the far left and on the far right (see Table 3.1 for party positions). Although the composition of governing coalitions typically shifts during a presidential term, for example, during Lula's two terms, the number of parties gaining cabinet positions was approximately nine. Between 2007 and 2009, ten parties from the left to the right (PT, PTB, PR, PMDB, PV, PDT, PSB, PP, PCdoB, and PRB) held cabinet posts. During Rousseff's first term, her coalition was even larger in size than Lula's and as heterogeneous as that of her predecessor. Such heterogeneous coalitions could exacerbate the problems of coalition unity. Even though a recent study shows an attitudinal convergence of Brazilian deputies on many fundamental questions (Power and Zucco 2012), the increase in governing coalition size and coverage in recent years appears to have shifted the major arenas of legislative conflict from that between government and opposition to that within the governing coalition.

Besides partisan differences, the literature on bicameralism indicates that bicameral incongruence is an important cause of legislative delay and gridlock (Tsebelis and Money 1997; Hiroi 2008a, 2008b). In Brazil, the upper and lower

Table 3.1 Brazilian parties from left to right, 1990–2009

Year												
									PL			
1990									PDC			
	PCdoB	PT	PCB	PSB	PDT	PSDB	PMDB	PTB	PRN	PFL	PDS	
1993		PT								PL		
	PCdoB	PSTU	PSB	PPS	PDT	PSDB	PMDB	PP	PTB	PFL	PPR	PRN
1997			PSB				PTB		PFL			
	PCdoB	PT	PPS	PDT	PMDB	PSDB	PR	PL	PPB			
2001					PMDB	PL						
	PCdoB	PT	PSB	PDT	PSDB	PTB	PFL	PPB				
2005		PT	PPS	PMDB	PTB	PFL						
	PCdoB	PSB	PDT	PSDB	PL	PP						
2009			PT				PMDB	PTB				
	PSOL	PCdoB	PSB	PDT	PV	PPS	PSDB	PR	PP	DEM		

Notes: Stacked parties, in any given year, indicate that the differences between their estimated positions are *not* statistically different at the 0.10 confidence level. All other adjacent parties are statistically different from one another.
Source: Based on data provided in an earlier version of Power and Zucco (2012).

chambers may well have different policy positions. The sources of bicameral incongruence include different electoral rules to select their membership. In Brazil, senators are elected by a majoritarian rule for an eight-year term and deputies by open-list proportional representation for a four-year term. The two houses also tend to differ on the political experiences of their members. Most of the senators have extensive political experiences; the Senate has had members who have served as presidents of the republic, vice presidents, ministers, governors, and federal deputies (Hiroi and Neiva 2013). Federal deputies' political experiences pale in comparison, although there are several members with long and distinguished political careers. The political experiences of senators tend to make them more sympathetic to issues related to public finance and administration than deputies. As such, the Senate has been considered more "*governista*" than the Chamber of Deputies, rendering more cooperation with the executive branch in the amendment and passage of bills, coming scratched from the lower house. However, this relationship may have changed recently, especially during President Lula's period. Research in Brazilian bicameralism is still scarce, but existing studies indicate that bicameral incongruence does affect both the speed and approval of legislative proposals (Hiroi 2008a).

HYPOTHESES

The interaction between Brazil's legislative institutions and procedures and policy positions of relevant actors generate interesting hypotheses. Our first hypotheses refer to presidents' ability to advance their policy agenda in Congress. As discussed earlier, presidents possess various agenda setting prerogatives and tools to move forward their legislative proposals and block legislation they do not support. In addition, presidents' allies in Congress usually occupy important positions endowed with additional positive and negative agenda setting powers, such as the leadership in the steering committee. We therefore expect high success rates of executive proposals relative to those of congressional proposals.

> *H1. Executive proposals are more likely to be approved, and approved faster, than congressional proposals.*
> *H2. The government's position will be on the winning side in most roll call votes.*

Despite the agenda setting powers that favor the president, there are many hindrances to proposal approval due to numerous hurdles built into the legislative process, such as qualified majority rules, multiple veto points in the committee stage, many instruments for legislative obstruction, requirement for concurrent approval of the two distinct houses of the legislature, and other intricacies of the legislative process. These rules provide abundant opportunities for the members of Congress to stamp their marks on the executive proposals. Hence, even if many executive proposals pass Congress, we expect that those bills, particularly major bills that propose significant change, will be altered by Congress.

> *H3. Congress will amend many executive proposals and most major bills initiated by the executive.*

In addition, as discussed in the introductory chapter of this volume, ideological distances between the key legislative actors have implications for policy change. Thus, we examine the ideological distances between legislative actors, not only the distance between the governing and opposition coalitions but also distances within legislative coalitions, in order to fully understand the legislative processes and outcomes. In Brazil, since coalitions are the major legislative forces, we need to examine the cohesiveness of legislative coalitions and coalition management. We define coalition cohesiveness as the ability of the members of the coalition to act in unity in legislative matters. Lack of cohesion within a governing coalition represents a smaller winset of the status quo because the distance between political actors within the coalition is high. Conversely, a cohesive coalition represents actors that are closer together and hence a larger winset. We expect that an uncohesive government coalition will create more bargaining difficulties and more obstruction, generating delay in legislative approval.

H4. The less cohesive the governing coalition, the more bargaining and obstruction there will be in the legislative process, leading to a greater delay in the passage of bills.

On the other hand, lack of cohesion in opposition coalitions would result in the opposite effect: a heterogeneous group of opposition parties may not be able to function as a unified front to counterbalance the forces of the governing coalition. In contrast, oppositions' ability to obstruct the legislative process and frustrate the governing coalition should be high when they are united. Given the massive institutional and resource advantage of the executive branch and its congressional allies that usually control the agenda setters' positions and majority seats, we expect that the oppositions' influence is observed mostly in obstructing the legislative process and delaying and amending proposals that will be approved.

H5. The more cohesive the opposition coalition, the greater its ability to engage in dilatory practices, leading to a greater delay in the passage of bills.

The distribution of patronage, especially in the allocation of cabinet posts among coalition partners, is presidents' essential tool for coalition management. Presidents strategically allocate ministerial portfolios as a means to construct a legislative coalition (Amorim Neto 2006). The distribution of cabinet positions affects the division of power among coalition members. The better distributed these resources, the more satisfied coalition members, and hence the fewer disputes there are internally. If parties participating in the coalition do not share these positions in a seemingly "fair" manner, dissatisfied coalition partners may impede or threaten to impede proposed legislation until satisfactory reallocation of these posts is undertaken (Amorim Neto 2002).

H6. The less proportional the distribution of cabinet posts among coalition partners relative to their legislative weights, the more bargaining and obstruction there will be in the legislative process, leading to a greater delay in the passage of bills.

The traditional literature on legislative conflict in presidential systems has emphasized government–opposition conflict. If a line separating the government and opposition exists in a meaningful way, such as along the line of ideological or policy disputes, and if there is an opposition large enough to override or attenuate the institutional advantages of the president, then the larger the distance between governing coalition and opposition, the less likely legislative proposals would be approved. The following hypothesis suggests how the ideological distance between the two coalitions affects legislative expediency.

H7. The greater the ideological divide between the opposition and the government coalition, the more obstruction there will be in the legislative process and hence the greater the delay in the passage of bills.

Brazil's legislature has a symmetric bicameral structure.[14] Legislative approval requires sequential examination by the two houses. There is no practice of a conference committee to resolve bicameral disputes, although bicameral joint committees are occasionally created.[15] Incongruence between the two houses is likely to lead to disagreements over policy change, which in turn should generate a greater delay in approval.

H8. The greater the incongruence between the upper and lower houses of Congress, the more time it will take for a bill to be approved.

DATA

We test the hypotheses using data on individual bills submitted to the Brazilian Congress between 1995 and 2003 and roll call votes that occurred in the Chamber of Deputies between 2003 and 2011.[16] The roll call data include all roll call votes that occurred during this period, covering the two Lula da Silva terms and the beginning of Dilma Rousseff's term. The proposal dataset covers the two terms of Fernando Henrique Cardoso (1995–8 and 1999–2002) and the initial year of Lula da Silva's first term (2003–6).

The proposal data track the fate of individual bills submitted to Congress between 1995 and 2003. The dataset consists of proposals for constitutional amendment and two types of statutory bills—ordinary and complementary. It does not include presidential decrees (provisional measures) because they are not bills. The dataset includes all executive and judicial proposals that were introduced in Congress. With respect to congressional proposals, the dataset includes all bills submitted and subsequently approved at least by the house of origin.[17] By this method, we are in practice examining *institutional* bills that passed the initial internal deliberation process. We thus call these bills "institutional" bills, and when referring to "all" bills in the subsequent discussion, we are referring to all of these institutional bills in our sample.

We are interested in the approval of bills and how long it takes for a bill to be approved. We converted the proposal data into monthly data and traced, in days, the histories of these bills from their introduction to Congress by assigning a series of 0s for each observational period until their approval, at which time a value of 1 is assigned. Bills that were terminated for reasons other than their passage (e.g., rejection, withdrawal by the author, or simply termination of deliberation at the end of a legislative period) are treated as censored at the time of the decision.[18] In the case of pending bills, their histories are traced until July 31, 2004, on which date they "exit" the dataset. This cut-off date was determined by the availability of data in the dataset.

ANALYSIS

To probe the hypotheses outlined in the previous section, we examine descriptive statistics and then statistically analyze the passage of time in Congress until a legislative proposal is approved.

Descriptive Statistics

Bills' fates in Congress likely depend on their salience. To measure issue salience, we first identified legislative issues that appeared on the first page and in the politics section of *Folha de São Paulo*, a leading newspaper in Brazil, during the first years of the first and second terms of President Cardoso and the first term of President Lula. We coded not only the explicit mention of a law proposal, but also more general issues that would be on Congress' agenda, such as "tax reform," and "social security reform." We then identified these issues with the specific bills dealing with the topics.

Table 3.2 presents the number of major bills mentioned by the *Folha* during the first years of the Cardoso and Lula administrations. First, it is interesting to

Table 3.2 Number of proposals mentioned by the media, 1995, 1999, 2003

Media mention	Cardoso—1994	Cardoso—1998	Lula—2002
Proposals not mentioned by the media	628	862	82
Proposals mentioned by the media	16 (8)	7 (1)	2 (2)

Note: The figures in parentheses represent executive proposals.
Source: Compiled by the authors.

notice the small number of such proposals, totaling only twenty-five cases of all institutional bills that were submitted during this period. This is partly due to the fact that Brazilian presidents often rely on issuing decrees, which effects instant change, rather than proposing bills, which will be subject to long congressional deliberation. Some of these decrees received intense media coverage, but they are not included in the table because they are not legislative proposals.

We also note that the majority of legislative action regarding major bills occurred during the Cardoso administration. This is not surprising given that Cardoso's legislative coalition during his first term was assembled based on a pact of economic modernization and reform. During the first year, a number of major constitutional amendments dealing with economic issues were proposed and subsequently approved.

In contrast, only two major bills were proposed during the Lula period in our dataset. This is partly because we only have one year of proposal initiation during the Lula government in our dataset. But it is also because the Lula government considered two constitutional amendment proposals (pension reform and tax reform) as its hallmark legislation and focused on the passage of these proposals within the first year.[19] Still, the number of mentions at the beginning of Lula's first term, in comparison to Cardoso's first term, is much lower.

Of the sixteen major bills considered during Cardoso's first term, the executive branch presented eight proposals. This is the highest level of activity by the executive branch during the period under investigation. During Cardoso's second term, of the seven major bills, the executive initiated only one. During Lula's first term, the executive branch originated both major bills. Thus, fourteen major bills originated in the legislative branch and eleven in the executive branch.

The passage rates of major bills indicate greater success rates of the executive branch compared to those of Congress. During the Cardoso periods, all but one major bill proposed by the executive was approved, whereas only one-half of the major bills initiated by the legislative branch were approved. Both of Lula's bills were approved. Hence, if we focus on the passage rates, the executive branch is twice as successful as the legislative branch in approving major bills.

In general, the executive branch is more successful than Congress in getting its legislation enacted. Figure 3.1 presents the proportion of institutional bills that were enacted by administration and origin.[20] During the first Cardoso term, 64 percent of all the executive proposals were enacted into law, compared to 29 percent of the congressional proposals. During Cardoso's second term, the enactment rate dropped for both branches; only 40 percent of the executive proposals and 20 percent of the congressional proposals were

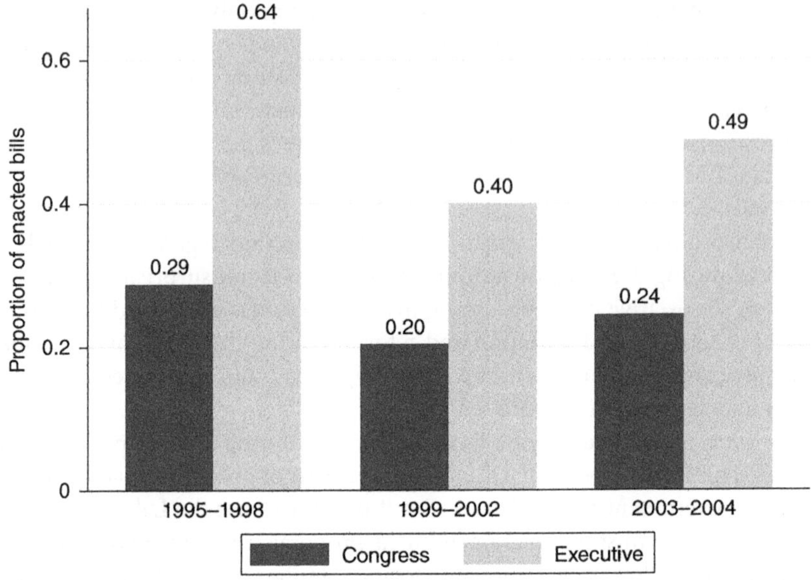

Figure 3.1 Proportion of enacted bills by origin

enacted. During the first nineteen months of Lula's presidency (January 2003 through July 2004) in the dataset, the enactment rates slightly improved: 49 percent for the executive proposals, and 24 percent for congressional proposals. Even though the enactment rates of the executive proposals pale compared to those of the Brazilian counterparts in Latin America (see other chapters in this volume), in all three periods, executive proposals fared much better than congressional proposals. Holding agenda setting powers pays off.

However, a simple passage rate may mask many challenges to bill approval. Figure 3.2 illustrates how long it took for bills to pass in Congress.[21] It shows that executive proposals tend to be approved much faster than congressional proposals. Still, only 15 percent of the executive bills are approved by Congress within the first three months after their introduction, and about a half stay in Congress for 840 days or longer.

We analyze the results of roll call votes in the Chamber of Deputies to evaluate whether the government is on the winning side of most votes. Table 3.3 presents the percentage of roll calls in which the position of the government leader is on the winning side when the roll call results in the approval or rejection of the proposal or procedural request. The column "total votes" indicates the absolute number of roll call votes of each type (obstruction, fast-track, and substantive) that were approved (in the first part of the

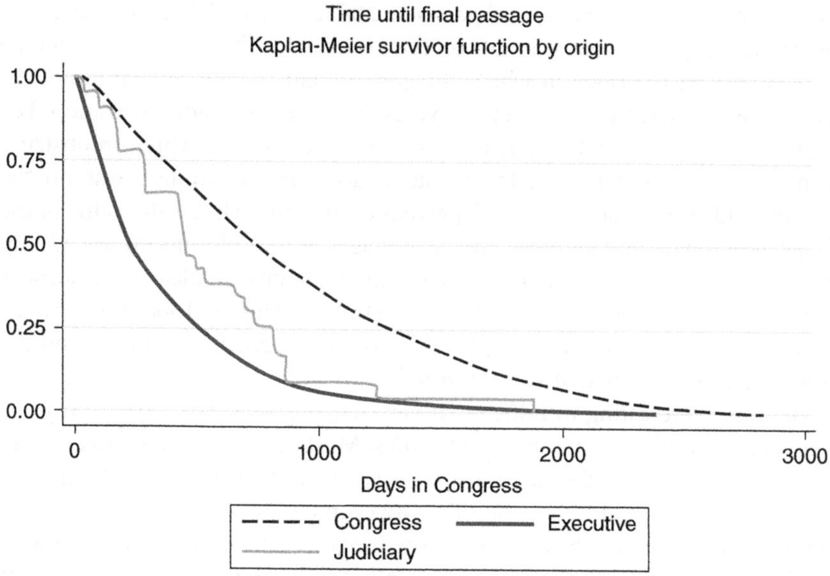

Figure 3.2 Time for passage of legislative proposals by origin

Table 3.3 Percentage of roll call votes in which government position is on the winning side, 2003–2011

	Lula I	Lula II	Rousseff*	Total votes (including those in which government is on the losing side)
	Approval and government yes vote			
Obstruction	85 (6)	50 (4)	–	15
Fast-track	82 (78)	76 (94)	100 (8)	227
Substantive	75 (83)	78 (154)	66 (6)	315
	Rejection and government no vote			
Obstruction	83 (122)	89 (149)	60(9)	347
Fast-track	75 (9)	57 (12)	–	33
Substantive	84 (53)	70 (54)	83(5)	146

Note: The figures in parentheses represent the number of times the government was on the winning side. The total votes column contains the total number of roll call votes in each situation for the entire period, covering all three administrations. It also includes roll call votes in which the government was on the losing side. For this reason, percentages and absolute values do not add up.

* It covers only one year (2011) of the Rousseff administration.

Source: Compiled by the authors based on data from the FSB Institute.

table) and rejected (in the second part of the table). This total includes roll calls in which the government was also on the losing side. The percentages include only values for the cases in which the government was on the winning side. These are calculated in relation to all votes of each type by administration. For example, during Lula's first term, there were seven roll call votes on obstructionist procedures approved by the floor, and the government was on the winning side for six of them, or 85 percent of the time. That is the value of the first cell in the table. Therefore, the percentages of the columns do not add up by row. The column with total values is included to give an idea of the number of votes of each type during each administration. Hence, Table 3.3 contains information that allows us to explore the use of obstructionist moves and the government's incidence of victory in roll call votes.

First, it is interesting to notice that very few obstructionist votes (only 15) were approved in the Chamber of Deputies. Most of these requests (347) were rejected. Nonetheless, obstructionist votes represent a third of all roll call votes (362 votes) in the entire period. The government is predominantly on the winning side when an obstructionist vote is rejected: 83 percent of the time in Lula's first term, 89 percent of the time in Lula's second term, and 60 percent of the time in Rousseff's first year. Interestingly, during Lula's first term, the government was on the winning side of 85 percent of the approved obstructionist moves, but this tendency decreases steeply in Lula's second term and Rousseff's first year. Still, absolute values of these votes for these years are very small. On the other hand, the government usually gets its way on fast-track moves and on substantive votes, both in approving bills and requests it favors and in rejecting those it opposes. The table thus shows that the government is usually on the winning side in all of these measures. Yet, it is also important to underline that the government's position is on the losing side in about one in five votes despite the tremendous institutional and resource advantages discussed previously.

Next, we examine our hypotheses on the role of Congress in influencing the lawmaking process. The dark-shaded bars in Figure 3.3 indicate the proportion of approved executive or congressional bills that received substitutive bills and/or floor amendments to all institutional proposals with executive or legislative origins.[22] It shows high levels of congressional activity in altering legislative proposals, with 60 percent of executive proposals and 46 percent of congressional proposals receiving substitutive bills and/or amendments in the plenary. Moreover, the light-shaded bars show that over 30 percent of approved executive and congressional proposals are amended through these means.

Among the major bills (which are not shown in the figure), 43 percent of congressional proposals and nearly all (90 percent) of executive proposals

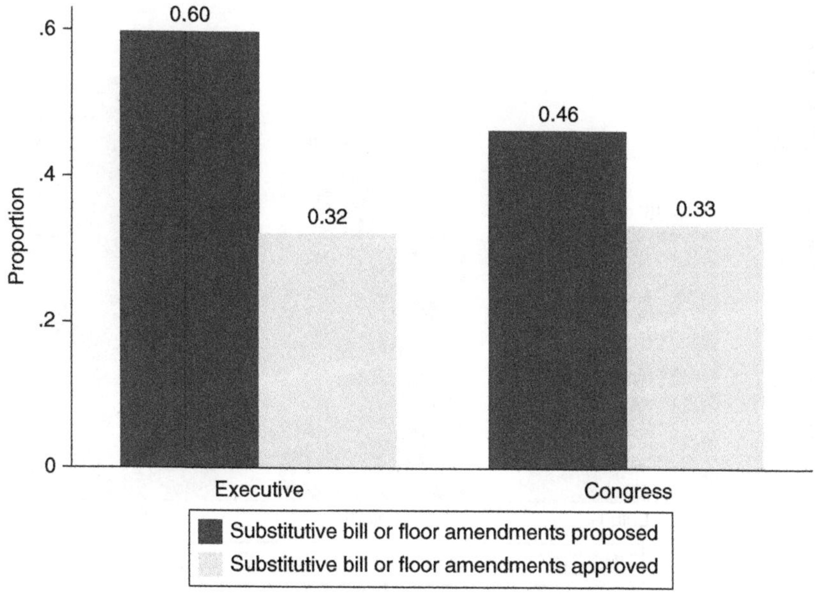

Figure 3.3 Proportion of approved bills that received substitutive bills or floor amendments

were amended. This provides strong support for H3. These data indicate that although Brazilian presidents may be quite successful in getting their proposals approved by Congress, a point demonstrated by the relative proposal approval rates, as we argued, they are far from completely dominating the legislative process. Congress amends many executive proposals and most major bills initiated by the executive. Therefore, even though Brazilian presidents may enjoy a high passage rate, they still must work with an active Congress that exerts significant influence on the content of legislation. Since many amendments occur in committees and since this measure does not capture committee amendments that were not incorporated in substitutive bills, the actual proportion of amended bills is even greater. The Brazilian Congress certainly is not a rubber-stamping institution.

Moreover, legislative obstruction is increasingly common in Brazil. Figure 3.4 indicates that the opposition is the main proposer of obstructionist moves, albeit the difference is not as substantive as one would expect, especially during the Lula administration. It is also interesting that many obstructionist moves are also born from within the governing coalition, which indicates potential trouble in its coalition management during the PT presidential administrations. Although legislative obstructionism from within the governing coalition diminished during the first year of Dilma Rousseff's term

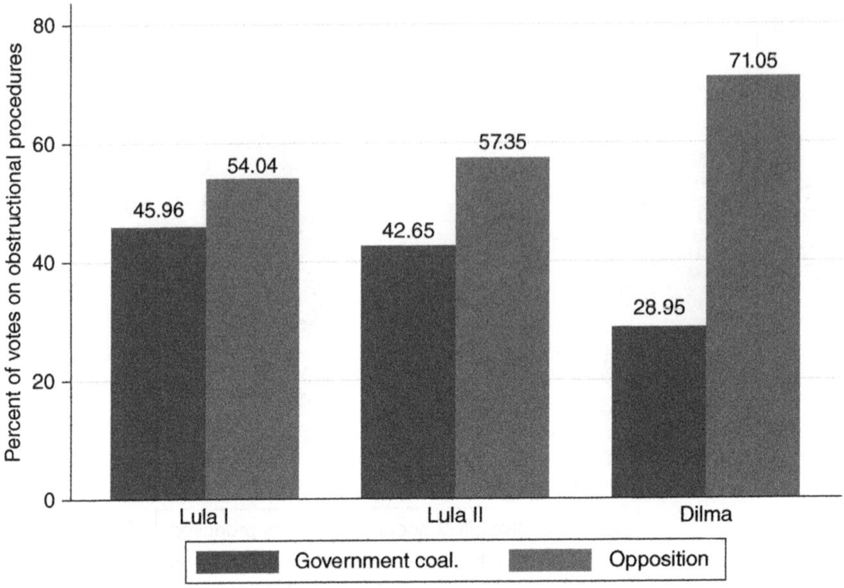

Figure 3.4 Percentage of obstructionist movements by coalition
Note: This covers only one year (2011) of the Dilma Rousseff administration.

(2011), available evidence indicates that the president faced a series of obstructions and rebellions by members of the governing coalition in subsequent years. Thus, the analysis of obstructionist movements suggests that oppositions are not the only challenges to Brazilian presidents. In fact, many challenges also spring from the legislative coalitions they put together with the intention to facilitate governing (Hiroi and Renno 2014).

Event History Analysis of Legislative Approval

As we have discussed, how long it takes for a bill to be approved is a great concern for many. Comparatively speaking, the legislative process in Brazil is slow. Figure 3.5 shows the Kaplan-Meier estimates of survivor functions for approved bills, rejected bills, and all bills in the sample. It indicates that most approved bills have their decisions made relatively "quickly" (given the Brazilian norm); approximately 80 percent of the approved bills have their passage within the first 1,000 days. In contrast, decisions to reject involve a rather prolonged process, with less than half of the rejected bills having their

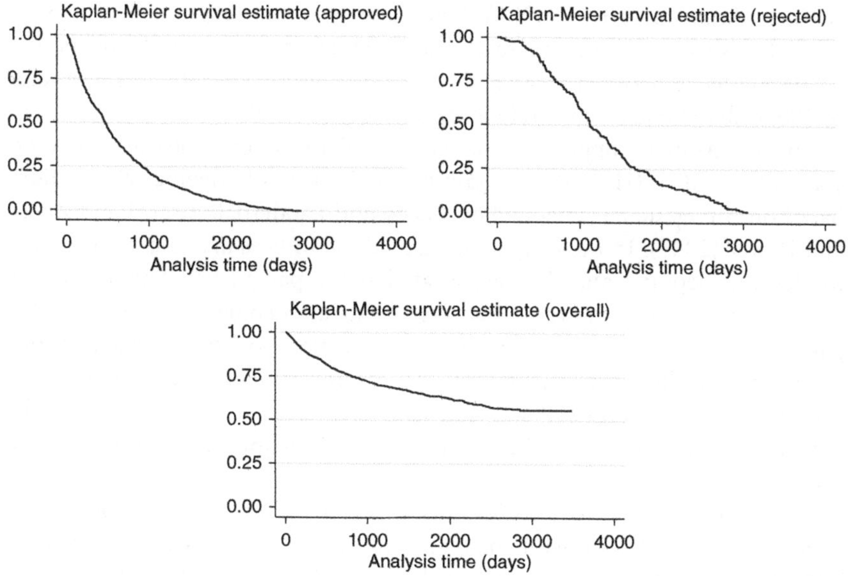

Figure 3.5 Kaplan-Meier survival estimates of bills in the Brazilian Congress, 1995–2004

deliberations concluded within 1,000 days of their initial introduction. However, some of the approved bills also suffered protracted deliberations in Congress: 4.5 percent of approved bills passed Congress after more than 2,000 days of their journey in the institution. These data demonstrate that there is a significant variation in the timing of their passage.

In this section, we test hypotheses 1 (executive proposals) and 4 through 8. Cohesiveness of the governing coalition (H4) and opposition (H5) is measured by the Rice Index of Cohesion, calculated by an absolute difference in the percentages of those voting yes and those voting no in a coalition. We computed a monthly index for each of these coalitions using every roll call vote recorded in Cebrap's legislative database for the Chamber of Deputies. We use the mean of the Rice Index during three preceding months because any particular month's index may reflect the nature of the specific vote taken rather than the degree of cohesion in general. We call these variables government coalition unity and opposition unity, respectively.

We use cabinet coalescence rates as a proxy for coalition management by the government (H6). Cabinet coalescence rates measure the proportionality in percentages between the shares of congressional seats in the Chamber of Deputies held by the parties in government and their ministerial shares in the cabinet (Amorim Neto 2002). When there is no correspondence between cabinet shares and legislative seats, the index takes a value of 0, and perfect correspondence between cabinet shares and legislative weights takes a value of 100. Cabinet coalescence rate is lagged by one month.

The government–opposition ideological divide is our measure of inter-coalition conflict (H7). It uses composite indices of ideological positions based on survey items generated by Zucco and Lauderdale (2011) and Zucco and Power (2009). In the original dataset, these indices are first calculated at the level of deputies and then aggregated at the party level. The ideological divide variable is the difference between the mean ideological positions of the parties that compose the governing or opposition coalition, lagged by one month. Finally, bicameral incongruence is our measure of the conflict between upper and lower houses (H8). It is measured by an absolute difference in the percentage share of seats held by the governing coalition in the upper and lower houses.

Coalition unity, cabinet coalescence rates, government–opposition ideological divide, and bicameral incongruence are all time-varying covariates. Thus, it is possible that the values of these variables change from the time of proposal initiation during the course of the deliberative process.

The analysis also includes the following control variables: judicial proposal, different majority requirements to approve a bill, whether or not bills were considered under the regime of urgency, whether substitutive bills were proposed, number of floor amendments submitted, issue salience of the bill, provisional legislation, and time to election. The number of floor amendments is logged. Issue salience is indicated by appearances in the *Folha de São Paulo* (see previous discussion), lagged by one month. Time to election counts the number of months until general elections. We estimate the timing of approval with Cox regression.

Estimation Results

The results of Cox regression analysis of the passage of bills are shown in Table 3.4. Variables that violated the proportional hazards assumption based on the analysis of Schoenfeld residuals were interacted with a natural logarithm of time. The results are interesting and revealing, but at the same time, we must be careful about generalizing these findings because the analysis is based on only nine years of record, mostly during the period of President Cardoso. Nonetheless, the results of the analysis support many of our hypotheses.

Table 3.4 Event history analysis of bills' passage in the Brazilian Congress, 1995–2004

Executive proposal	5.51***
	(0.87)
Executive proposal*ln(t)	−0.78***
	(0.14)
Government coalition unity	0.01
	(0.01)
Opposition unity	−0.01***
	(0.003)
Cabinet coalescence	0.27***
	(0.06)
Cabinet coalescence*ln(t)	−0.04***
	(0.01)
Ideological distance	0.16
	(0.27)
Bicameral incongruence	3.66***
	(1.36)
Control variables	
Judicial proposal	−0.09
	(2.41)
Judicial proposal*ln(t)	0.22
	(0.38)
Supermajority	0.47**
	(0.23)
Absolute majority	−0.16
	(0.21)
Urgency	9.48***
	(1.14)
Urgency*ln(t)	−1.23***
	(0.18)
Substitutive bill	−1.99***
	(0.68)
Substitutive bill*ln(t)	0.26**
	(0.11)
Floor amendments (logged)	−0.69**
	(0.28)
Floor amendments *ln(t)	0.17***
	(0.05)

(*continued*)

Table 3.4 Continued

Issue salience	6.34***
	(1.25)
Issue salience *ln(t)	−0.78***
	(0.22)
Provisional legislation	1.43***
	(0.23)
Month to election	−0.01*
	(0.004)
N	66,134
Wald Chi-Square	708.71

Note: The estimation used Cox regression with the Efron method for ties. Entries are coefficients. Robust standard errors clustered on individual bills are in parentheses. * p<0.10, ** p<0.05, and *** p<0.01, two-tailed tests.

As expected, how well coalitions are managed influences the speed of legislation. The coefficient of cabinet coalescence is positive and significant, indicating that greater proportionality in the allocation of cabinet positions among coalition partners contributes to swifter bill approval. However, the negative coefficient of this variable interacted with time suggests that this effect wanes with the passage of time. In other words, proportional allocation of cabinet posts has greater influence initially, but as bills linger in Congress without decision, its effect diminishes.

The analysis also reveals that a united opposition is a major hindrance to legislative approval and significantly slows the deliberation process. On the other hand, neither the cohesiveness of the governing coalition nor the ideological distance between the governing coalition and opposition has a statistically significant impact on the timing of passage. In addition, the analysis shows effects of bicameral incongruence that are contrary to our hypothesis and findings by prior research. We find that during the period under investigation, bicameral differences in the governing coalition had a positive, not negative, effect on proposal passage. One possible explanation is related to the peculiarities of the time being analyzed. The variable's positive coefficient may be an artifact of large majorities President Cardoso enjoyed throughout his two terms. That is, the variable may be reflecting the degree of an oversized coalition in one of the houses, which is likely to help bills' passage, rather than the effect of a bicameral divergence.

Finally, as we already know from the analysis of descriptive statistics, the Cox regression analysis confirms that executive proposals are more likely to have faster approval than congressional proposals, demonstrating the importance of agenda setting powers. Interestingly, the analysis also shows the diminishing effect of executive proposals over time; with the passage of time, executive proposals tend to lose the advantage of being executive proposed.

To summarize, our data analysis found support for hypotheses on executive proposals (H1), coalition management (H6), and opposition unity (H5). It points to the importance of analyzing agenda setting powers and politics within coalitions.

CONCLUSION

In this chapter we explore how various institutional and partisan factors influence lawmaking in Brazil, a paradigmatic case of coalitional presidentialism. Using data on legislative proposals and roll call votes, we test implications of the analysis of institutional prerogatives, policy distances between major actors, and the interactions between these factors.

Our empirical analysis confirms a significant agenda setting advantage of the executive branch in advancing its legislative agenda. However, executive proposals do not pass unscarred by Congress or without the long and arduous process of bargaining and legislative obstruction. The evidence clearly indicates that the legislative branch has an appetite for amending legislative proposals, and obstruction and delay are more common than previously acknowledged.

Comparison of Brazilian presidents with other Latin American presidents indicates that the approval rate of executive proposals in Brazil is the lowest of any Latin American president examined in this volume. The difficulties of dealing with wide coalitions with actors that have very different goals and preferences severely limit what the president can get passed in the normal legislative process. It is through the use of agenda setting powers, particularly provisional presidential decrees, that the record of the Brazilian executive comes closer to those of other presidents in Latin America.

All in all, however, the Brazilian case seems as one in which the institutional mechanisms for agenda setting allow for legislative bills to be approved, permitting a certain degree of governability. Yet, this does not happen, as once thought, based exclusively on the wishes and powers of the executive branch. In fact, the institutional design of the legislative process creates opportunities for shared responsibility over lawmaking between the executive and legislative branches.

NOTES

1. Some scholars even claim that the allocation of positions in the cabinet indicates a shared policy platform and agenda between all members of the coalition, instead of simple patronage (Figueiredo and Limongi 1999). However, evidence of this shared agenda among coalition members has not been sufficiently demonstrated.
2. This excludes legislative decrees called *decretos legislativos*.
3. Strictly speaking, both the constitution and the internal rules of Congress refer to sessions. When considering deadlines, we use sessions and days interchangeably.
4. The government has less flexibility with constitutionally defined transfers.
5. See, for example, "Uso abusivo de MPs contraria Congresso," *Jornal do Brasil*, January 29, 1995, p. 3; and "Congresso limitará edição de MP," *Jornal do Brasil*, October 23, 1995.
6. During the 54th legislature, the Chamber of Deputies had twenty permanent committees with predefined jurisdictions, thirty-six special committees to deal with specific topics and constitutional amendments, and eight external committees, which followed some external event. Congress also has the prerogative to install a Parliamentary Committee of Investigation (Comissão Parlamentar de Inquérito—CPI), with a limitation of five functioning CPIs in any given year. Congress can also create a Joint Parliamentary Committee of Investigation (Comissão Parlamentar Mista de Inquérito), which congregates senators and federal deputies.
7. Six percent of the chamber members or leaders representing this number may request a roll call vote to the steering committee.
8. Rapporteurs have shorter deadlines to produce materials considered under priority or urgency regime. No extension is allowed for the materials under urgency regime. Extensions may be granted to materials considered under ordinary or priority regime for up to one-half of the original term.
9. In the Chamber of Deputies, conclusive power may *not* be used for bills of complementary law, constitutional amendments, codes (including electoral and criminal codes), bills of popular initiative, committee proposals, Senate proposals, bills amended by the Senate, bills that have divergent committee reports, and bills under urgent consideration. In the Senate, terminative power *may* be used in international treaties, Chamber bills that were approved by conclusive power, and other types of proposals except constitutional amendments.
10. Testing this hypothesis requires distinct data that we do not have at this point. We thus put this on the agenda for future research.
11. For exceptions, see Pereira and Mueller (2000), Ricci and Lemos (2004), Santos (2002), Santos and Rennó (2004), and Santos and Almeida (2005).
12. The Senate has more simplified procedures.
13. It would also be interesting to verify the success rate of bills with discharge petitions in comparison to bills that follow the normal course.

14. Even though Brazil's bicameral congress is in principle symmetric in the distribution of prerogatives, the bicameral relationship becomes asymmetric with respect to the processing of statutory law proposals. In such cases, the first house where the proposal is originally introduced has an overriding power over the reviewer house's amendments (Hiroi 2008a).
15. Joint committees produce reports, and often bills, but these committee proposals still need to be examined separately and sequentially and are open to amendments.
16. The proposal data come from Hiroi (2008a) and roll call votes from Cebrap (2011). The periods of data coverage are different because these data were coded at different times. Although they cover different years, each dataset has unique information that is useful for our analysis. Moreover, our hypotheses do not require testing using data from the same period.
17. In other words, this selection method identifies and considers institutional proposals. Executive and judicial proposals introduced to Congress are institutional proposals because they cleared internal deliberation processes within these branches prior to their introduction to Congress. We define Chamber and Senate bills as institutional proposals when they passed the first house where they were introduced. Essentially this method establishes equivalency between executive, judicial, and congressional proposals by helping to remove the bills that were proposed simply for the sake of proposing (which many members of Congress do). See Hiroi (2008a) for detailed information on the dataset and selection procedure.
18. Censoring bills that are terminated for reasons other than approval basically uses the same approach as the latent survivor time approach to estimate competing risks. In the latter, the event of interest is assumed to occur eventually if time went on long enough without the "failure" from other types of event. Based on this assumption, observations are censored when cases experience other types of event. This is the approach we use in estimating the approval duration model. We also attempted to estimate a rejection model. However, due to the fewer cases of rejection, the model did not converge.
19. The Lula government indeed concentrated its effort on the passage of these two proposals to the extent that it led to an illegal legislative support-buying scheme called *mensalão* (big monthly stipend), arguably the biggest scandal involving the executive and legislative branches.
20. Readers are reminded that the denominator includes, respectively, all executive or congressional institutional proposals introduced to Congress during each specified period. Thus, in addition to enacted bills, it includes bills that are still pending at the end of the period as well as bills that were withdrawn, rejected, appended to other bills, totally vetoed, or terminated for other reasons.
21. As discussed in the previous section, the figure is based on the data coding passage as the event of interest and all other outcomes as censored.
22. The data include only amendments submitted on the floor. Amendments proposed in committees are reflected if they are adopted by rapporteurs in their substitutive bills.

4

Presidential Power, Legislative Rules, and Lawmaking in Chile

Eduardo Alemán and Patricio Navia

Under Chile's constitutional structure, the executive branch has a prominent role in the lawmaking process. A strong executive characterized the constitution of 1925, and subsequent constitutional reforms (eight between 1943 and 1971) further reinforced presidential authority. Written in 1980 under the tutelage of Augusto Pinochet's military government, the current constitution has remained in place through the return to democracy. Major reforms were undertaken in 1989, before the democratically elected government took power, and again in 2005.

The 1980 constitution established a regime type that has struck many scholars as severely biased in favor of the executive branch. It has been called, for instance, "reinforced presidentialism" (Cea 1992), "super-presidentialism" (Shugart and Carey 1992: 129), "exaggerated presidentialism" (Siavelis 2000), and "ultra-presidentialism" (Godoy 2003). The president is typically portrayed as the foremost proponent of major legislation (Londregan 2000; Alemán and Navia 2009). Several institutional prerogatives have allowed presidents to pursue an active role as proponents of major legislation.[1] Less noted, however, is how the distribution of positions inside Congress has severely constrained presidential decision-making. There is also scant scholarship on the institutions that structure the bill-to-law process within the legislature.

In this chapter we analyze the distribution of legislative agenda setting power in Chile. We specify which institutions are actually at the heart of the president's legislative authority, and how agenda setting power is distributed inside the Chilean Congress. As noted in the introduction to this book, the impact of agenda setting depends not only on a series of institutional capabilities, but also on the positions of legislative actors. We discuss how the distribution of partisan positions during the Concertación era (1990–2010) constrained institutionally powerful presidents. Lastly, we present an empirical analysis of some of the implications of our argument about legislative agenda setting, with particular attention to the passage of major bills.

Our analysis confirms the conventional wisdom that presidents propose most major bills, and shows that presidential bills are more likely to pass and travel faster to enactment than congressional bills. But the analysis also shows that presidential bills are regularly subject to amendments before becoming law. Presidents are deeply engaged in protecting their bills and bargaining with legislative actors throughout the amendment process. We also show the importance of last-stage institutions—conference committees and presidential vetoes—in improving the positions of committees and the executive. Lastly, we show that the implications of agenda control in Congress are also reflected in voting behavior. We examine individual roll rates in roll call votes in the Chamber of Deputies, controlled by the governing coalition, and the Senate, then tied between the opposition and the government coalition. The analysis shows significant differences between chambers, reflecting the presence and absence of a majority capturing agenda setting offices.

The rest of this chapter is divided into four parts. The first part discusses the institutional features that allocate rights over the legislative agenda. The second part concentrates on the positions of major legislative players in the period following the transition to democracy. The third part examines the empirical record, while the fourth one concludes.

AGENDA SETTING INSTITUTIONS

The constitutional organization of Chile is characterized by three institutional veto players—the president, the Chamber of Deputies, and the Senate—alongside a Constitutional Tribunal.[2] Each of them is endowed with veto power. The president can be overridden in matters of law when both chambers muster the two-thirds majority required for overcoming a presidential bloc veto. Similarly, a president with the support of two-thirds of one chamber can override the other chamber in matters of law. Neither scenario, where one institutional veto player is bypassed by the two others, has actually taken place since the return to democracy in 1990. The distribution of partisan seats has made this an unlikely event.

In stark contrast to the US model of presidentialism, Chile's institutional structure provides broad agenda setting powers to the president. The right to introduce a bill or an amendment can affect the options ultimately considered by the plenary, but only as long as the proposals can reach such a stage in the legislative process. Who controls consideration of bills—scheduling power—is also crucial. Within Congress, agenda power is centralized in leadership posts controlled by the chamber's majority. These offices exercise control over the flow of legislation. Congressional committees are also powerful within their own jurisdiction. Neither permanent committees nor the congressional leadership, however, can prevent the president from compelling Congress to attend a bill. In the next two sections we describe the formal allocation of agenda power.

Presidential Prerogatives

Constitutional provisions give the president various tools to influence the passage of bills and a high degree of control over economic policy-making. While the institutional framework allocates several powers to the executive branch, three prerogatives stand out in matters of agenda control: (i) wide authority over tax and spend legislation; (ii) extensive amendment rights, including the right to introduce amendatory observations to vetoed bills; and (iii) authority to force the scheduling of bills for plenary debate. Together, these prerogatives make the president the most prominent agenda setter.

On almost all legislation dealing with government expenditures and tax matters, the executive is the constitutional first-mover and can preserve the status quo by keeping the gates closed. The constitution gives the president the exclusive right to introduce bills that establish or modify taxes, public salaries, public services, administrative functions, collective bargaining, pensions, and social security. Likewise, the president alone can introduce bills or amendments that demand government expenditures. While the president is required to initiate the budget bill every year, Congress is restricted in the types of changes it can introduce, and the default outcome if Congress does not approve the budget is the president's original proposal. Congress cannot increase or diminish the estimates of revenue included in the budget bill and can only introduce changes that reduce expenditures, except those established by permanent law (Baldez and Carey 1999).

It must also be emphasized that this authority over money bills and related amendments provides the president with a useful bargaining tool. For instance, every individual or partisan actor seeking to push forward a bill or amendment with spending attached to it needs to negotiate to get the explicit support of the executive branch. Moreover, once the executive chooses to introduce an amendment in an area where it has exclusive jurisdiction, it is often a take-it-or-leave-it proposal; legislators are restricted with the type of counter-amendments they could offer (i.e., only those reducing/redirecting spending). The president's right to introduce amendments to legislation being debated in Congress extends beyond "tax-and-spend" bills to other areas of policy. Presidents tend to use amendments to fight fire with fire as well as to solidify consensual bargains. The former may occur, for instance, when the president disagrees with parts of the bill as reported by the committee or when amendments introduced by legislators appear likely to pass a floor vote and make the president worse off. Unlike individual amendments, which must be pre-filed and discussed by the committee with jurisdiction over the bill, those introduced by the president are sometimes brought directly to the floor. These amendments must also be germane to the bill in question.

Amendment powers are reinforced by the frequent participation of members of the executive branch (ministers and others) in committee deliberations. The members of the cabinet have the constitutional right to participate in congressional sessions where they enjoy speaking privileges. Cabinet members also have the obligation to appear when Congress demands it. In practice, some of the most substantive interaction between ministers and legislators occurs during the committee deliberation phase, before a bill is reported to the floor for final passage. One would be hard pressed to find a relevant executive bill that passed Congress without repeated visits from members of the executive branch to a committee or a minister participating in floor deliberations.

After Congress passes a bill, the Chilean president has another key agenda setting tool. In addition to the typical block veto, which allows the president to reject the entire bill and Congress to override with a qualified majority of two-thirds of members, the president has the constitutional right to introduce take-it-or-leave-it amendments last.[3] This prerogative enables presidents to respond to unwanted policy changes with an alternative proposal, making it a much more effective tool than the block veto, which can only be used to protect the status quo (Tsebelis and Alemán 2005). The counter-proposal ("observations") presented by the president can be accepted or rejected by a simple majority, but a qualified majority of two-thirds in each chamber is needed to insist on the original version of the bill. If the president's amendments to the bill are not accepted and Congress cannot override the veto, then the bill, excluding the sections altered by the president, is the default outcome.

The president can also affect the congressional schedule by using motions of urgency, which compel Congress to act within a short period of time. Presidents can attach three types of urgencies to bills: *immediate* imposes a three-day deadline; *suma* a ten-day deadline; and *simple* a thirty-day deadline. Urgencies are used to force a choice in the face of contentious disagreement, as well as to speed up the approval of more consensual or already-negotiated bills. Presidents can also withdraw and renew these urgencies, and they often do it when congressional leaders signal that more time is needed to reach an agreement.[4] *Suma* or *immediate* urgency requests identify those proposals prioritized by the government (Alemán and Navia 2009). Executive urgencies influence passage rates. In a prior work, we have shown that executive bills prioritized by the government through urgency procedures are significantly more likely to become law (Alemán and Navia 2009). Executive bills with *simple* urgency requests are not necessarily more likely to pass than bills without an urgency motion but they are more likely to be reported by the committee with jurisdiction in the chamber of origin. Any type of executive motion of urgency increases the odds of approval of bills initiated by legislators.

To sum up, the contemporary institutional setting grants the Chilean president broad rights over the legislative agenda. These prerogatives include being the monopoly agenda setter on money bills, as well as having the opportunity to be the last-mover on every bill. These prerogatives, coupled with the rights to influence the timing of bills through the urgency process and to introduce ordinary amendments (fighting fire with fire or cementing broad consensus), provide the Chilean president with sufficient agenda setting power to become the most prominent actor in lawmaking.

Some features of this institutional structure were already in place before the military coup of 1973, such as the ability to introduce urgency motions and amendments, including observations to vetoed bills. Presidential authority over spending legislation had been established in the 1925 constitution and tightened with the constitutional amendment of 1943 (Article 45), which restrained Congress from adding appropriations to executive bills, creating new public services, or setting wages in the public sector.[5] The president, however, had less control over tax bills, and legislators were still allowed to initiate private laws providing pensions and other individual favors, which they did habitually. Also relevant for the particularistic achievements of legislators was the use of omnibus legislation, *leyes misceláneas*.[6] But these practices ended with a constitutional reform in 1970.

Agenda Setting in Congress

Inside the Chilean Congress, two sets of offices possess agenda setting power: the leadership committees (chamber and partisan), which control bill scheduling, plenary time, and committee assignments; and permanent committees, which have substantial influence over the amending process and the opportunity to make take-it-or-leave-it proposals to the plenary at the conference stage.

The congressional leadership has power over resources sought out by legislators: plenary time and assignment to coveted committees. It can facilitate or obstruct legislators' proposals and career advancement. In the Chamber of Deputies, the majority-elected directorate, called Mesa, has the authority to fast-track bills to the plenary floor under a procedure (*tabla de fácil despacho*) that severely curtails debate, avoids the normally required second committee report, and forces an immediate vote on the bill and any related amendments.[7] The Mesa crafts the daily schedule (*orden del día*) after consultation with the leaders of the legislative party blocs (Jefes de Comités Parlamentarios). This party leadership group shares with the Mesa the power to bring consensual proposals to the plenary floor through another fast-track procedure (*tabla de despacho inmediato*).[8] In the Senate, the chamber's president is the only actor formally responsible for crafting the daily schedule, but leaders of the legislative party blocs have the right to alter it by scheduling matters to be attended at a future date. The president of the Senate has the power to fast-track bills to the plenary floor in a manner similar to the lower chamber's Mesa.

Legislators care about their committee assignment. They provide an opportunity to influence policy and advance their constituents' interests. Committee chairmanships are coveted positions, and membership in the most sought out committees is considered to be quite prestigious. The distribution of seats inside permanent committees must follow the respective party shares in the chamber, but the lower chamber's Mesa and the upper chamber's president have the power to decide over individual assignments in their respective chambers. Recommended committee assignments are considered approved by the chamber unless the proposal is challenged to a no-debate majority vote in the plenary floor. While most legislators retain their membership in one of the two committees to which they were originally assigned, it is common for legislators to switch assignments at least once. After the initial distribution of legislators into committees, every petition to reassign a legislator to a different committee has to be supported by the leader of the legislator's party bloc.

Party leaders also have influence over the distribution of end-of-day speaking time (*incidentes*), which is allotted to parties according to their share of chamber seats. This time is rather valuable to legislators because it gives them the opportunity to promote their constituents' interests from the plenary floor. It is a visible platform for position taking. Legislators use it, for example, to speak in favor of a local cause, advance a chamber resolution, demand governmental action, or pay tribute. In general, the issues addressed reflect local rather than national policy matters. It is not a platform to debate bills, but it is still an important one for electorally motivated legislators.

Permanent committees have substantial authority over narrow policy jurisdictions.[9] They most often have to report bills submitted to them, but still have substantial *positive* power to affect the content of legislation. Bills can be forced out of committee by the executive, through an urgency request, and by the chamber's authorities, through its agenda privileges. Individual legislators in the Chamber of Deputies can force a bill out of committee if a motion passes with majority support, while in the Senate a bill must be debated within sixty days, if two of the five members of a committee demand it. Despite the inability to kill bills by refusing to report them, committee members have the institutional tools to protect bargains reached inside the committee from unraveling after a bill is reported to the floor.

In Chile, all amendments must be sent to the permanent committees with jurisdiction over the bill before the plenary debate for final passage (*discusión en particular*) takes place. This strict pre-filing requirement forces legislators to reveal any intended changes, giving the committee the chance to decide whether to respond to the amendment with a counter-amendment of its own (i.e., fighting fire with fire). Legislators whose amendments were rejected during committee deliberations can request a floor vote when the bill is debated for final passage, but only if they gather enough endorsements from other legislators (two party bloc leaders in the lower chamber and ten senators in the upper chamber).[10]

Perhaps the most important source of agenda setting power for members of permanent committees stems from their participation in conference committees (*comsiones mixtas*). Conference committees are established with the purpose of resolving bicameral differences on legislation.[11] The conference committees have an equal number of deputies and senators and decide by majority rule. Only members of the committee with original jurisdiction over the bill can be assigned to conference committees: the Senate's delegation is made up of all committee members, while the delegation from the Chamber of Deputies is usually composed of one-third of the committee members (selected by the Mesa).

Conference committees have the power to make a take-it-or-leave-it proposal to both chambers of Congress. Moreover, conferees have the discretion to alter all parts of the bill with germane amendments, including matters formerly agreed upon by both chambers.[12] So, even if proposals are modified in ways unwanted by the committee, their members often have another chance at the bill in the conference process. While conference committees must report the bill (i.e., they lack ex-post veto), they have significant proposal power at the concluding stage of the legislative process. The conference stage gives Congress an opportunity to improve its bargaining position vis-à-vis a strong executive. For example, Alemán and Pachón (2008) examine the possible interactions between conference committees and the executive. Through a series of spatial examples they show that despite the wide veto and amendment capabilities of the executive, there is still the possibility for conference committees to anticipate such actions, and strategically select a response. So, conference committees make last proposals considering not only the preferences of legislators in each chamber, but also the potential executive responses that may follow. In the end, the committee can search for an alternative that would pass under closed rules and would not generate a subsequent amendment (*observation*) by the president.

To summarize, inside the Chilean Congress the offices endowed with significant agenda setting power include the directorate (lower chamber Mesa and Senate president), the leadership committee made up of party bloc chiefs (*líderes de comités*), as well as permanent and conference committees. The first two exercise general control over the flow of legislative proposals to the plenary floor, while the latter control the flow within their respective jurisdictions. These agenda setters can delay and even exclude bills from reaching the floor, but they cannot do it against the wishes of the executive. Committees are endowed primarily with positive agenda setting power over their assigned policy areas. The possibility to fight off unwanted amendments with their own counter-proposals and the right to have a second go at a bill during the conference stage make up the basis of committee power. However, committees are not independent of the party leadership that controls their composition. Their membership (and the membership of conference committees in the lower chamber) is selected by those same offices that enjoy scheduling power. Individual legislators need the support of the leaders of their legislative parties to get good committee assignments, have access to speaking time in the plenary floor, and have an opportunity to see their proposals and amendments considered amid the significant time constraints that characterize all national congresses.

PARTISAN POSITIONS AND PRESIDENTIAL SUPPORT

The ability to exercise control over the legislative agenda depends not only on the formal procedures discussed previously, but also on the position of relevant legislative actors. In Chile, party fragmentation has prevented any one party from gaining a majority of seats in both chambers of Congress. Since the early 1960s, the number of parties represented in the Chilean Congress has varied between seven and eleven in the Chamber of Deputies and between four and seven in the Senate. The transition to democracy gave way to two stable competing alliances: the center-left Concertación and a center-right Alianza (it has changed names several times). The competing coalitions were originally formed towards the end of the military regime with the goal of winning the 1988 plebiscite, which asked voters whether they approved another eight years of military rule.

Since the return to democracy, the two coalitions have won almost all seats to both chambers of Congress. The first four presidents elected after the end of military rule were members of the Concertación coalition—Patricio Aylwin (1990–4), Eduardo Frei Ruiz-Tagle (1994–2000), Ricardo Lagos (2000–6), and Michelle Bachelet (2006–10). This center-left coalition included the Christian Democratic Party (DC), the Socialist Party (PS), the Party for Democracy (PPD), and the smaller Radical Social-Democratic Party (PRSD), while the center-right opposition included the National Renewal Party (RN) and the Independent Democratic Union (UDI). In 2010, the Concertación lost the executive to the center-right coalition, making Sebastián Piñera (RN) the first conservative president since the early 1960s. In 2014, the Concertación, allied with the Communist Party under a new coalition (named Nueva Mayoría), returned to the presidency.

Concertación presidents enjoyed a slight majority of seats in the Chamber of Deputies until Michelle Bachelet's presidency, when a few defections made the governing coalition lose its majority. In the Senate, however, the Concertación was in the minority until 1998, when it tied with the opposition. During this time, non-elected senators (including former military officers from the dictatorship era) strengthened the bargaining power of the center-right coalition. The constitutional reform of 2005 got rid of the non-elected senators and in the subsequent election the Concertación won a slight majority of Senate seats. However, a series of defections during the 2006–10 period cut short their hard-won majority status. President Sebastián Piñera (2010–14), who won the executive for the center-right coalition for the first time since 1990, was elected without a majority of seats in either chamber.

The lack of unified government has not been the only incentive governments have to negotiate with the opposition. Special super-majority requirements, codified in the constitution, have also promoted consensus building on many substantive policy areas. For instance, laws that interpret constitutional provisions (*interpretativas*) require the support of three-fifths of each chamber's members, laws that complement the constitution (*orgánicas*) require four-sevenths, and others that legislate on any matter mentioned in the constitution require an absolute majority. The distribution of seats and super-majority requirements meant that the government coalition had to negotiate with the opposition. Even when slim majorities were needed, the government had to reach out to at least a few opposition legislators. If the opposition voted together, it could veto Concertación proposals.

Analyses of the contemporary Congress tend to agree about the ideological ranking of legislative parties. Within the center-left Concertación, the PS is further to the left of the PPD, which is itself positioned to the left of the more moderate DC. Inside the center-right Alianza, the RN is consistently ranked as more moderate than the UDI. In terms of legislative behavior, analyses of roll call votes have shown that parties are disciplined, competition is bipolar, and coalitions act in a unified manner in roll call votes (Carey 2002; Alemán and Saiegh 2007).[13] Presidents have always been rather moderate, arguably closer to the center of the ideological left-to-right spectrum than the average legislator of their coalition.

Political parties exert significant influence over the careers of individual legislators. Chileans vote in an open list, selecting individual candidates rather than parties, but which two candidates end up being on the ballot is the result of bargaining among coalition party leaders. In order to be on the ballot, aspirants first need to receive their party nomination, and then they need their party to successfully bargain with other coalition members to secure a place in the two-member list for the given district. Parties want to nominate candidates that can win and thus, aspirants need to show they are strong in that district. However, strength—measured as potential electoral support or financial resources to run a campaign—is a requirement, not a guarantee for a party and coalition nomination. Party leaders hold significant power in deciding which candidates and which districts they will defend as they bargain with other parties over the list of coalition candidates in the sixty districts for the Chamber of Deputies and nineteen districts for the Senate. Aspirants are expected to have exhibited party loyalty.

Parties also exert significant control over incumbent legislators. Incumbents have relatively high name recognition and can sometimes build a personal vote base. Two out of three incumbents usually win re-election (Navia 2008). Because the main competition is within lists—not between lists—candidates have to run against other candidates from like-minded political parties. As more than 90 percent of the districts are equally split between the Concertación and Alianza coalitions, to secure their seats, incumbents normally want to prevent their own coalitions from nominating strong challengers in their districts. Thus, electorally motivated incumbents seeking to prevent challenges at the next election also have incentives to avoid antagonizing the party leadership during the legislative sessions. Parties are more likely to defend disciplined legislators and cede districts of unruly legislators when they bargain with other coalition members over the formation of the list of candidates for the next election. Politicians do have the potential to run as independents in their districts—occasionally some do and even a few incumbents whose parties cede their districts in negotiations with other coalition members run as independents. However, since votes are tallied by party lists, independents—who cannot run on lists—need to get a higher vote share to secure a seat. The threshold to run as an independent is not excessively high—petitions legally signed by a number higher than 0.5 percent of voters in the last election in that district. Most incumbents can easily meet the requirements. However, getting elected as an independent is much more difficult. Less than 3 percent of all legislators elected since 1989 have run as independents.

Despite all this, unity has not always been perfect. In the first few years after the transition to democracy, party discipline was strongest. In recent years, signs that party attachments are weakening among voters—the percentage of Chileans who identify with political parties has fallen from a high of 75 percent in the early 1990s to a low of about 40 percent by 2010—may have lowered incentives to act in a disciplined manner. In addition, right-wing Chilean politicians are typically less committed to enforcing party discipline, partly a reflection of their history of discrediting political parties during the Pinochet administration. An ongoing debate among the right over the role of parties, the tensions between party discipline, and the use of conscience votes (i.e., *free* votes) reflects right-wing politicians' view that party discipline belongs to class-based parties and not parties that promote individual freedom and reject class warfare (Allamand 1999; Huneeus 2001; Angell 2003; Correa Sutil 2005; Allamand and Cubillos 2010).

In the 2005 election, tensions within the Alianza coalition led to a division between the UDI and RN in the presidential election. Though the Alianza had a single list of legislative candidates, it ran with two presidential candidates. Since legislative slates are not required to be associated with a presidential candidate, both RN and UDI had their own presidential candidates. Former presidential candidate Joaquín Lavín, a UDI leader who narrowly lost the 1999 election, and businessman and former senator Sebastián Piñera, an admittedly moderate RN leader, faced each other in the first round of the election, turning that contest into a sort of informal Alianza primary. Piñera won more votes than Lavín and went on to lose against Concertación's Bachelet in the run-off for the presidency. Yet, Piñera secured the leadership position in the Alianza, which allowed him to run unopposed in the Alianza presidential ticket in 2009, when he defeated the Concertación candidate in a run-off election, putting an end to twenty years of center-left government.

During the Bachelet administration (2006–10), there were more party defections by legislators than in all the previous sixteen years of democratic rule. Three senators (in the thirty-eight-member chamber) resigned from their parties, two from Concertación parties and another from an Alianza party. In addition, five deputies resigned from the Christian Democratic Party more than a year before the end of the Bachelet administration to form a new centrist party, the Regionalista Party (PRI). In the last year of the Bachelet administration, an additional group of one senator and three deputies resigned from Concertación parties to join other groups or run as independents. The defections observed during the Bachelet administration have been associated with the electoral implications associated with the fall in party identification among Chilean voters (Morales and Navia 2010).

In conclusion, despite being endowed with significant institutional powers, Chilean presidents have been constrained by legislative players. The lack of unified government and super-majority requirements to change various policies has meant that presidents needed to rely on more than just the support of their own coalition partners. Party leaders have significant influence over legislators: they can facilitate the advancement of their policy proposals, provide them with precious speaking time, and reward them with prestigious positions. Additionally, party leaders can be a powerful force, furthering or hindering legislators' political careers. While unity within the governing coalition helps the president, unity within the opposition means that presidents are less likely to be able to rely on a few dissident legislators to consistently reach working legislative majorities. Overall, presidents operate in a constrained environment, pressured not only to rally consensus among various partners but also to reach out to non-coalition members with ideologically distinct positions.

PATTERNS OF LAWMAKING

This section examines some of the implications derived from the institutional and positional context described before. We address four aspects of agenda control: (i) the proposal power of presidents; (ii) the amendment process without unified government; (iii) the usage of presidential vetoes and conference committees; and (iv) voting behavior in the plenary.

Are presidents the chief lawmakers in Chile? The discussion of institutional prerogatives highlights the central place given to the executive in terms of initiating legislative proposals and being able to compel Congress to discuss such bills. Given the president's right to be the first mover on several substantive areas of policy, the extensive technical resources of the executive branch, and the electoral motivations to advance a governmental policy program, we expect major policy proposals to be more likely to originate in the executive than in Congress. Anecdotal evidence suggests that the executive is the chief proposer of major legislation, despite the fact that most bills introduced originate with members of Congress. This preponderant role for the executive in bill initiation is commonplace in parliamentary democracies, but not in the US Congress. Given the president's right to influence the legislative agenda by compelling attention to particular bills, we also expect major executive bills to travel to enactment faster than congressional bills.

These expectations may be seen as highly favorable to the executive, yet we have underlined the positional constraints within which Chilean presidents had to operate. Opposition actors should be particularly empowered in a context of minority government, which reduces the executive's control over the legislative agenda. As we noted before, every administration in the period 1990–2013 has had to reach out to congressional players outside the governing coalition to win legislative passage of their bills. Super-majority requirements for several important proposals have made cross-coalition bargaining necessary. In addition, the level of uncertainty surrounding the passage of most bills has not been trivial—not fewer than six parties in two chambers and at least a few senators and deputies opened to the possibility of crossing the coalition divide have complicated legislative bargaining. As a result, we expect presidential bills to receive frequent congressional amendments—some friendly and others not—and eventually incorporate a number of them before enactment. Given differences in the composition and control of each chamber, we also expect bicameral disputes on major bills to occur often. Conference committees should be formed frequently to address major bills.

The ability to make the last proposal before final congressional passage and the fact that such proposals cannot be amended any further by legislators provide substantial agenda power to conference committees. Coming at the end of the process, conferees are also likely to have better information about the preferences of pivotal actors in both chambers and the president than during committee deliberations. Legislators confronting this take-it-or-leave-it bill have to ask themselves whether they prefer the conference committee proposal to the status quo, and whether the president is likely to veto the bill in any manner. But conferees should have anticipated the latter possibility too.

Presidents are also advantaged by their last-stage agenda power. When vetoing a bill, Chilean presidents have several options. They can veto the entire bill, delete parts of it, or introduce new germane amendments in the form of observations (i.e., additions or modifications). One of the main implications from the work of Alemán and Tsebelis (2005) on agenda setting in Latin America is that these amendatory observations provide presidents much more leeway to favorably influence bill outcomes than absolute (bloc) vetoes. When presidents decide to veto a bill, we expect them to opt for the former mechanism.

Lastly, we address floor voting behavior. We have argued that the governing coalition has substantial positive agenda setting power to influence the content of bills faced by legislators. The governing coalition also has gatekeeping power over several areas of policy, either through the president's exclusive initiation rights or through the leadership's influence over committees and calendars. The relatively high level of party unity, particularly in the lower chamber, also makes the effort of trying to force into the calendar bills unwanted by most members of the majority coalition a rather costly position-taking strategy.

The consequences of agenda control should be manifested in floor voting behavior. For the cartel model, developed by Cox and McCubbins (2002) with the US Congress in mind, the unconditional veto power in the hands of the leadership of the majority party should be evident in roll call votes: the majority party should never be "rolled." That is, we should not observe bills passing that are opposed by the majority of the majority party. Given the agenda setting powers held by the Concertación coalition, and the incentives legislators of the government coalition had to remain loyal to the party, we should not see instances where the majority coalition is rolled. The absence of majority coalition roll rates is what Alemán (2006) showed using final passage votes from the 1997–2000 period.

The implications of agenda control should also be manifested in the voting records of individuals. In the Chamber of Deputies, where the government coalition controlled the offices with agenda setting power, individual roll rates for legislators from the government coalition should be significantly lower than those of legislators from the opposition. Deputies from Concertación should not be likely to oppose items scheduled for a vote. The expectations for the Senate, however, are different. Because neither coalition could monopolize the offices with agenda setting power, individual roll rates should reflect ideological positions rather than coalition differences. So, legislators from moderate parties within each coalition should be rolled less often than legislators from more ideologically extreme parties. We examine empirically these two hypotheses:

H1. In the Chamber of Deputies, legislators belonging to the Concertación should be significantly less likely to end on the Nay side of votes receiving a majority of Yea votes than legislators from the Alianza.

H2. In the Senate, ideology should have a greater effect than coalition affiliation in determining who ends on the Nay side of votes receiving a majority of Yea votes.

In the next section we examine a dataset that includes a sample of "major bills," as well as the entire record of bills introduced between 1990 and early 2006. The set of major bills was collected in the following manner: any legislative proposal mentioned on the front page of the newspaper *El Mercurio* at some point during the first year of an administration was considered a major bill and included in the dataset. We look at three periods, each associated with the first year of the democratic administrations that governed Chile between 1990 and early 2006: Aylwin (March 1990 to March 1991), Frei Ruiz-Tagle (March 1994 to March 1995), and Lagos (March 2000 to March 2001). We found a total of 163 major legislative proposals mentioned on the front page over the three periods. This includes executive initiatives as well as congressional initiatives. Of those proposals, 157 were actually introduced as bills in Congress. Some of these proposals were introduced right away, while others were introduced later in the president's term.[14] A few bills become front-page news—major bills given our criteria—several years after being introduced.

In addition, we present information from the entire record of bills introduced between March 1990 and March 2006, which was collected from congressional sources.[15] The analysis of roll call votes centers on the 2002–6 period for the lower Chamber and on the 2004–6 period for the Senate. The latter data were compiled from information made available by the Chilean Congress on its website.

The Chief Proposer

The number of major bills initiated by the executive (E) and members of Congress (C), together with the number of major bills passed, appear in Figure 4.1. Figure 4.2 shows the total number of bills initiated between 1990 and 2005.[16] The first figure lends support to the notion that in Chile major policy proposals originate mostly in the executive branch. While the gap seems to be narrowing over time, in these three cases presidents greatly outperform legislators.

Among this sample of major bills, we find several landmark laws. Some of those initiated by President Aylwin include proposals for major political and administrative decentralization, abolishing the death penalty, extending press freedoms, reforming labor laws, and shortening the presidential mandate. Major initiatives introduced by President Eduardo Frei include new regulations for private healthcare providers, a new banking bill, an education bill dealing with school subsidies and teacher rules, a penal reform, and a new sports bill. Examples from President Lagos' set of major bills include a reform to compulsory military service, a series of transportations bills, a new unemployment insurance benefit, campaign finance reform, and a bill introducing new financial regulations targeting tax evasion and taxing capital gains.

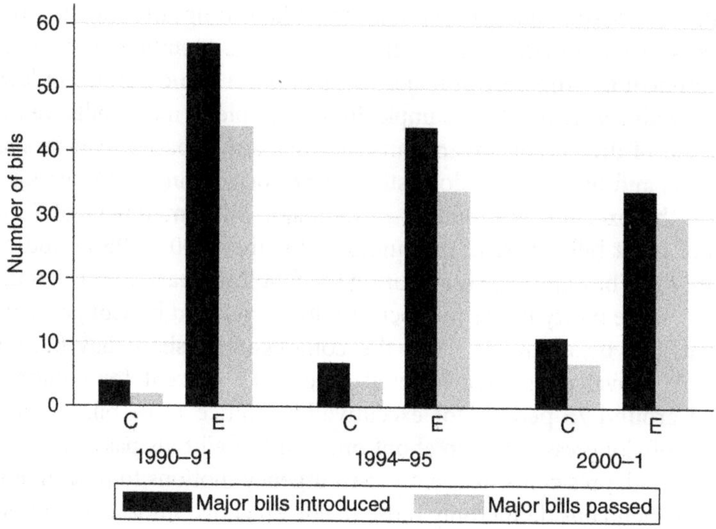

Figure 4.1 Bill introduction in Chile, major bills introduced and passed

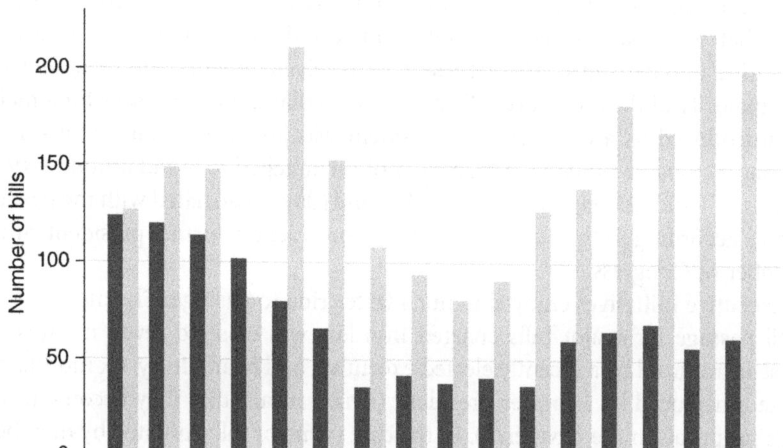

Figure 4.2 Bill introduction in Chile, all bills introduced, 1990–2005

Two initiatives—the budget bill and the bill setting the salaries of state employees—were introduced by all three presidents. Members of Congress are less prominent as proposers of major legislation, yet some significant laws also originate with legislators. For example, in our sample of major bills we find the legalization of divorce, an organ transplant bill, anti-tobacco regulations, HIV prevention, and penalties for domestic violence originating in Congress.

While the executive introduces most major bills, members of Congress introduce most bills overall. The numbers for the 1990–2005 period appear in Figure 4.2. They illustrate how during the first four years after the transition there was some parity in the number of bills introduced by Congress and the president, but beginning in 1994 the congressional share has been much greater. Approval rates have hovered around 15 percent for congressional bills and around 75 percent for executive bills. Since 1994, bills initiated by members of Congress make up about one-third of all bills passed.

As expected, presidents frequently used urgency motions to push major bills forward. When considering only those major executive initiatives that became law, we find that the executive attached some form of urgency motion to 72 percent of successful major bills, and the most severe forms of urgencies (*suma* or *immediate*) to around half of them. The incidence of urgency motions among major executive bills is greater than that reported for all bills (Alemán and Navia 2009). Urgencies were also used, although at a lower frequency, with several of the major bills introduced by members of Congress.[17] When we look at major bills that were passed very promptly—in less than 100 days—we find only executive initiated bills. All of these bills received urgency motions, and the vast majority of the most severe form.[18] The median time of passage for a major bill introduced by a Concertación president was just over seven months if the bill had a *suma* or *immediate* urgency motion attached to it and around sixteen months if it did not. Figure 4.3 shows the time (days) associated with the passage of bills according to the author: the current president, a former president, and a member of Congress.

Executive initiatives enjoyed a much faster ride to passage. The median time until passage for major bills enacted into law was close to seven months for those introduced by a recently elected executive, and nearly forty-six months for those introduced by a former president (which meant that they become front-page proposals in the next term). In the case of major bills initiated by members of Congress, the median time until passage was close to sixty-two months, which is more than the four-year term deputies are elected to serve. With regard to all bills passed, the median time for executive-initiated bills was ten months, while the median time for congressional-initiated bills was two years.

To sum up, most major bills originate in the executive branch, which confirms the conventional wisdom on this matter. Less noted, however, is

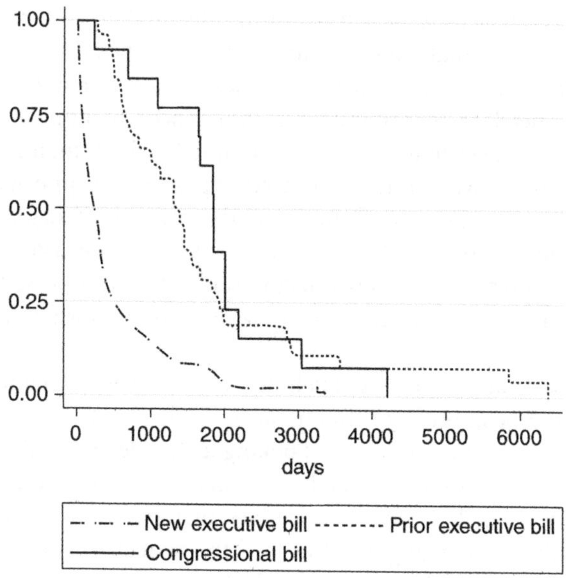

Figure 4.3 Time until enactment, major bills passed—Kaplan-Meier survivor function

that such executive bills are most often helped by agenda setting tools that force them onto the congressional calendar. Presidents regularly apply urgency motions to navigate major bills towards enactment, making full use of their right over plenary time. As expected, laws (major or otherwise) that originate in the executive branch travel towards enactment faster than laws introduced by legislators.

Amending Bills: Constraints of Minority Presidents

We have argued that in Chile, the opposition coalition could block governmental proposals. On constitutional matters this was evident early on. The Alianza blocked the passage of several constitutional reforms, as well as more than twenty Concertación-initiated bills to reform the electoral system. Those constitutional reforms that succeeded ended up including substantive opposition amendments. Take the case of the constitutional reform on regional and local administration, enacted at the end of 1991 (Law 19,097). The successful bill, deemed by President Aylwin the most important proposal of the entire twentieth century on the subject of the territorial administration of Chile, was introduced in the opposition-dominated Senate seven months after this chamber had explicitly rejected his prior bill on the subject.[19] In its final form, the bill included substantive amendments on electoral procedures and administrative organization that were sought out by the opposition parties.

The cross-partisan support behind President Lagos' major initiatives also illustrates the need to incorporate the preferences of opposition senators. Fourteen of his sixteen major bills that became law had unanimous or near-unanimous support, while one other faced opposition by an eclectic group of senators from both coalitions.[20] In the end, only one of Lagos' major bills confronted a divided (*general*) vote in the Senate: the tax evasion bill. This bill received the support of only Concertación senators, but it passed nonetheless because RN senators facilitated passage by deciding to abstain, and few UDI senators showed up to vote against it.

The cross-partisan support built behind President Lagos' major initiatives is indicative of the positional constraints faced by Concertación presidents following the transition to democracy. Looking at the details of the bills passed, we observe that most were amended in substantive ways. In our examination we found only a small group of initiatives that passed without substantive changes introduced in Congress: three of the sixteen major bills President Lagos initiated passed without any amendments at all, and one other was only superficially amended. Three bills were in areas where the executive had monopoly proposal power and the other was a very short (one-page) human rights proposal negotiated with the opposition before being introduced and supported by all parties.[21]

The Senate, where the Concertación government lacked a majority, could always reject government proposals. The opposition coalition in the Chamber of Deputies could also veto proposals when special majorities were required. This happened, for example, in January 2001 when the government's campaign finance reform bill, pushed forward by a series of executive motions of urgency, was defeated in the floor of the Chamber of Deputies because supporters could not reach the super-majority required for passage (four-sevenths of the membership). While major bills introduced by the president generally receive the support of the parties making up the presidential coalition, this is not the case for every bill. For example, the bill readjusting the salary of public employees sent by President Lagos to Congress at the end of November 2000 ended up passing the Senate with the support of a floor alliance of some government and some opposition legislators, despite the opposition of a few disgruntled Christian Democratic senators who broke ranks.

Examining the details of bills also allows us to appreciate the deep involvement of the executive in the amendment process. In all major bills we observe members of the executive participating in committee deliberations, and very often participating in floor debates. Ministers are prominent actors on the plenary floor, defending bills and arguing against unwanted amendments.

It is also remarkable that the executive often introduces amendments to its own bills, seeking to negotiate its way to approval. Most major bills introduced by the executive are subsequently subject to executive amendments. Sometimes these amendments are proposed to satisfy demands from the opposition or from government legislators, and sometimes to fight off modifications introduced or likely to be accepted by the committee with jurisdiction over the bill. President Lagos, for instance, sent amendments modifying sixteen of the nineteen major bills he introduced. These took place while the bills were in the committee deliberation stage.

The involvement of members of the executive branch on the amending process and the veto player status of the opposition can both be grasped in the speech given by Minister of the Interior José Miguel Insulza (later OAS chief) on the floor of the Chamber of Deputies, as the government bill on campaign finance reform was going down in flames because of a lack of sufficient support:

> This is not a bill where the will of the majority was imposed without respect for the opinion of the minority. On the contrary, among the articles [of the bill] that did not meet the required quorum—because the minority refused to vote—there are some that they requested. Among them, it is worth mentioning those related to the conduct of public services during the electoral period and those having to do with limits on advertisement. [...] There are articles where the executive introduced amendments precisely because of requests from deputies from the opposition—not from the government or from *Concertación* [deputies]—which were approved by unanimity in committee. Even to this day, the executive was willing to introduce amendments at the request of members of the opposition; none from *Concertación*. Consequently, it has become clear that [the opposition] has no intention to set any limits to campaign spending.[22]

In summary, major bills initiated by the executive are subject to substantive amendments before being enacted into law. We do not find a shred of evidence of a rubber-stamping Congress at play. Despite the executive's strong formal powers, congressional actors regularly force policy changes on executive bills. As expected, presidents use their agenda power to protect bills during the amending process. They habitually offer amendments of their own and send members of the executive branch to participate in committee deliberations.

Conference Committees and Amendatory Vetoes

Permanent committees are prominent players in crafting major legislation, and often exercise their influence through the conference process. Bicameral incongruence fosters the formation of conference committees. Disagreement between chambers appears to be more prevalent with more salient bills. In our sample, of those major bills that became law, 46 percent went through a conference committee. When we look at all bills introduced between 1990 and 2005 that eventually became law, we find that close to 14 percent of those initiated by the executive and just over 23 percent of those initiated by legislators went to a conference committee.

Aware of their crucial importance in the lawmaking process, parties seek to staff conference committees with fellow partisans and allies. Alemán and Pachón (2008) have shown that in Chile's Chamber of Deputies, the majority coalition always has a majority of the five conference committee delegates. In the Senate all five committee members go to conference; while some permanent committees had a majority from the government coalition, others had an opposition majority.

Both chambers of Congress most often approve the legislative proposals of conference committees. This is shown in Figure 4.4, which illustrates the fate of the conference committee proposals related to major bills, by period examined. In all but one of the cases, the conference committee presented one take-it-or-leave-it proposal. In one other case, it decided to divide the vote into two (and lost one). In most instances the proposals advanced by conference committees are passed by wide margins, which implies support from members of both coalitions. Occasionally, however, conference committee proposals are defeated.

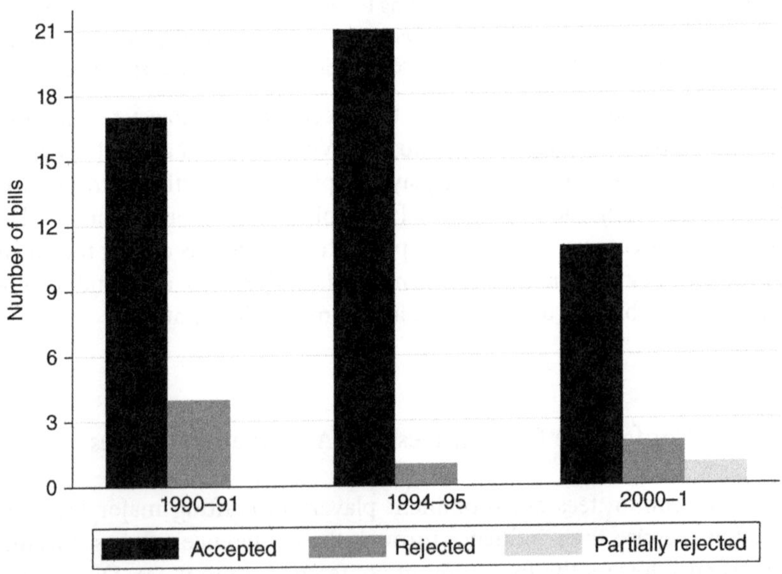

Figure 4.4 Major bills in conference committee

Regarding the seven conference committee reports that did not pass, the events surrounding them illuminate this last stage in the lawmaking process. On only one occasion was the conference committee called to resolve a bill dispute after one chamber, the Senate, had completely rejected it. The calling of a conference committee in such an instance is in the constitution, although in practice it occurs infrequently. After one chamber completely rejects a bill, the success of a conference committee proposal on that matter is unlikely (Alemán and Pachón 2008). In this particular case, the conference committee proposal was very close: it won half of the Senate votes. In the other six cases, conference committees were called to resolve differences between two versions of a bill. In all of these instances, qualified majorities were required for passage. Conference committees almost won on two occasions, when their proposals gathered a majority of Yea votes but failed to reach the super-majority required by the constitution. On two occasions, proposals were rejected unanimously by the lower chamber, and in the other two there were divided votes.[23] Lastly, it is important to note that in four of the conference committee proposals that were rejected, the executive intervened with an amendatory veto primarily to resolve the inter-chamber dispute.

Overall, the record shows that vetoes issued by the president were always of the amendatory type, never absolute vetoes. The total number of major bills in our sample that received amendatory observations is twenty-two (about 19 percent of those passed). All of these proposals became law, and the executive was able to make improvements in each one of them. In fifteen of these cases, all of the executive amendatory observations were approved by Congress, and in the other seven cases there was partial approval.

In short, bicameral differences often prompt the formation of conference committees, and this occurs more frequently with more salient bills. When presidents decide to veto a bill passed by Congress, they always prefer to respond with amendatory observations, rather than with a bloc veto. Both conference committees and presidents exhibit a high degree of success in getting their take-it-or-leave-it proposals to become law. By utilizing these agenda setting instruments, they are able to affect the proposals faced by Congress in a manner that makes policy outcomes more acceptable to them.

Voting Behavior

Lastly, we examine some of the implications of agenda control for roll call votes. First, we review coalition roll rates in the Chamber of Deputies. Next, we move on to focus on individual votes in both the Chamber of Deputies and the

Senate, where we expect to observe differences in terms of who wins and who loses as a result of who controls the congressional agenda.

Coalition roll rates in the Chamber of Deputies

We begin calculating roll rates for each coalition in the Chamber of Deputies between March 2002 and March 2006. If the floor agenda is in the hands of the chamber's majority coalition, as we argue, then we should observe no bills passing that are opposed by the majority of the Concertación coalition. In Chile, as in most Latin American countries, a general vote in support of passage is taken before discussing and voting the particular sections of the bill and related amendments. After voting on the details of the bill there is no final vote on the bill as a whole as amended by the floor. As a result, there are many "final-passage" votes on each bill: first, the general vote on the bill, and then usually various votes on parts (e.g., articles) of the bill and related amendments.[24] In the United States, for example, there is a final vote on the bill as a whole after the amending process, which is used to calculate roll rates. Thus, to calculate coalition roll rates in Chile's Chamber of Deputies we begin with more encompassing categories.

We examine all 2,145 roll call votes where Yeas were greater than Nays plus Abstention. In regard to the minority coalition, the number of votes with more Alianza deputies voting against than in favor or abstaining is 327, which is 15.4 percent of the total. The number of Yea votes that have more Concertación deputies voting against than in favor or abstaining is sixty-five, which is 3.1 percent of the total. Prima facie, these results do not differ much from those found for majority and minority parties in the US House of Representatives. Cox and McCubbins (2005) shows that roll rates in the presence of a majority party tend to be around 5 percent. However, further examination reveals that even these majority coalition defeats are not actually examples of the final-passage rolls as characterized in the literature on the US Congress. Eight of those votes did not meet required qualified thresholds and ultimately failed to pass, and twenty-six votes related to declarations or other types of motions, not actual bills. The rest of the votes, thirty-one in total, were amendments to small parts of bills that a majority of voting Concertación deputies had supported on the plenary floor.

This means that the number of bills that passed the Chamber of Deputies against the wishes of a majority of the majority coalition is zero—the only majority coalition rolls that took place between March 2002 and March 2006 were related to small amendments to welcomed bills. Such a result, we believe, confirms the view that the majority coalition has sufficient agenda control to block passage of bills disliked by the majority of its members.

Individual roll rates

To further evaluate the implications of agenda control for floor decisions, we move on to examine individual roll rates in both the Chamber of Deputies and in the Senate—where the competing coalitions were tied. We hypothesized a different distribution of individual roll rates given the different position of agenda setters: in the lower chamber, where agenda setting offices were in the hands of parties in the government coalition, opposition legislators should be on the losing side significantly more often, while in the split Senate, where neither coalition fully controlled the agenda, the ideological moderates of both coalitions should be the advantaged ones. The dataset from the Senate covers fewer years (August 2004 to March 2006) and has fewer roll call votes (249 where Yea votes are more than Nay votes plus Abstentions) than the one from the lower chamber. The results, grouped by party, appear in Figure 4.5. The top panel (a) shows the results for the Chamber of Deputies, while the lower panel (b) shows the results for the Senate.

In the Chamber of Deputies, members of the government coalition were significantly less likely to be rolled than members of the opposition. Concertación deputies were rolled on average 9 percent of the time, while Alianza deputies were rolled on average 36 percent of the time. Differences within coalitions are illuminating. Inside the opposition, deputies from RN were less likely to be rolled than deputies from UDI or independent deputies affiliated with the Alianza—their roll rates were about 11 percent lower than those of their right-wing partners. Within the government coalition, there were no differences between the roll rates of DC, PPD, and PRSD deputies. Socialist (PS) deputies had roll rates that were on average slightly higher (close to 3 percent) than those of PPD and DC deputies. However, those leftist deputies in the Socialist Party were significantly less likely to be rolled than the right-wing deputies in UDI (average roll rates are lower by 28 percentage points) or the right-wing independents associated with the Alianza coalition.

In the Senate, there is no significant difference between the individual roll rates of government senators and those of opposition senators. On average senators were rolled in 19 percent of instances. When we look at the partisan affiliation of senators, we find no statistically significant difference between the average individual roll rates of Christian Democrats (DC) and those of members of the opposition parties (RN or UDI), even though the latter have slightly higher averages. Socialist senators (PS) and the appointed "institutional" senators on the far right (INSTA) had similar rates, which were significantly higher than those of other senators (by about seven percentage points).

Overall, the results lend support to our expectations. While the average roll rate for deputies (22 percent) is very similar to the average roll rate for senators

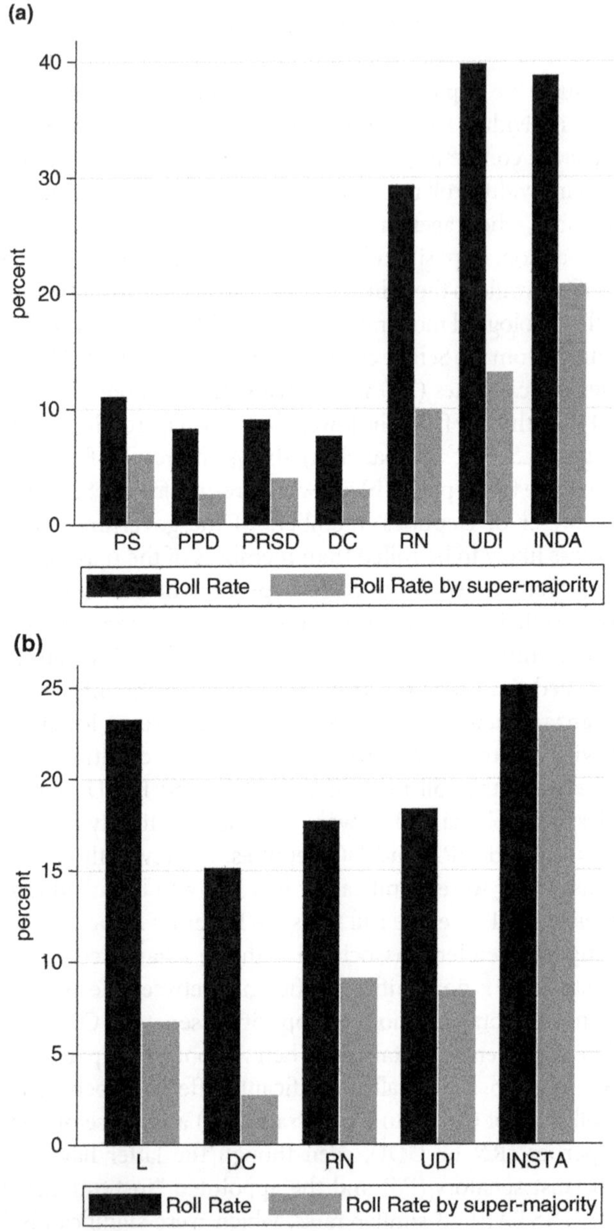

Figure 4.5 Chile, individual roll rates by party

(a) Chamber of Deputies, 2002–2005

(b) Senate, 2004–2005

(19 percent), the pattern of winners and losers is different. In the lower chamber, deputies from the government coalition have reaped the benefits of controlling the offices with agenda setting power. In the Senate, however, the lack of agenda control has led to similar results across coalitions, with extremists as the main losers within each coalition.

It is also illuminating to focus on non-unanimous lopsided votes because they reflect who loses in cross-coalitional arrangements. If, instead of focusing on Nay votes where a majority voted Yea, we focus only on those where a qualified majority of more than four-sevenths of the membership voted Yea, the results for the Chamber of Deputies are maintained (with lower overall rates). In Figure 4.5, the average individual roll rate by super-majority for each partisan group is captured by the gray bars. In the Senate, however, there is no significant difference between the individual super-majority roll rates of leftist Senators (L) and those of other parties. The more habitual losers in these cases were the appointed senators on the far right. Christian Democrat (DC) senators, positioned closer to the center, were significantly better off, on average, than legislators from the right-wing coalition.

Looking at the revealed ideal point of legislators sheds further light on our last few propositions. To this end, we run a series of regression analyses where the dependent variable measures individual roll rates and the main independent variables measure the distance between the legislator and the median of the government coalition, as well as the distance between the legislator and the median of the chamber. Our measures of distance come from bill co-authorship data. To get ideal points we use the procedure advanced in Alemán et al. (2009), which specifically focuses on deriving revealed preferences from bill co-sponsorship matrices. Given that individual roll rates are derived from roll call votes, the use of co-authorship data gives us a source to derive legislators' positions without relying on floor voting behavior. The actual measure is the first dimension (normalized to fall between −1 and 1) after running principal components (with singular value decomposition) on the agreement matrix derived from co-authorship data. The overall fit and correlation between this measure and conventional assessments of ideological positioning is higher for the Chamber of Deputies than for the Senate, but in both cases the measure picks up clear differences between coalitions and across partisan groups. The regressions also include controls for tenure (i.e., *freshmen*), and membership in the chamber's directorate (i.e., Mesa). The results appear in Table 4.1.

The results show that in the Chamber of Deputies as distance to the median of the government coalition increases so does the roll rate. While the predicted individual roll rate is 6.5 percent for a legislator positioned at the median of the government coalition, it is 43.8 percent for a legislator positioned at the

Table 4.1 Distance and individual roll rates, OLS

	Chamber of Deputies				Senate			
	indiv. roll rates		super-majority		indiv. roll rates		super-majority	
	#1	#2	#3	#4	#5	#6	#7	#8
Distance to median from the government coalition	**0.23***** (0.01)	**0.31***** (0.03)	**0.07***** (0.01)	**0.09***** (0.02)	**−0.03** (0.03)	**−0.14** (0.13)	**0.05** (0.04)	**−0.19** (0.17)
Distance to median legislator	~	**−0.12***** (0.04)	~	**−0.03** (0.02)	~	**0.12** (0.13)	~	**0.27** (0.17)
Freshmen	**−0.03**** (0.01)	**−0.03*** (0.01)	**−0.01** (0.01)	**−0.01** (0.01)	**0.02** (0.03)	**0.03** (0.03)	**−0.04** (0.04)	**−0.03** (0.04)
Chamber's Directorate	**−0.06***** (0.02)	**−0.05***** (0.02)	**−0.01** (0.01)	**−0.01** (0.01)	**0.01** (0.04)	**0.02** (0.04)	**−0.06** (0.06)	**−0.04** (0.06)
Constant	**0.11***** (0.01)	**0.13***** (0.01)	**0.04***** (0.01)	**0.05***** (0.01)	**0.20***** (0.02)	**0.19***** (0.02)	**0.07***** (0.02)	**0.06***** (0.02)
R^2	0.78	0.80	0.46	0.47	0.03	0.04	0.05	0.10
Observations	121	121	121	121	49	49	49	49

Standard errors in parenthesis.

median of the opposition coalition. The results also show that members of the Mesa and deputies in their first term are less likely to be rolled. If, instead of using the individual roll rates with a majority cut-off as the dependent variable, we use those super-majority rolls previously mentioned, the significant effect of distance to the median legislator of the government is maintained. The model for the Chamber of Deputies has a very good fit, explaining most of the variance in the data. The regressions for the Senate data, however, have a very poor fit, and none of the independent variables is statistically significant.

In short, this section has shown that the implications of agenda control in the Chilean Congress are reflected in the voting behavior of its members. Differences in results between the Chamber of Deputies and the Senate are the consequence of differences regarding who controls the offices with agenda setting power. Majority control in the lower chamber leads to significant advantages for legislators in the center-left coalition, while in the split Senate there are no significant differences between the two coalitions, and those with slightly higher roll rates are leftist senators from the government coalition and appointed senators on the right-wing opposition.

CONCLUSION

This chapter has examined several aspects of agenda control inside the Chilean Congress. We have specified the institutional foundation of presidential agenda setting authority, and underlined the distribution of agenda setting power inside Congress. The institutional framework portrays a president endowed with significant negative and positive agenda setting power, which reflects a model of constitutional presidentialism substantively different from the one associated with the United States.

In addition to delineating the institutional distribution of power, we have argued that presidents operated with serious positional constraints due mainly to the lack of unified government and super-majority requirements for changes on several substantive policy areas. This had policy consequences: most major presidential bills passed with substantive amendments incorporated during committee deliberations. The amendment process, seldom discussed by the Chilean legislative literature, is highly consequential for the content of bills. Agenda setters need to be engaged. As we have shown, presidents, as well as permanent congressional committees, can mitigate unwanted changes to desired bills towards the end of the legislative process, at the conference and veto stages. Lastly, we presented the first comparison of legislators' voting records in the lower and upper chambers of Chile, and demonstrated that control over the offices with agenda setting power impacts who wins and who loses.

In conclusion, understanding legislative agenda setting helps to explain patterns of lawmaking. This chapter contributes to the understanding of agenda setting authority in Latin American presidential democracies. Specifically, we have examined Chile to determine how formal prerogatives interact with positional constraints. Our results complement prior legislative works, illuminate the implications of legislative institutions, and provide new evidence that underlines both the lawmaking consequences of agenda control and the positional constraints with which agenda setters have to operate. The active legislative role of presidents and the peculiarities of agenda control in Chile illustrate the important and consequential institutional variations that exist within presidential systems.

NOTES

1. Available evidence also shows that Chilean presidents are generally successful at seeing their initiatives become law (Alemán and Navia 2009; Saiegh 2011).
2. The Tribunal can only address constitutional issues and cannot be overridden by the president or Congress.
3. These must be germane to the bill in question.
4. A vote compelled by an executive urgency request may not necessarily be the final passage vote, but it is intended to move the bill forward.
5. As conservative senator Francisco Bulnes noted, some of the limitations established by the reform of 1943 were also circumvented by still allowing congressional initiatives to set wages in the private sector, which in turn had the effect of forcing readjustments in the public sector (cited in Brahm García et al., 2002: 180).
6. The lack of clear germaneness rules for amending bills gave legislators the ability to transform executive initiatives into more complex bills addressing a variety of matters sought by legislators.
7. A majority vote in the plenary, called by a leader of a party bloc, can remove an item from this *tabla de pronto despacho*. The Mesa, with the unanimity of the leaders of party blocs, can also fast-track bills under a process called *tabla de despacho inmediato*.
8. Unanimity of the leaders of party blocs is required for such a fast-track schedule to be applied.
9. Among all the permanent committees, the Public Finances committees (Hacienda) of each chamber stand out. Not only must all tax-and-spend bills be directed to the Public Finances committees, but any other bill that has some financial implication also must be referred there.
10. Committees can still protect their own positions by making appropriate counterproposals when needed.
11. In Chile conference committees (*comisiones mixtas*) are formed under two different circumstances: one is after the chamber of origin rejects the amendments introduced by the revising chamber (constitutional Article 68) and the other is after a revising chamber rejects a bill approved by the chamber of origin (Article 67). In the period prior to the military government, conference committees played a less relevant role in policy-making, partly because the constitutional rules in place were different. Under the 1925 constitution, the formation of conference committee was optional and the shuttling of bills between chambers could go on for more rounds than under the (contemporary) 1980 constitution.
12. Moreover, no formal procedure exists to force conference committees to address particular indications from the parent chambers (as is the case in the US Congress).
13. Evidence from final passage votes has also shown that in the Chamber of Deputies the Concertación is never "rolled," that is, bills always passed with the support of most members of the coalition (Alemán 2006).

14. In very few cases (4 percent) there are major proposals advanced publicly by the executive that were never actually introduced as bills.
15. For the post-1989 period, data are available electronically from the website of the Chilean Congress. For the earlier period we collected data from several yearly records in the *Diario de Sesiones* and the related *Historia de La Ley*, available at the Library of Congress in Santiago, Chile.
16. The dataset starts in March 1990 and goes until February 2006, when the congressional period ended.
17. Around 62 percent received some form of urgency and 31 percent received either *suma* or *immediate* urgencies.
18. The budget bills under Frei and Alwyn were also passed promptly but under a timetable where the default is the president's bill—they were not declared urgent by the executive.
19. See the transcripts from the debate in the *Diario de Sesiones del Senado*, August 7, 1991, p. 9.
20. This refers to the initial vote in the *general* phase.
21. Two of the financial bills were also very short (one was just half a page, and the other two pages long).
22. Speech given on January 16, 2001 (*Diario de Sesiones*, p. 20).
23. It is worthwhile to note that the eight failures in terms of conference committee reports of major bills occurred in the Chamber of Deputies.
24. The voting process usually includes the "general" and "particular" phases, but on occasions, usually when there are no amendments offered, the general and particular vote can be taken together.

5

The Unrealized Potential of Presidential Coalitions in Colombia

Royce Carroll and Mónica Pachón

Historically, the Colombian executive wielded considerable control over the policy-making process, even when the president lacked legislative support. Before the adoption of the constitution of 1991, this was possible chiefly due to extensive decree powers which allowed the president to routinely bypass a legislative process that was mostly composed of locally oriented legislation initiated by deputies. The 1991 reforms curtailed unilateral executive power, making the president much more reliant on legislative support. However, throughout the 1990s the party system became even less accommodating to the executive as parties increasingly fragmented and a pattern of extreme individualism continued (Shugart et al. 2007). Without unilateral avenues or strong congressional party support, the president faced constant legislative resistance. The perceived failures of the political system ignited a debate on the need for electoral reform aimed at encouraging a stronger party system, which finally passed in 2003 and significantly reduced party fragmentation in the House and Senate (Pachón and Shugart 2010).

Along with electoral reform, multi-party coalitions have emerged in which presidents increasingly include members of various parties in the cabinet. However, parties have not served as firm building blocks for linking such coalitions to control of the legislative process. Despite major changes to the party system and a major reform to the electoral system, parties remain individualized and with weak programmatic foundations. These factors operate in conjunction with legislative rules that greatly empower individual members of Congress. As a result, coalitional presidentialism in Colombia has yet to serve as an effective means to coordinate between legislative parties and the executive branch.

In this chapter, we analyze the current Colombian legislative process in terms of the input and output of the legislative agenda during the four presidential periods from 1998 to 2014. Our sample includes all bills introduced in Congress during this period, with a subset of "major" bills coded as those mentioned in the media—specifically those appearing on the front page of the largest national newspaper (*El Tiempo*). During this time, the electoral and party system has changed significantly, while presidential constitutional power and the internal rules of Congress have remained unchanged. Importantly, changes in Colombia's party system have coincided with the formation of multi-party coalition cabinets designed to facilitate executive–legislative relations instead of ad hoc legislative coalitions. Such presidential coalitions have been associated with executive–legislative coordination in the policy-making process, especially in Brazil (Figueiredo and Limongi 2000; Amorim Neto 2002). Colombia's recent party system changes have indeed produced coalition building between legislative parties and the president. However, we show that the growth in such coalitions does not lead to any additional advantages for these presidents because inter-party coalitions do not translate into a means to organize the legislative process. First, legislators face incentives to focus on developing personal constituencies rather than supporting their party's collective agenda. Second, unlike in Brazil, decentralized formal institutional rules in Congress empower deputies to influence both the agenda and the content of bills, which affects the legislative efficiency of the governing coalition. As a result, legislative bills continue to predominate in legislative output, deputies from parties in the coalition have no advantages over others in passing legislation, and executive failures remain just as frequent despite large and increasingly formalized coalitions.

The first section of this chapter discusses the institutional features that allocate rights over the legislative agenda, focusing on the powers of the president and the features of the chamber that empower individual deputies. The second section examines the characteristics of the party system and coalition patterns, focusing on the recent changes brought about by the 2003 electoral reform. The third part discusses the empirical record with regard to the introduction and passage of legislation. We find that the dramatic changes in the party system, though bringing coalitions designed for more cooperative executive–legislative relations, have not produced substantial changes in the president's or coalition parties' ability to efficiently control the legislative agenda relative to the ad hoc bargaining that preceded it. Following Alemán and Tsebelis in the introduction of this volume, the absence of cohesive majority governments in Colombia requires that we focus on the details of agenda setting institutions and the incentives of legislative actors to better understand policy outcomes.

THE INSTITUTIONS OF AGENDA CONTROL IN CONGRESS

The Mesa Directiva in each chamber presides over the bill scheduling and is in charge of leading the debate according to the House and Senate rules. The Mesa is composed of a president and two vice presidents, each with one-year terms and without the possibility of re-election. Despite the short terms for the members of the Mesa, and the practice of formal votes to replace these positions after each year, the parties in Congress reach a negotiated agreement on which members will hold these positions across the entire presidential term before the first legislative session begins. On the floor, the Mesa president also is in charge of ensuring that bills are actually voted on, as widespread absenteeism means that active mobilization is needed to form a quorum and the Mesa president has the power to sanction members. Such mobilization is also necessary to protect executive bills from amendments.

While controlling the legislative leadership in each chamber is important, it by no means enables party negotiations within the coalition to control the agenda. First, unlike other countries with presidential coalitions, such as Chile or Brazil, no formal institutions exist in Colombia's Congress to empower or even recognize party leaders. Only since 2010, under Santos, has even an informal effort emerged to integrate Mesa and party leadership and better coordinate among governing parties. This produced the Mesa de Unidad Nacional, an informal body in which the president and his ministers discuss and decide the legislative agenda with the presidents of all parties in the coalition (Prieto 2011). This arrangement was intended to facilitate integration between the formal leaders of parties, the executive coalition, and the agenda setting process.

By far the most important institutions governing the legislative process in practice are legislative committees. All bills are required to go through the committee stage and neither the Mesa nor the floor can discharge bills; thus, it is imperative for the executive coalition to attempt to influence at least the most important committees. Members of the seven permanent committees in the Senate and in the House of Representatives are chosen through negotiation among parties and can serve the entire term. Historically, legislators with the most clout and prominence tend to get their preferred committee assignment and to become chairs (Pachón 2003). Each committee's president (chair) is formally elected by the committee but these too are assigned in practice by informal negotiation for one-year non-renewable terms. Committee presidents decide on the agenda of each committee and choose the *ponentes* (rapporteurs) for the bills assigned to the committee.[1] Being a *ponente* gives a legislator the advantage to propose changes to the bill even before the debate is opened to the members of the committee. The informal practice is that the proposal made by the *ponente* is voted on in the committee, not the original text proposed by the author.

Primarily as a result of these considerable powers, legislators in Colombia can delay and influence all bills that go through the legislative process. Negotiations among party leaders in the coalition and the president are no guarantee these hurdles can be overcome.[2]

Formally, the president has several powers to influence the agenda. First, the president holds the right of exclusive introductory powers in certain policy areas. Second, the president has the means to expedite the consideration of bills. Third, the president has urgency powers, such that Congress is required to begin committee deliberations and decide on priority bills within thirty days. The president can also freeze the agenda until a decision is taken, reducing the ability to delay consideration.[3] In addition, the president can call for joint sessions of the House and Senate committees, which reduces the time of deliberations and limits amendments and dilatory strategies.[4] Finally, the president can use extraordinary sessions during the legislative recess for Congress to debate the executive's priority bills.[5] Together these powers have the potential to ensure priority for executive initiatives, but by no means allow the president to bypass efforts by members of Congress to impede executive bills.

Once executive bills are on the agenda, the president must still work to restrict amendments from altering legislation, as the bills are fully open to committee or floor amendments throughout the process. Open amendment rights can be used by any members and often are employed by members to claim credit for a modification of an executive bill. Further, the executive branch cannot itself propose amendments except through members of their coalition in Congress.[6] Conference committees provide a venue for presidents to counteract deputy interference in the content of legislation but, depending on their makeup, this process can just as easily work against executive interests (Alemán and Pachón 2008). For these reasons, even with a majority coalition, the president cannot easily control all aspects of the legislative process for executive bills, much less legislative initiatives.

Meanwhile, the president lacks unilateral power to resort to decrees except under temporary emergency situations, the constitutionality of which is determined by the Constitutional Court.[7] Although the Court may allow decree power to be exercised before review, even for months, states of emergency do not provide an alternative to statutes. As such they have been used infrequently.[8]

In sum, the institutional and political circumstances within the Congress make it extremely difficult for the president to control the policy-making process without consistent cooperation from a coalition in Congress. Overall, consistent with the expectations of Alemán and Tsebelis in the introductory chapter, formal agenda setting powers are insufficient for presidents to overcome the challenges stemming from heterogeneous legislative coalitions in combination with decentralized chamber rules.

THE POLITICAL PARTY SYSTEM IN THE COLOMBIAN LEGISLATURE

The Colombian political party system has changed significantly since the 1991 constitution. While the Liberal and Conservative Party (PCC) still initially dominated, the electoral system—which lacked any restrictions on the number of lists per party—led to extreme electoral fragmentation (Archer and Shugart 1997; Crisp and Ingall 2002; Crisp and Desposato 2004). This resulted from both decentralization reforms that promoted localized parties and a low effective threshold to earn seats in the legislature (Cox and Shugart 1996; Rodriguez Raga 2002; Moreno and Escobar-Lemmon 2008; Avellaneda and Escobar-Lemmon 2012). The Senate began employing a single national district, which was intended to encourage more nationally oriented senators (but see Crisp and Desposato 2004) and certainly enabled small parties to gain representation. In the years following the reform, Colombia incrementally moved from a highly personalistic two-party system to having more than seventy-two legally recognized political parties and movements, which made it increasingly difficult for the president to form the coalitions that became necessary in the absence of decree power (Gutiérrez 2007; Cárdenas et al. 2008). Multiple party membership (known as "double militancy") allowed traditional party leaders to form party-like movements with independent political campaigns and no accountability to traditional party directorates. Analyzing the traditional political parties from 1991 through 2002, Roll (2005) identified at least six different factions of Liberals (the nominal plurality party) with just a small percentage of the members holding the official endorsement and, in the context of unrecorded votes, little party discipline. Roll observed that "the members of the traditional political parties in the House of Representatives are mostly interested in finding resources for their regions and consider party positions as secondary with respect to their main objective" (Roll 2005: 48).[9]

Extreme party system fragmentation was persistently criticized by the public, non-governmental organizations, and members of the political elite. In 2003, the electoral system was reformed to an open-list system[10] from one that functioned as a multi-member plurality system with candidates effectively independent from one another.[11] This reform naturally had a significant impact on the aggregation of the political party system, as parties had to limit their lists to only one per district, as well as reach a 2 percent threshold to win representation in 2010, and 3 percent in 2014 (Pachón and Shugart 2010). As politicians joined larger party lists, a less fragmented multi-party system took shape. To illustrate, in 2002, fifty-three parties in the House had two or fewer seats, comprising 38 percent of all seats. By 2010, only six parties won representation in the House with fewer than three seats. Under the open-list system, the members of parties continued to reflect diverse personal constituencies, but the unification into single entities nevertheless coincided with potentially more meaningful roles for parties in the political system, including the possibility for multi-party presidential coalitions.[12]

Presidential Coalitions

Given the power that legislators have to shape the agenda, especially in terms of blocking and delaying legislation, the president has a strong incentive to form stable relationships with a coalition of deputies in Congress. During the period under study, presidents attempted to form a variety of coalitions using cabinet appointments and negotiating with legislative parties. These have grown in their size, depth, and formality across the four presidential periods under study. As described in Table 5.1, Pastrana's coalition, called the Alliance for Change (La Alianza por el Cambio), was made up of the PCC, a faction of Liberal Party dissidents, and a number of independent legislators. His coalition quickly fell apart in the aftermath of the defeat of his 1999 electoral reform proposal and a subsequent corruption scandal in Congress. He was only able to rebuild his coalition by joining with a significant number of Liberal Party legislators in exchange for giving them a more prominent role in the cabinet. In addition to having the weakest coalition, Pastrana is also the least popular president in the sample, with initially 27 percent approval during his first coalition period and only about 20 percent after his coalition breakdown.

Table 5.1 Presidential coalitions and political support in Colombia, 1998–2014

		Mean presidential approval	Parties included in the congressional coalition	House Seat %	Senate Seat %
Pastrana	1998–2000	27.75%	Conservative Party, Liberal faction, several independent movements and indigenous representatives.	58.40%	52.90%
	2000–2001	20.75%	Conservative Party, several independent movements and indigenous representatives.	38.60%	28.40%
	2001–2002	20.60%	Liberal faction, Conservative Party, and several independent movements and indigenous representatives.	58.40%	52.90%
Uribe I	2002–2005	71.21%	Conservative Party, Cambio Radical, Liberal faction, Alas Equipo Colombia, Convergencia Ciudadana, Colombia Democrática, and Colombia Viva.	65.10%	58.80%
	2005–2006	71%		62.61%	66.97%
Uribe II	2006–2007	70.10%	Conservative Party, Cambio Radical, U Party, Alas Equipo Colombia, Convergencia Ciudadana, Colombia Democrática and Colombia Viva.	62.43%	68.80%
	2007–2008	75%		63.43%	70.93%
	2008–2009	73.30%	Conservative Party, U Party, Alas Equipo Colombia, Convergencia Ciudadana, Colombia Democrática and Colombia Viva.	51.96%	57.38%
	2009–2010	68%		52.63%	55.14%
Santos	2010–2011	69.50%	Conservative Party, U Party, Liberal Party, Cambio Radical	83%	73%
	2012–2014	43.70%	Conservative Party, U Party, Liberal Party, Cambio Radical, and Green Party.	84%	78%

Source: Author estimates based on data from Congreso Visible and Invamer Gallup.

President Uribe's first congressional coalition from 2002 to 2006 marked a watershed moment in the party system. First, while Uribe's coalition was also very fragmented, it was composed of the new parties that emerged as the traditional Liberal and Conservative parties lost support. Second, Uribe won office as an independent, consolidating the division of the Liberal Party on which he had earlier built his political career.[13] With the subsequent passage of the electoral reform and Uribe's successful re-election, the political system reorganized as a new party composed of his supporters, Partido de la U (or U Party), was created, simplifying the process of coalition formation after the 2006 election. During this time, many observers characterized Uribe's coalition as a "steam-roller Congress," with critics even suggesting there was insufficient attention to minority views (e.g., Uprimny 2009), although such impressions were heavily influenced by Uribe's public popularity. Uribe's effort to seek a constitutional amendment allowing him a third term shook the unity of the coalition, however, resulting in the loss of Cambio Radical's support. Nonetheless, Uribe's popularity remained as strong as in the beginning of his term, with a 71 percent mean approval rate, and his popularity maintained these levels or improved throughout his second term.

Despite the existence of congressional coalitions in both Pastrana and Uribe administrations, the nomination of the cabinet remained a largely separate process from congressional organization. Most cabinet members during this time could be considered "independents" or technocrats despite their formal association with a political party since they had at most a very loose connection to their parties in Congress. President Santos, historically a Liberal and former Defense Minister of President Uribe, ran as the candidate from the U Party in 2010. After his victory,[14] Santos was able to obtain support from the Conservative (PCC), Liberal, and Cambio Radical parties to build a grand coalition—Unidad Nacional (Hoskin and Pachón 2011). This cabinet coalition is known to have involved policy negotiations in exchange for legislative support. Notably, to obtain the support of the Liberals, Santos made a major concession on compensation for victims from the civil conflict, a prominent Liberal proposal that had been opposed by Uribe. The Conservatives preserved influence over rural policies, such as subsidies to coffee producers. A program for housing for the poor was given priority due to the inclusion of Cambio Radical, who obtained the Housing ministry. Given the size of the coalition seat share, the negotiations within the coalition held the potential to substantially reduce legislative bottlenecks for the government agenda. Santos also began with strong public support—in his first two years he had an average approval rating of 69 percent, However, Santos lost much of his support after 2012, with his approval falling to 43 percent when he pursued a constitutional reform to streamline the justice system that resulted in an embarrassing failure.[15]

The small leftist PDA, in opposition throughout the Uribe period, remained the most visible ideological opponent of the president. Other small but influential parties, such as the Partido MIRA and the Green Party, also obtained representation in the House and Senate with only a handful of seats.

The Programmatic Nature of Parties and Patterns of Roll Call Voting

Here we illustrate some of the recent patterns in the party system by examining the distribution of preferences across the parties as well as their aggregate voting patterns. Figure 5.1 displays a series of density plots of the distribution of preferences of legislators in the House using the basic dimensional space underlying responses to elite survey data[16] for the period 1998–2010, estimated jointly via the Bayesian implementation of Aldrich–McKelvey's scaling method (Aldrich and McKelvey 1977; Hare et al. 2015).[17] The placements derived from the University of Salamanca's elite survey data suggest that nominal party groupings corresponded with at best very loose ideological differentiation in both Pastrana's administration and Uribe's first term. Yet, the parties are ranked intuitively, with Liberals containing a tendency towards "left" self-placement. In addition, the Uribista faction of the Liberals that formed after 2002 tended to identify roughly to the right of the "official" faction.

Compared to either of those periods, the period 2006–10—the first after the electoral reform—produced programmatic inter-party differences. In this period, members of the U Party[18] and especially Cambio Radical show considerable internal heterogeneity.[19] Among the other parties, ideological positions are much clearer, however. The members of the Liberal and PDA political parties, especially the latter, position themselves on the left and have less internal variance than the centrist parties. Similarly, unlike the other parties associated with the governing coalition, the PCC is composed mostly of members that place themselves clearly on the right of the ideological spectrum.

In contrast to the survey data just presented, roll call voting reflects the end result of the party influence on members as well as the indirect influence of legislative organization on the agenda and therefore the set of choices available to legislators. Thus, the apparent differences between roll call–based measures and survey based measures can be taken as an indication of these organizational effects in the House. In Figure 5.2, we present a histogram of ideal points based on the first dimension Optimal Classification coordinates (Poole 2000; Poole et al. 2009)[20] of all recorded roll call votes cast during the latter part of the 2006–10 period, when recording began.[21]

Roll call voting under Uribe (2009–10) appears to reflect a polarized chamber in which the differences between the centrist deputies and those on the right within the governing coalition are not clearly visible. Instead, the PCC, the U Party, and to a lesser degree Cambio Radical are not distinguishable and concentrated on the "right" (i.e., government) side of the spectrum. Meanwhile, parties outside the coalition—Liberals and the PDA—are positioned at various

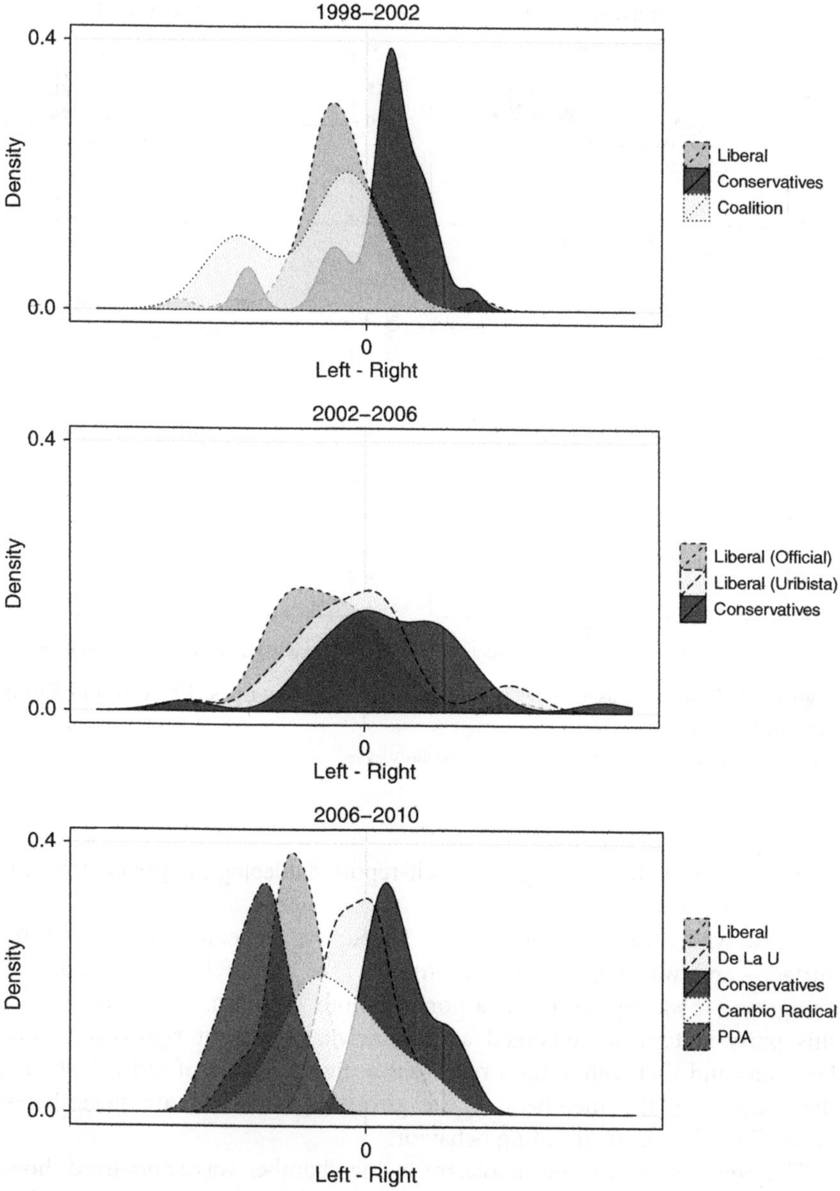

Figure 5.1 Scaled deputy ideological self-identification in the House of Representatives, 1998–2010

Source: Author estimates based on data from the PELA Survey, Universidad de Salamanca.

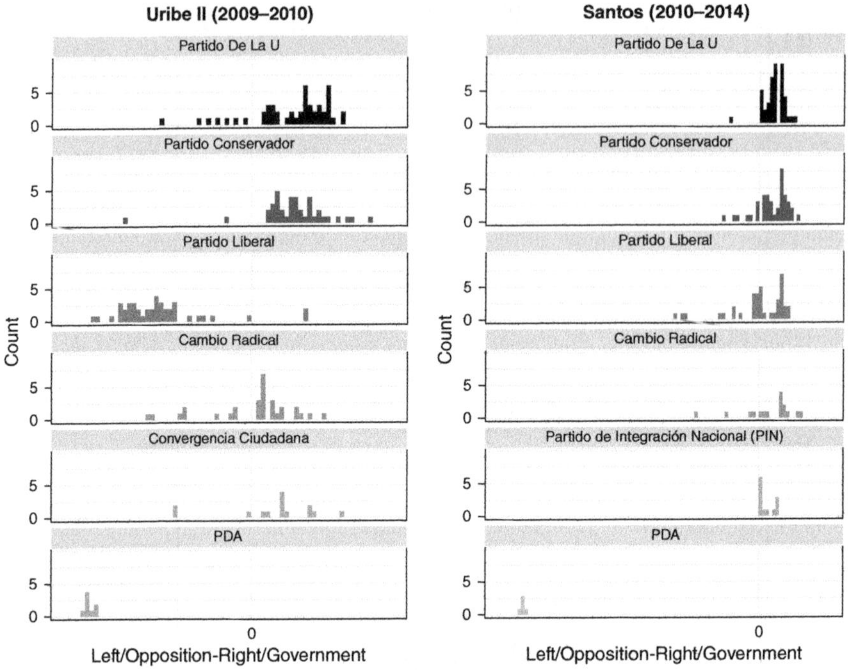

Figure 5.2 Roll call–based ideal points of Colombian deputies, Uribe II and Santos administrations

Source: Author estimates based on data from Congreso Visible.

points on the left, reflecting their self-reported ideological preferences and opposition posture.

Thus, while the coalition behind Uribe was generally rightist on the surface—and was opposed consistently by the center left and far left in Congress—it was by no means a homogeneous coalition. While the PCC in this party system has emerged as a somewhat coherent right-wing force, Uribistas and their other allies represent a diverse group of individuals. For the most part, the members of the governing coalition are nevertheless generally in line in their voting behavior.

The emergence of some bipolarity in the chamber was short-lived, however. As described previously, Santos formed an even broader coalition than Uribe. This coalition nominally incorporated all major parties, unifying the parties associated with Uribe's governments with the largest opposition party in the previous term, the Liberals. The unipolar distribution of voting patterns by party from this term captures the dynamic of a centrist coalition formed around the president. As cabinet partners, Liberals are no longer distinguished from the government, reflecting both their coalition membership and policy movement by the government to incorporate Liberal positions. Meanwhile, the political right is best represented by the most conservative members of the PCC.[22] The only party functioning as a consistent opposition in voting patterns is the small leftist Polo Democrático. Further, Santos' coalition coincides with an internal consolidation of the most ideologically diverse governing parties, De la U and Cambio Radical, each of which had contained groups of members opposed to the government during Uribe's second term.

Taken together, it is apparent that the parties in Congress have developed programmatic differences although floor voting is chiefly a function of government membership and does not illuminate inter-party differences. In the next section, we show that even these dramatic changes have not led to aggregate changes in patterns of lawmaking.

PATTERNS OF LEGISLATIVE ACTIVITY

We now examine how the institutional setting interacts with the political actors involved in the policy-making process in Colombia. We focus on the four most recent legislative periods—1998–2014—and distinguish local, national, and major bills from others in terms of legislative introduction, success, and productivity.

Who Introduces Legislation?

At the introduction stage, a large number of bills come from the legislature. Executive introduction has, overall, been stable at roughly 10–12 percent of all bills in the period considered in this chapter. Figure 5.3 displays the total number of bills introduced by each branch and chamber during the period in question, divided by two-year periods under each president. The general patterns among branches are stable across time, both in the proportions each branch introduces, as well as total bills during the period. One of the biggest exceptions to this stability takes place in the most recent period, during the last two years of Santos' term. This period of inactivity coincides with the large-scale failure with the justice reform mentioned earlier and the subsequent crisis that it generated within Congress (Escandón 2013).[23]

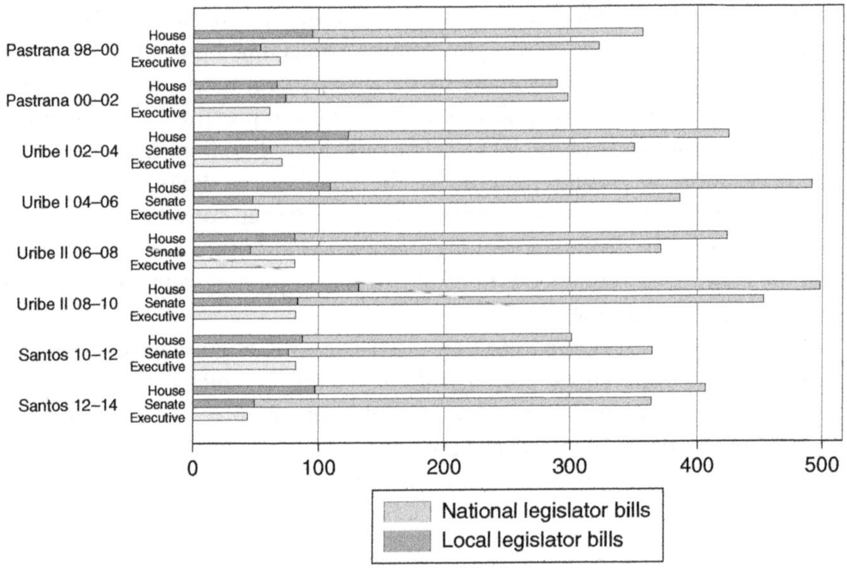

Figure 5.3 Bills introduced by branch and chamber, 1998–2014

Source: Author calculation based on data from Congreso Visible.

In terms of patterns across parties, these vary little across time when taking into account party sizes, but it is noteworthy that two small non-government parties—MIRA and PDA—account for a substantial amount (293 and 227 respectively since 2002) of total bills introduced despite very small seat shares. Each of these parties is associated with efforts to take positions using legislative introduction.

An important source of variation in the Colombian Congress is whether bills deal with national or local policy, which we would expect to vary with changes in the party system and coalition patterns. To examine this, we follow criteria similar to Taylor-Robinson and Díaz (1999) to classify bills as "local" and "national." A bill intended to target a municipality, a hospital within a certain region, or some economic sector in a particular region is considered "local." Bills with no specific targets modifying a code, or creating a social benefit for a broader group of citizens who fulfill certain criteria are considered "national" bills.[24]

For the most part, whether national or local, the bulk of bills can be interpreted as the independent activities of individual deputies. While the vast majority of bills introduced deal with some aspect of national policy, about 13 percent of deputy bills are local in nature.

Who Passes Bills?

So far we have discussed simply legislative activity, without regard to viability. Here we show how many of the bills introduced actually make it to the floor and have a chance of approval. Figure 5.4 shows the fate of bills by presidential period separated by branch of origin. There are four categories shown: first, those bills that could not make it out of an initial committee stage; second, those that passed one chamber and failed in committee in the second chamber; third, bills that died in the plenary floor in either chamber; finally, all bills that made it through the legislative process.[25]

The vast majority of legislative bills—over 70 percent on average—fail to pass the committee stage, although this has declined slightly over time. For the executive, this number is much lower at 21 percent (excluding treaties), the notable outlier being the second part of Uribe II discussed in the following. While on average 66 percent of the executive bills pass, this figure is only 17 percent for legislators.

Although floor failures for executive bills indicate at least some weakness in mobilizing support on the floor, the committee stage is the dominant reason executive bills fail. Despite the efforts of the president to bargain with parties

Figure 5.4 Fate of bills introduced by each branch, 1998–2014

Source: Author calculation based on data from Congreso Visible.

and control both the Mesa and committee memberships, the coalition is routinely insufficient to ensure that executive bills receive floor consideration. In addition to these weaknesses in positive agenda power, the coalition is not always reliable in ensuring bills opposed by the president do not reach the floor. One high-profile example was the bill known as the Victim's Law, pushed by the Liberals when in opposition during the second Uribe term. This bill proposed compensation to victims of the ongoing civil conflict. Despite the president's opposition, Liberal Party leaders introduced the bill and were able to obtain floor majorities in two rounds of debates in 2008 and 2009.[26] In short, negative agenda control often did not successfully serve executive interests even under the large and more organized coalition of Santos.

While there are some distinctions across terms, there is no apparent trend in favor of presidential success or any systematic correspondence to the type of coalitions formed. However, one major deviation occurs during Uribe's second term, when despite high public approval, the president faced a very high rate of bills failing in the first stage. This period coincided with two extraordinary events that affected relations with Congress. The first was an intense confrontation between the president and the courts in which seventy-three members of Uribe's coalition were under investigation for ties to illegal groups. These events forced many legislators to leave Congress and thirty were prosecuted and detained. With their seats threatened by new legislators, incumbent legislators were concerned about their own status in these investigations and the coalition's ability to facilitate movement through the legislative process by coordination with Congress was weakened (Pachón 2009). When Uribe's attempt to deal with these matters using decree power was stopped by the Constitutional Court, a subsequent effort to pursue statutes without coordination with coalition members led to another set of stalled initiatives. The second major event disrupting executive–legislative coordination was the controversy surrounding Uribe's attempt to be re-elected to a third term. Though ultimately unsuccessful, this issue led to conflict between parties in the coalition as well as within them (Ungar 2008; Congreso Visible 2009), most visibly precipitating the departure of Cambio Radical from the governing coalition.

We next examine more closely how presidents and legislators have varied in their ability to ensure the passage of bills and how the type of legislative bills corresponds to their success. First, looking again at presidential success, Figure 5.5 shows the predicted success rates from probit estimates of enactment as a function of type and administration (see Table 5.A1 in the Appendix) from 1998 to 2014 for executive and legislative bills (both House and Senate). Contrary to a frequent characterization of Uribe's coalition as "steamrolling," executive success overall did not change from Pastrana to

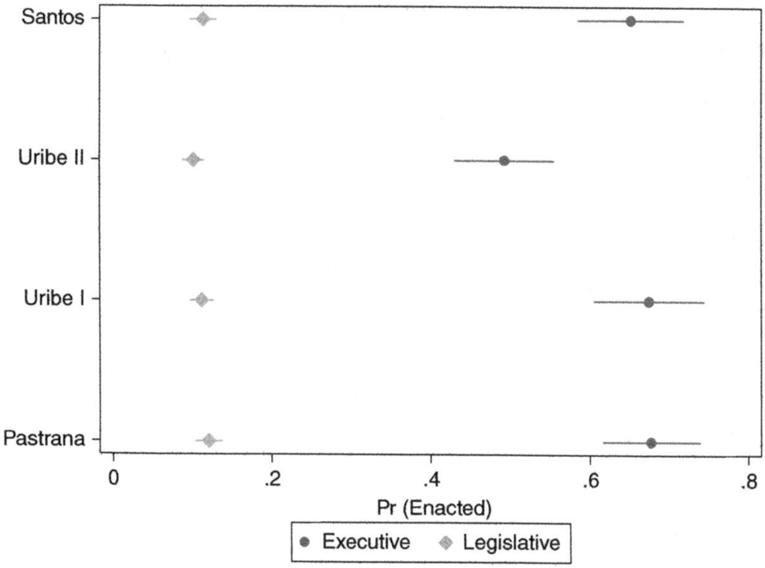

Figure 5.5 Predicted success rates from all bills introduced by the executive and legislators, 1998–2014

Source: Author calculation based on data from Congreso Visible.

Uribe's first term and actually declined sharply in Uribe's second term. While more than 67 percent of the total bills introduced by Pastrana's administration were passed, Uribe's success reduced to 62 percent in his first term, and to only about 50 percent in his second, a statistically significant drop. Santos' term, meanwhile, restored but did not exceed the previous rates of success under Uribe and Pastrana, despite much more formal efforts to organize a multi-party coalition.[27]

While the change in the party system may not have led to clear differences in executive success, differences might yet be apparent in the success of bills from legislators. To allow us to identify any such pattern, we examine legislative bills during this period allowing the probability of success to vary by author's coalition status, by president, and by the national–local emphasis of the bills. Figure 5.6 shows the predicted success rates based on a probit model interacting dummies for each presidential term both with dummies for the government coalition status of each author party and dummies for the local or national content of the bill (see Table 5.A2 in the appendix). To identify the coalition status of bill authors we consider both formal party affiliation and position towards the government. The latter is necessary to differentiate two groups of Liberals, those supporting the governing coalition under Pastrana

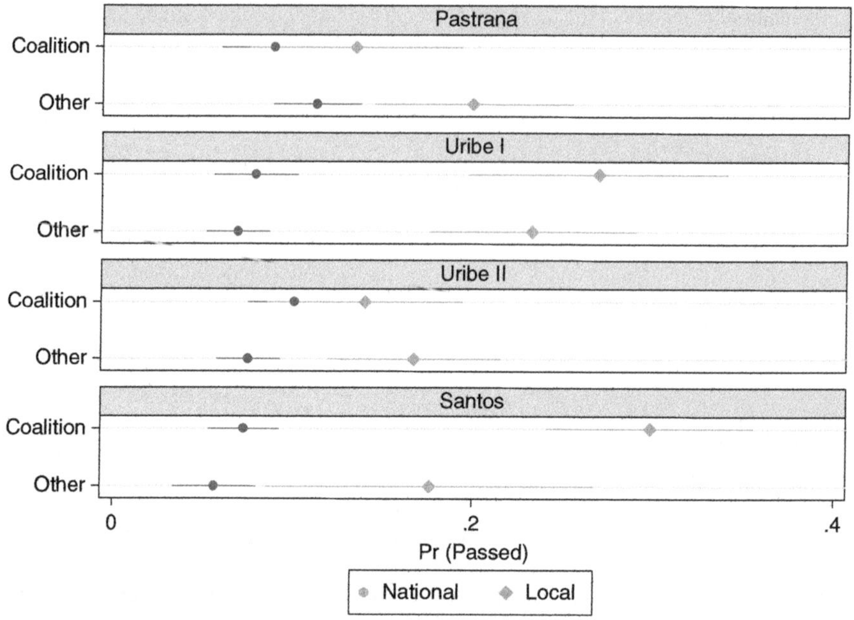

Figure 5.6 Predicted success rates from all bills introduced by legislators, by coalition status and type, 1998–2014

Source: Author calculation based on data from Congreso Visible.

and Uribe's first term and those known as the "oficialistas" who followed the party line and opposed those presidents. Bills that have more than one sponsor are classified according to the affiliation of the majority of sponsors.

First, a clear pattern is present that local bills have a much higher passage rate than national bills. One reason for this is that local bills do not provoke the policy conflicts associated with national policy, thus there are fewer political barriers to passage. Second, coalition status of the author does not greatly affect probabilities of success for bills, although there is some difference present among local bills under Santos. Across terms, the probability of success for national bills changes little. The main source of variation comes from changes in the success of local bills across time, where legislators of all types had much greater success rates on local bills during Uribe I.

To examine how these successes translate into the overall output of the legislature, we show the aggregate numbers of bills produced from the executive and the legislature, broken into two-year periods. Figure 5.7 shows the total legislative productivity by scope and branch of origin, over two-year

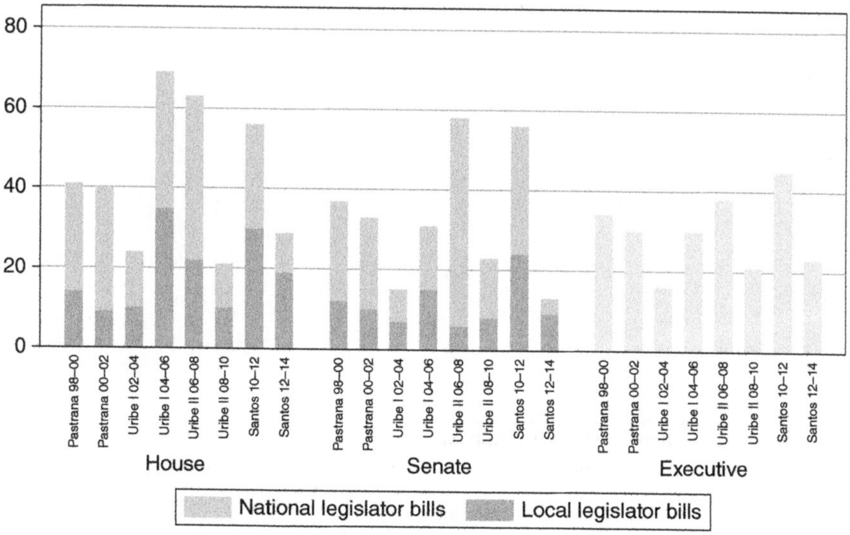

Figure 5.7 Overall legislative productivity, 1998–2013

Source: Author calculation based on data from Congreso Visible.

periods within each term. Although success rates are low due to the large number of bills introduced, legislators are nevertheless responsible for the vast majority of the total legislative output. Even when considering just national bills, legislative bills consistently rival the quantity produced by the executive. But the greater emphasis on local bills is apparent in that they constitute the majority of successful bills at any given time in each house. In fact, not only do the House and Senate both have a tendency to introduce local bills, the Senate actually has considerably more success in passing them. Again the dramatic drop-off in productivity in the final years of Uribe's second term is clear. The difference between the first and second half of Santos' first period is also noteworthy, with the latter being much less productive for all types of bills, and Senate bills declining most dramatically. Still, there are no apparent differences in the emphasis on national or local bills.

Introduction and Enactment of Major Bills

While we have separated local from national bills, only a few "national" bills are broad in their scope and political salience. Figure 5.8 shows

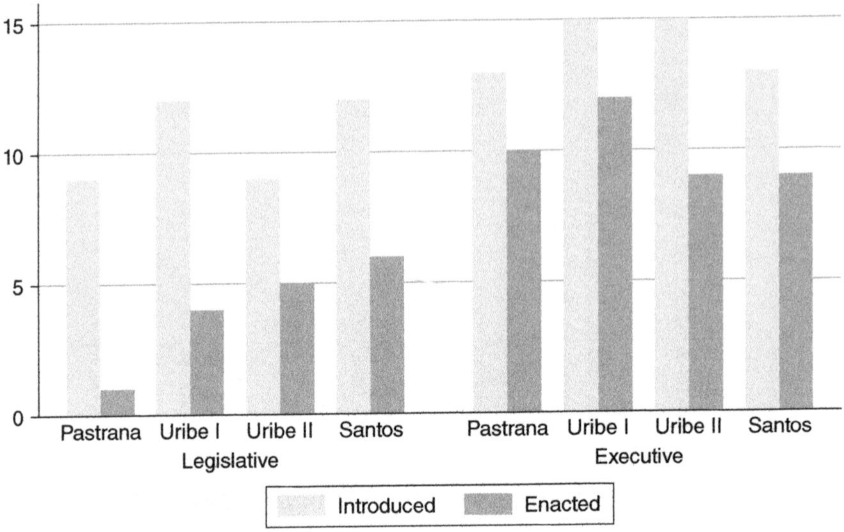

Figure 5.8 Introductory and enactment patterns on major bills, 1998–2012
Source: Author calculation.

patterns of introduction and enactment of "major" bills, defined here as those mentioned in the media—specifically those appearing in the front page of the largest national newspaper (*El Tiempo*). By this definition, the executive has introduced ten to fifteen major bills per year, despite very different coalitions and political contexts. From the executive side, aside from several treaties, these bills typically include major campaign promises, routine but important bills such as the budget, and bills that respond to major events. Legislators' major bills are almost as frequent. The major bills from legislators mainly reflect efforts to respond to current events or concerns of the public, especially concerning violence or fatalities due to lack of regulation or enforcement. Some deal with structural reforms such as the electoral system or other constitutional changes. All of these bills are classified as "national."[28]

About 70 percent of executive major bills are enacted, consistent with our analysis that all four presidents have generally managed a similarly moderate degree of control over the legislative process even if under widely varying circumstances and using different means.

While both legislators and the executive have the capacity to produce bills prominent enough for major media coverage, enacted laws on these topics have been far less frequent for legislators. This was particularly apparent during Pastrana, though successful major legislative bills have been increasingly common since Uribe's era.

While this may reflect the elements of a more party-oriented legislature, one must interpret this pattern with caution. First, the sample is quite small. Second, the nature of these bills must be taken into account. For example, widely publicized bills increasing prison terms for drunk drivers, imposing the death penalty for sexual crimes, and regulating church leaders have been successfully enacted, but tend to reflect the ability of politicians to appeal to public support for popular policies rather than attempts to associate parties with broad policy solutions. Thus, even when accounting for notoriety, there are arguably important qualitative differences in the types of major laws successfully pursued by legislators and the president.

One way to illustrate the more controversial nature of executive proposals is to examine the amendment process of bills, which captures the conflict among legislators on the content of the bills. The closest systematic proxy for the amendment process in available data is the number of floor votes per bill, which is only available since 2009. The logic of this measure is that, given the open amendment rule currently used in the legislature, major bills would be subject to significant efforts at modification, while less important bills would go through the legislature with less debate and amendments. Thus, to do this, we divided the sample of bills for which we have votes into those that are legislative, executive, and major executive. Although this illustration is limited, we note that there is a significant difference between legislative and executive bills in terms of effort at amendment. While the major legislative bills during this time have only 3.3 votes on average before passage, this is lower than even ordinary (non-major) executive bills, which have thirteen votes on average. We interpret this as suggesting that the types of major bills getting passed from legislators are not especially controversial in terms of the main policy disputes among parties. Meanwhile, the major *executive* bills during the same time have received an average of thirty-two votes per bill, which suggests that these bills are drawing a far greater number of amendments than major bills coming from legislators.

CONCLUSIONS

The post-1991 era of Colombian politics has been characterized by tremendous change in the formal structure of executive power, shifting much greater responsibility for national policy to the legislature. Without the ability to pursue a unilateral course, presidents have incentives to work with legislative parties in order to control the legislative agenda. After a period of extreme fragmentation, the emergence of nominal partisan support surrounding Alvaro Uribe suggested a move in the direction of more stable and party-based executive–legislative coalitions. Presidential support in the form of negotiated multi-party majorities has grown considerably, especially in the aftermath of the 2003 electoral reforms and with the Santos coalition in 2010, which clearly involved negotiations over policy in exchange for legislative support. Still, this apparent change in the basis for presidential support obscures a great deal of continuity in the capacity of executives to control the agenda, even across widely varying political situations.

The main reason for this, we argue, is that the rules of Congress continue to empower individual deputies at the expense of parties. While parties appear to be stronger on the surface compared to Colombia's fragmented "hyper-personalistic" era, the incentives for individual politicians to act as independent players in the legislative process remain firmly intact, despite a major change to the electoral rules. In conjunction with very decentralized legislative rules that allow individual deputies considerable ability to delay, modify, and otherwise complicate the passage of bills, presidents must expend substantial resources to control the legislative agenda. Without centralized legislative rules, such as those Figueiredo and Limongi (2000) argue are critical to enabling presidential coalitions in Brazil, negotiations among parties are insufficient to ensure control over outcomes in the Colombian Congress. While the executive continues to be the main source of major bills, and executive initiatives are certainly more likely to pass than legislative bills, these advantages do not change substantially across varying political circumstances, both in terms of public support and coalition size.

Taken together, our findings suggest that parties in Colombia have yet to institutionalize as a means for presidential coalitions to organize Congress. Larger, more formal governing coalitions under Uribe and Santos did not improve the executive's ability to avoid losses on executive initiatives, despite a persistent effort to maintain control of legislative institutions and some high-profile successes. In fact, Uribe's ability to ensure passage of executive bills actually declined near the end of his tenure in office when a series of events destabilized congressional politics. Santos' term, meanwhile, with the broadest and most formalized coalition, has produced executive and coalition advantages no better than those under Pastrana's politically weak minority coalition.

While insufficient to result in major changes to patterns of legislative outcomes, there is some evidence that legislative parties have become more important. First, we note that there is some indication of greater ideological differentiation emerging in Congress since 2006, despite the centrism and opportunism characterizing many politicians associated with the presidential coalition. The case of the Santos coalition suggests that inter-party bargaining on national policy is more important than ever for organizing legislative support. In addition, the Colombian Congress has been actively involved in the promotion of major bills—those most salient in public discourse—and those authored by legislators have been viable since 2002. Thus, some pieces are in place for presidential coalitions to translate into legislative control.

Finally, it is important to note that bill-level statistics understate the substantive impact of the legislature in policy-making via the amendment process. Even more than the bill-level patterns noted, amendments are an arena where individual politicians can be highly effective. Although we cannot systematically analyze this with available data, the share of "successful" executive bills should be interpreted with some caution as a direct indicator for the executive's influence over the legislative process.

APPENDIX

Table 5.A1 Effects of origin and term on the success of executive initiatives, probit estimates

DV = Passed	Coef	S.E.
Executive	1.629***	(0.098)
Uribe I	–0.044	(0.060)
Uribe II	–0.103*	(0.060)
Santos	–0.038	(0.063)
Uribe I X Executive	0.036	(0.145)
Uribe II X Executive	–0.378***	(0.133)
Santos X Executive	–0.032	(0.142)
Constant	–1.169***	(0.044)
Observations	7,007	

*** p<0.01, ** p<0.05, * p<0.1

Table 5.A2 Effects of author coalition status and type on the success of legislative initiatives, probit estimates

DV = Passed	Coef	S.E.
Coalition	–0.263	(0.172)
Uribe I	0.114	(0.138)
Uribe II	–0.119	(0.139)
Santos	–0.084	(0.204)
Coalition X Uribe I	0.377*	(0.225)
Coalition X Uribe II	0.148	(0.234)
Coalition X Santos	0.662**	(0.262)
National	–0.368***	(0.119)
Coalition X National	0.127	(0.206)
Uribe I X National	–0.382**	(0.167)
Uribe II X National	–0.104	(0.166)
Santos X National	–0.282	(0.238)
Coalition X Uribe I X National	–0.172	(0.274)
Coalition X Uribe II X National	0.148	(0.277)
Coalition X Santos X National	–0.400	(0.312)
Constant	–0.845***	(0.100)
Observations	6,153	

*** p<0.01, ** p<0.05, * p<0.1

NOTES

1. Like the Mesa Directiva, committees also have vice presidents that lack formal power over the committee agenda and are assigned to minor parties.
2. There is also a formal restriction against amendments that would imply additional expenditures. This restriction applies equally to the introduction of new pieces of legislation. Nonetheless, when deciding on the constitutionality of bills vetoed due to their budgetary implications, the Constitutional Court interpreted the constitution so as to empower legislators with budgetary initiative (Salazar 2011).
3. In our analysis, we cannot account for patterns of the use of these powers because systematic data on when these powers were invoked are not available.
4. Some bills such as the Annual Budget are required by law to be debated in joint sessions for the Third and Fourth Committees from both the Senate and House.
5. From June 20 to July 20 and from December 16 to March 16.
6. This is, of course, impossible to oversee as the amendment is signed off by legislators only. Typically, members of the executive branch will be present on the

floor while bills of their interest are being debated and this way they can ensure the text is close to their own preferences.

7. In addition, it is important to note that many bills and all treaties require automatic review by the Constitutional Court as well before taking effect. Even bills without an automatic review can be challenged by any citizen as unconstitutional in procedure or content. Consequently, the Court plays an important role in the enactment of policy (Rodriguez-Raga 2011). During the period discussed in this chapter (1998–2014), the Court issued an average of 278 decisions on the constitutionality of legislation (Constitutional Court 2013).
8. In the period under consideration here, President Pastrana used his decree power briefly in 1999, and it was used again in 2002, 2003, and 2008 by President Alvaro Uribe. President Juan Manuel Santos used it during the state of economic and social emergency in late 2010.
9. "(…) los miembros de los partidos tradicionales de la Cámara de Representantes están ante todo interesados en conseguir recursos para sus regiones, consideran las posiciones del partido político secundarias respecto de este objetivo" (Roll 2005: 48).
10. The system also optionally allows parties to choose closed lists.
11. This system is sometimes referred to as "personal list" or "quasi-SNTV."
12. Even before the 2006 election, Congress enacted a bill called the Ley de Bancadas, which attempted to give party leaders instruments to enforce party discipline. The bill was intended to mandate that parties should vote together in the legislature and also gave privileges to party leaders over members in scheduling hearings, speaking on the floor, and rapporteurs' appointment. The law allowed for exceptions but left it to party organizations to develop sanctions for disloyalty. The application was therefore unenforceable and parties did not follow it in practice. Further, the notion of party leader privileges over members was later declared unconstitutional. Still, the law has had at least one major consequence in that the Court cited this bill as the basis to declare unconstitutional the referendum for Uribe to run for a third term due to a lack of party loyalty on the vote (see Londoño 2008; Ungar 2008).
13. Carroll and Shugart (2007) suggest that Uribe's rise outside the traditional party system can be taken as a form of "endogenous evolution," in which party system change responded to failures of democratic institutions. The electoral reform itself, meanwhile, was a consequence of this change but also produced a series of exogenous effects on the party system (Pachón and Shugart 2010).
14. Santos' opponents included a coalition of independent politicians under the label of the Green Party, and candidates from the Conservative, Liberal and Cambio Radical, and Polo Democrático Alternativo (PDA) parties. Santos obtained 46.68 percent of the vote, followed distantly by Antanas Mockus from the Green Party with just 21.51 percent of the vote.
15. During the conference committee, text that had been previously deleted was added that included privileges for congressmen and other public employees currently under investigation. Santos' administration only realized this afterwards and ultimately had to oppose enactment in that form.
16. Survey data come from the University of Salamanca Proyecto de Élites Parlamentarias de América Latina (PELA) (1998, 2003, and 2006 Colombia surveys).

17. This method recovers a single dimension reflecting the underlying self-placement scale data while accounting for individual differences in perception of the meaning of ideological placements. This is done by incorporating information on deputies' responses regarding the perceived ideology of the presidential candidates and parties in each period. All periods make use of the common stimuli (parties and candidates) such that their left–right self-placements are comparable across periods.
18. Officially named Partido Social de Unidad Nacional, created in 2005, the U Party was a coalition headed by congressmen supporting the re-election bid of Álvaro Uribe Vélez.
19. For clarity, only the six largest parties are shown. One excluded small party called Convergencia Ciudadana was affiliated with the governing coalition and resembles Cambio Radical in both position and internal variance.
20. The Optimal Classification scaling algorithm estimates of voter locations and divisions between the majority and minority votes provide the best fit among a set of dichotomous choice data. The result is a set of positions that can be taken to identify the basic underlying differences in a set of voting patterns among legislators.
21. We consider only Yeas and Nays here, dropping abstentions (when legislators go to the floor but do not vote). Colombia is atypical in its extreme degree of non-voting in the chamber, as about 30 percent of legislators on average are recorded as present on the plenary floor and still do not vote. Although legislators are not allowed to abstain formally, this has become an informal widespread practice (see Aroca and Guevara 2013). In this sense, parties are far less "disciplined" than the figures suggest. Our emphasis here, however, is on party-level behavior with regard to inter-party similarity and government support when formal votes are cast.
22. An emerging tendency towards rightist opposition to Santos is also reflected in the fact that former president Uribe and close allies subsequently have become publicly opposed to the government from the right.
23. Escandón (2013).
24. Because of the importance of these local bills, this simplification focuses on the clearest distinction in the sample of legislation, but the "national" category used here is heterogeneous.
25. Since we are focused here on the stages of the legislative process leading up to the floor, this category excludes cases in which the floor voting in each chamber was successful but the final enactment was blocked by a conference committee, presidential veto, or by the Constitutional Court.
26. The strategy of the government in this case, was to heavily amend the bill to undermine its effect in case it passed. The bill died after the conference committee version proposed to eliminate certain amendments that changed the bill's original intent (Osorio 2010a, 2010b).
27. It should be noted that highest executive success rates observed in this period are comparable to the average reported by Cardenas et al. (2008) for all presidents

1991–2003, as well as those before 1991—both periods known for highly inefficient executive–legislative relations (Shugart and Carey 1992; Archer and Shugart 1997).

28. Besides electoral reforms, major bills include a constitutional amendment to prohibit the re-election of the Attorney General, an amendment to change the system by which the Central Bank's Board of Directors is elected, a Minority Rights bill, and the Legislator's Ethics Code, among others.

6

Parliamentary Agenda Setting in Latin America

The Case of Mexico

Ma. Amparo Casar

The purpose of this chapter is to analyze how formal institutions and the actual distribution of seats within Congress determine the relative power of the executive and parliamentary factions in the lawmaking process and its outcome. In particular, it examines the agenda setting power of the president and its ability to push or block bills vis-à-vis that of Congress.

This chapter challenges the idea that Mexican presidents are chief legislators or privileged actors in the domain of the legislative process. At the same time, it argues against the idea that opposition parties systematically work against presidential bills, that under minority governments the win rate of presidential bills is low, and that executive–legislative relations are doomed to failure. Despite a reduction in the win rate of presidents after the switch from majority to minority status, the overall passage rates of presidential bills are not particularly low, especially when compared to the passage rates of other presidents in Latin America who formed majority coalitions, such as those in Colombia and Brazil. Moreover, as in Chile and the United States, broad and oversized coalitions have been the rule, but when the major parties are divided, the most common alliance has been between the president's party and the median party, as hypothesized by Alemán and Tsebelis in the introductory chapter.

This study provides evidence to support the theses that as plurality in Congress has developed, this branch of government has become a decisive player in legislative matters, that party-sponsored bills contribute more to the total change in legislation than those of the executive, and that presidential bills, contrary to what happened during the hegemonic and dominant party system years, are subject to major amendments.

FROM A HEGEMONIC PARTY TO A PLURALITY SYSTEM

Until the Mexican political system became an electoral democracy where access to power was finally rooted in free and fair elections and the principles of certainty of rules and uncertainty of results were established, legislative powers conferred by the constitution to both the president and Congress were inconsequential. During the long period characterized as a hegemonic and then dominant party system (1940–97), Mexico had unitary governments where the president's party held absolute majorities in both houses of Congress, almost all governorships, and control over all local legislatures. The hegemonic party, the Partido de la Revolución Institucional (PRI), held at least 70 percent of the Chamber of Deputies until 1985. Remarkably, it was not until 1988 that the PRI lost its first senatorial seats and until 1989 its first governorship (the northern state of Baja California). Unitary governments were coupled with full allegiance to the president by members of his party and episodes of indiscipline on the part of congressmen or insubordination on the part of local executives were seldom found.[1] Table 6.1 shows the distribution of seats in Congress from the mid-1940s to the mid-1990s.

Unequal access to power precluded not only the emergence of divided or minority governments but also the surfacing of a meaningful opposition capable of blocking or, at least, checking presidential power. In addition, unconditional discipline by party members meant that presidents could take for granted congressional support and need not worry about local legislatures obstructing their constitutional reforms. In sum, the absence of free and fair elections created a long-standing situation in which the president's will was constrained neither by party indiscipline nor by the need for coalition building.

Table 6.1 Distribution of seats in Congress, 1946–1994

	Senate							
	1946	1955	1964	1970	1982	1988	1991	1994*
PRI	100%	100%	100%	100%	100%	94%	95%	74%
	Chamber of Deputies							
	1946	1955	1964	1970	1982	1988	1991	1994
PRI	96%	94%	83%	84%	75%	52%	64%	60%

* Number of senators grows from 64 to 128.

Sources: Casar (2001); Instituto Federal Electoral (2007).

After two decades of piecemeal electoral change, Mexico was transformed into a multi-party system and in 1997 encountered a situation long present in most presidential systems: that of minority governments. Powers contemplated in the constitution began to matter. Although changes in executive–legislative relations began to occur before 1997, this year became a landmark because for the first time the president's party lost its de facto lawmaking powers and the president was forced to build congressional coalitions for any legislative action he wanted to endorse.[2] Cooperation between the executive and legislative branches of power became necessary to produce policy outcomes.

Plurality in Congress had several consequences. First and foremost, the absence of a majority for the president's party created the conditions for legislators to deploy their legally granted powers. All of a sudden, it became clear that the Mexican presidency was not as powerful as it used to appear and that its previous strength derived not so much from its constitutional powers but rather from its full control over representative and administrative posts, including the fate of political careers. The characterization of Mexico as a case of hyper-presidentialism was rooted not in the constitutionally granted powers of the president but in the dominant position of his party that monopolized all electoral and administrative posts at both the national and local levels.

In consequence, the president ceased being the chief legislator and Congress acquired a centrality not seen before in Mexico's modern history. For the first time in decades the executive had to compete as an agenda setter, faced constraints to further its legislative agenda, and found itself defenseless in face of a majority unwilling to abide by its preferences. These facts thoroughly transformed executive–legislative relations.

Second, changes in the distribution of power affected not only both branches of government and their relations but also the behavior of parties. For different reasons, both the president's party and opposition parties lost their unitary line of command. As soon as democracy made inroads, parties became internally divided among three components: the party organization represented by its internal directive bodies such as executive or national committees; the parliamentary party; and the party in government, that is, those representatives who held executive positions either at the federal or state and local levels. Making these three party components work in the same direction has proved difficult and detrimental for stable and productive relations between the legislative and executive branches of power. Intra-party disagreement and conflicts turned out to be an obstacle for settling disputes, reaching decisions, and upholding covenants.

Third, the lawmaking process became not only more cumbersome but also more prone to open conflict. Policy-making became less centralized and concentrated, and a number of political actors who had had practically no say in the heyday of the PRI became crucial.[3]

Finally, plurality disclosed the weak spots and impracticalities of the constitution and congressional internal rules, which were previously concealed. This was due, essentially, to the fact that the Mexican transition—in contrast to what happened in most Latin American countries—was not accompanied by the drafting of a new constitution.

The internal organization of Congress revealed itself unsuitable in a context of plurality. Congress rules were drafted when the PRI was the hegemonic force in both chambers and there was no need to negotiate the integration of governing bodies or committees, to establish minority rights, to regulate intercameral relations, or to avert deadlock.[4] Since the appearance of minority governments, parliamentary agreements became necessary to overcome critical situations regarding the composition of Congress' governing bodies, the selection of the House and Senate speakers, committee composition, agenda setting powers, floor voting, and distribution of resources.

In sum, the advent of electoral democracy in Mexico revealed the weaknesses of an executive whose power was grounded not on the constitution and congressional rules but on a hegemonic and disciplined party and on unwritten rules and practices. Institutional rules allocating agenda setting power and the positions of legislative parties became important to understanding legislative outcomes in Mexico only after the demise of unified one-party rule. This point is consistent with the view of Alemán and Tsebelis presented in the introductory chapter.

INSTITUTIONAL CONSTRAINTS: EXECUTIVE'S AND CONGRESS' ROLES

The president's and Congress' roles in the lawmaking process—including their agenda setting power—is determined by: (1) institutional prerogatives that structure the bill-to-law process; (2) the relative position of the president's party in Congress; (3) the command/allegiance the executive holds over its party; and (4) the degree of party discipline.

The first defines formal powers of law-making and includes not only constitutional norms but also Congress' internal rules (Ley Orgánica del Congreso and Reglamento Interior) and is analyzed in this section. The next three determine each actor's—president and parties in Congress—bargaining power at pushing through or obstructing their respective political agendas and will be examined in the following sections.

The Executive's Role

The Mexican constitution does not provide the executive branch of government with a privileged role in the lawmaking process. It never did but, as argued earlier, until the advent of democracy and the appearance of minority governments it did not matter. Once formulated and presented before Congress, presidential bills were sure to pass regardless of their nature. The same was true in any other area where presidential action required the consent of Congress, such as appointments, treaties, or authorization to leave the country. The problem was that the changes brought about by the democratic transition left formal executive prerogatives basically unchanged, when not diminished.[5]

In contrast with many other presidents in Latin America, the Mexican executive is relatively weak in terms of its formal legislative powers. It does not have areas of exclusive initiative—save the budget bill, it holds no emergency decree powers; its veto power is deprived of partial enactment; and, during the period under analysis, it did not have urgency powers.[6] All these characteristics have reduced minority presidents' policy influence.

The Mexican president can act proactively by introducing legislative proposals. However, he has no more formal weight in terms of bill initiation than the other players that hold this prerogative: legislators and state legislatures.[7] Neither the constitution nor the Ley Orgánica del Congreso (LOC) gives executive bills primacy in consideration over those of other initiators.

For the five legislative periods (1997–2012) under analysis, urgency powers that allow presidents to present initiatives that Congress must approve or reject in a certain time frame were not an instrument held by Mexican presidents in any of the modalities found in countries such as Brazil, Chile, or Uruguay. The most the president could do was encourage Congress to consider or focus on his bills. Moreover, the appeal to the population as a means to press legislators, that is, the strategy of "going public," has been rather limited since consecutive re-election for legislators was prohibited in the Mexican political system until 2014 and executive re-election is still barred (Kernell 1986).[8] Mexican presidents also lack the power of urgency or provisional decrees. Through this power other Latin American presidents are able to legislate without previous approval by Congress, by enacting policies with the force of law unless and until Congress repeals them (Colomer and Negretto 2005).

As important as the power of introducing bills is that of rejecting those approved by Congress. Conditions and procedures to do so are crucial for they define the strength of the veto power granted to the president. As Tsebelis and Alemán (2005) rightly argue, a veto is not only a negative power but, under certain conditions, provides the president with an important tool to shape legislation. Out of the different modalities described by them, the Mexican executive has block veto and the right to present amendatory observations.[9] Bills vetoed by the president require a two-thirds majority in both chambers to be overridden. If the president includes amendatory observations, the bill returns to the chamber of origin, where they can be approved by a simple majority and continue the regular legislative process.

To sum up, the Mexican constitution does not grant wide legislative powers to the executive branch. In fact, the only proactive powers in the hands of the Mexican president are those of initiation, being the gatekeeper in the budget bill, making amendatory observations in case of a veto, and, as of 2012, tagging bills for urgent consideration. Save for the latter, all these have been permanent features of the institutional setting. Some other prerogatives of the executive were barred from the constitution, for example, summoning Congress to extraordinary sessions or appointing the Attorney General without congressional approval. Many other powers simply disappeared as Congress became a plural institution since they derived from the privileged position of the president's party, which, as said before, held an overwhelming majority of seats in both houses of Congress. A notable example of the latter was the president's prerogative of appointing the speakers of both the House and the Senate. In contrast to the Latin American constitutional trends, in Mexico successive reforms have reduced rather than extended executive powers. The only exception is the introduction of urgency bills, albeit with no *afirmativa ficta*.

The Congress' Role

Although a de facto weak institution before the advent of electoral democracy, constitutionally speaking the Mexican Congress has always been a fairly strong institution. As such, it was endowed with several agenda setting powers. These, however, have only recently been used to their full effect.

The first and obvious one is that legislators have the right to introduce any kind of bills except for that of the budget proposal, which is reserved to the president. They can do so as individual legislators, jointly, or as parliamentary factions.

Agenda setting prerogatives are centralized in two governing bodies: the Mesa Directiva and the Party Leadership Committee (Junta de Coordinación Política, JUCOPO) of each chamber. A president, three vice presidents, and a secretary of each parliamentary faction constitute the Mesa Directiva of the Lower House. It is elected each year by two-thirds of the floor with the provision that its president must rotate on a yearly basis among the three major political parties represented in the House. Rules for the Senate are very similar save for the case of the president, who, although elected on a yearly basis—in this case by simple majority—can be re-elected and does not have to rotate among parliamentary factions.

Leaders of all parliamentary factions compose the JUCOPO in both chambers. If there is a majority party, it will occupy the JUCOPO's presidency for the entire legislature; if not, in the Lower House it will rotate on a yearly basis among the three major parties and in the Senate among those parliamentary factions that have at least 25 percent of total seats.[10]

These bodies have the power to schedule the discussion of bills and floor voting; to conduct floor debates, including assigning turns and time to speakers; to establish fast-track procedures;[11] and to suspend, extend, or adjourn floor sessions—that is, to control the flow of legislation. They are also in charge of negotiating and proposing the integration of the standing committees (including who is to preside over them) and to convene extraordinary sessions of Congress. Finally, they have the prerogative to draft the congressional budget and to distribute resources among parliamentary factions and committees.

Committees are integrated on a proportional basis according to share of seats but no party is allowed to have more than half of its members. Resolutions involve tough negotiations since they require a majority to issue a report and many are subject to revision once they reach the floor.

Nonetheless, power lies with the head of the committee, who, apart from receiving and distributing resources from the governing bodies, is in command of drafting the agenda and of summoning and adjourning sessions. This means that committees' presidents are able to kill a bill by failing to report it out. However, it must be pointed out that, in the end, the JUCOPO has the power to decide which bills are to obtain consideration.[12] Although internal rules establish that committees have to issue reports in five days or ask for an extension, in reality time limits have never been enforced.[13]

Regarding the internal workings of parliamentary groups, power lies in the leader of each faction who holds high discretionary powers over appointments and all kinds of resources sought by individual legislators.[14] Apart from the non-consecutive re-election clause still in operation and closed lists for proportional representation (PR) seats, the concentration of power among parliamentary leaders reinforces discipline within factions. Undisciplined legislators have a hard time not only in terms of career advancement but also in terms of being able to legislate.

In sum, governing bodies of Congress have both strong negative and positive agenda control powers (Cox and McCubbins 2002). They have the unhindered capacity to block bills from being reported and then being debated and voted in the floor. Additionally, they have the faculty to propose legislative initiatives in all areas—except the budget—and amendments to those of other initiators. In this sense, Congress standing for either the promotion of policy changes or the maintenance of the status quo is decisive.

The most noticeable, if not the only, check on the agenda setting power of each house of Congress is the other house. Contingent on the distribution of power and depending on the unity of parties between each house, the co-legislative chamber may turn out to be the only institution capable of exerting blockage of bills.[15] This check has sometimes been exploited by the executive to delay or even block an unwanted bill.

DISTRIBUTION OF POWER CONSTRAINTS AND THE IDEOLOGICAL SPECTRUM

Distribution of power and the positional structure of parliamentary factions within Congress are as important as formal rules and procedures in the lawmaking process. It determines the power of the president's and opposition parties to push through or block preferred/opposed legislation.

Mexico cannot be characterized as a fragmented party system in spite of the fact that since 1979 the number of parties in Congress has averaged seven. According to the Tagaapera index, which calculates the number of effective parties, Mexico effectively has 2.9 parties (Bernal 2009) and stands at the lower end of the spectrum of Latin American party systems (Saiegh 2010). Nonetheless, since 1997 no party has been able to gain the majority of seats in either chamber.[16] Mexico is thus a clear case of a plurality-led Congress with the president's party alternating between being the first or second minority. Table 6.2 shows the share of seats for the president in each chamber and the number of parties from 1997 until 2012.

The president's party position has varied greatly. Zedillo maintained sufficient partisan support to obstruct the passage of bills in both houses for

Table 6.2 President's party position in Congress, 1997–2012

LVII Legislature (1997–2000)	LVIII Legislature (2000–2003)	LIX Legislature (2003–2006)	LX Legislature (2006–2009)	LXI Legislature (2009–2012)
President's party 1st minority in Lower House (48%)	President's party 2nd minority in Lower House (41%)	President's party 2nd minority in Lower House (30%)	President's party 1st minority in Lower House (41%)	President's party 2nd minority in Lower House (29%)
President's party majority in Senate (60%)	President's party 2nd minority in Senate (36%)	President's party 2nd minority in Senate (36%)	President's party 1st minority in Senate (41%)	President's party 1st minority in Senate (41%)
5 parties	8 parties	6 parties	8 parties	7 parties

Note: No legislature, except LVII legislature in the Senate, had a majority; they were all plurality-led governments.
Source: Own elaboration from Casar (2000); <http://www.diputados.gob.mx>.

constitutional reforms and in the Senate for all other legislation. Additionally, in the Chamber of Deputies he only needed eleven extra votes to pass any piece of legislation. In contrast, Fox held the power to obstruct only constitutional reforms in the Chamber of Deputies during the first half of his administration. Finally, Calderón had sufficient support in the Senate to block constitutional reforms during his whole administration and in the Lower House during the first term of his administration. The share of seats for each party in Congress from 1994 to 2012 is shown in Figures 6.1a and 6.1b.

Presidents have also been constrained by the positional structure of parliamentary factions. The Mexican party system is essentially composed of a center party (Partido Revolucionario Institucional, PRI), a center-right party (Partido Acción Nacional, PAN), and a center-left party (Partido de la Revolución Democrática, PRD). It should be expected that the centrist party, the PRI, would be in a better position to find support at either side of the ideological spectrum. As will be shown in this chapter, data support this conjecture: the PRI has been part of most winning coalitions. Nonetheless, in exceptional circumstances, the two parties on opposite sides of the spectrum have coalesced against the center party. Such was the case during Zedillo's second legislature (1997–2000) when the PAN and PRD coalesced against the PRI in what became known as the G4.[17] The ideological ordering of parties and their legislative strength are shown in Figure 6.2.[18]

Arguments put forward so far lead to the conclusion that Mexican presidents do not have extensive legislative prerogatives and have few resources to

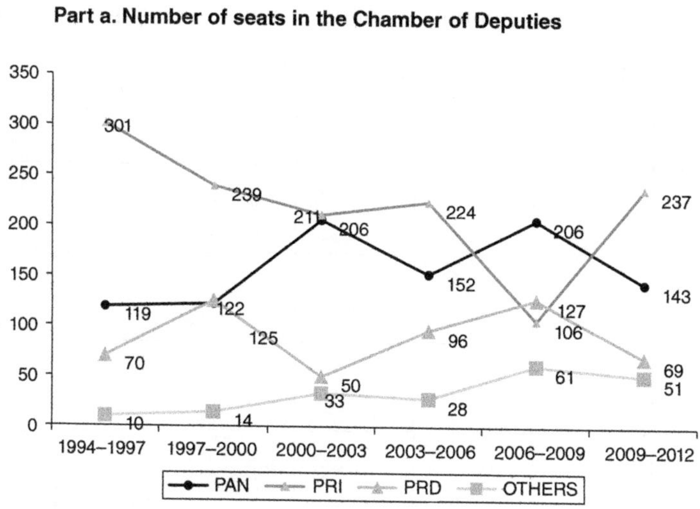

Figure 6.1a Distribution of seats in the Congress, 1994–2012, number of seats in the Chamber of Deputies

Sources: Casar (2000); <http://www.diputados.gob.mx>.

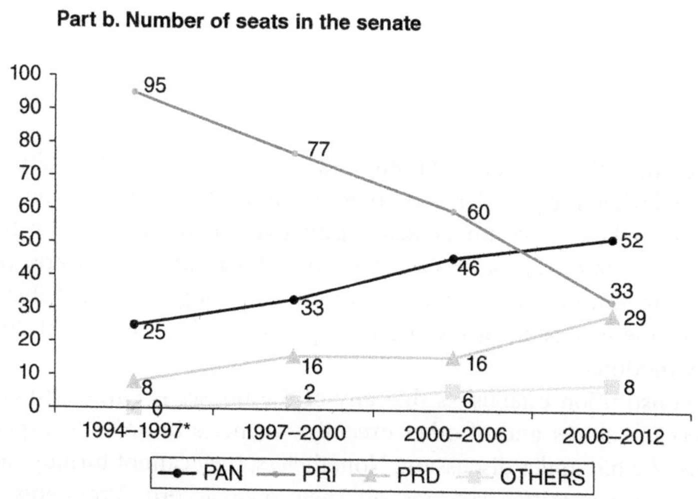

Figure 6.1b Distribution of seats in the Congress, 1994–2012, number of seats in the Senate

Note: In 1997 a reform to renew the Senate by halves every three years was passed. The reform was revoked the following year.

Sources: Casar (2000); <http://www.diputados.gob.mx>.

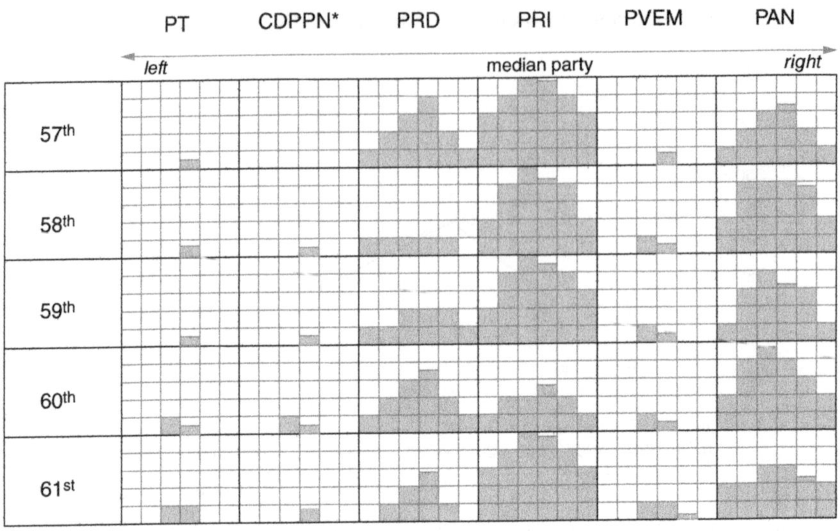

Figure 6.2 Generally accepted party positions in the ideological spectrum and distribution of power in the Chamber of Deputies

* In 2011, the CDPPN changed its name to Movimiento Ciudadano (MC); ▪ = 10 seats.

Sources: Own elaboration with data from <http://www.diputados.gob.mx> and <http://www.senado.gob.mx>.

influence the attention, deliberation, and approval of bills. This situation is aggravated when the president's party is in a minority situation. Except for the budget, presidents have no exclusive initiative, no privileges regarding the treatment of their proposals as against those of legislators, no decree powers, no rights to summon extraordinary sessions of Congress should they deem necessary the extension of the ordinary period, and, until August 2012, no urgency motions.[19]

The constitution establishes that any of the houses is entitled to convene members of cabinet and of other executive agencies in order to explain the contents of a bill under discussion. Nonetheless, they cannot turn up in either the floor or committee sessions on their own accord. Presidents attend Congress when they take the oath on the first day of their term and, as a rule, each 1st of September to deliver a state of the union address on the opening day of the first period of each legislative year.[20]

To these institutional features must be added a distribution of power in Congress that is unfavorable to the president's party and solid party cohesion and discipline that force block negotiations and compromises.

In contrast, Congress holds the key to most variables that shape the bill-to-law process: scheduling and plenary time power, control over resources, jurisdiction over committee assignments,[21] and the right to extend legislative periods to attend their agenda priorities. In fact, the only limit faced by Congress, other than the mobilization of public pressure by the executive, is the presidential power to veto a piece of legislation and making amendatory observations.

In sum, there are no reasons to presume the president is the major bill initiator, let alone the chief lawmaker. On the contrary, given his underprivileged position we should expect serious difficulties in enacting his legislative program. In addition, one should also anticipate a sustained effort by the president to build a governmental coalition or, in its absence, the formation of ad hoc coalitions with parliamentary factions close to his ideological position. Compared to hegemonic or predominant party systems (as was the case in Mexico), in a multi-party system with no majority for the incumbent, one should expect smaller coalitions and lower win/lose ratios. However, to show a consensus façade, presidents can attempt to build larger coalitions at the cost of "vote buying" (Saiegh 2011) either through patronage or supporting some opposition parties' bills.

More generally, the fundamental change away from presidentially dominated single-party government that took place after 1997 should have enhanced the role of Congress in lawmaking. If this is correct, then we should observe the following implications: an increase in the use of veto power compared to the era of unified governments, which should help minority presidents block and amend (through observations) bills passed by Congress; an increase in obstructive behavior towards presidential bills; privileged attention to legislators' initiatives; and frequent amendments of executive initiated bills. In the following section we examine the empirical evidence to assess these assumptions.

AGENDA SETTING AND LEGISLATIVE OUTCOMES

Given both the institutions and the distribution of power discussed previously, what, then, are the consequences for legislative outcomes and the relative success of the executive and Congress in setting the agenda? The empirical record of bills introduced between 1997 and 2012, that is, for a period characterized as a *plurality-led congress* (Calvo and Sagarzazu, this volume), is used to answer these questions; the conclusions are confirmed through the examination of a sample of major bills.[22] The analysis includes bills and their results, floor voting behavior and coalitions, and all presented and superseded vetoes.

Although the executive has never been the sponsor of most bills (Nacif 2006), the number of bills presented by actors different from the executive has certainly soared since plurality came about. There has been a marked change in the number and proportion of bills initiated by parties. In the LII legislature (1982–5), when Mexico still had a dominant party, 55 percent of bills in the Lower House were initiated by legislators or state congresses[23] and 45 percent by the executive. In contrast, during the last legislature (2009–12), 99 percent of all bills have been initiated by legislators or state congresses and just 1 percent by the executive. In absolute numbers, the executive passed from sponsoring 139 bills in 1982–5 to just 32 in 2009–12, a decrease of 77 percent. The number of bills introduced by the executive and other actors, as well as their respective approval rate, is shown in Table 6.3.

The approval rate of bills has seriously decreased in the fifteen-year period of minority governments. Part of this reduction is explained by the "farcical" soaring of bill proposals, the majority of which—as their initiators well know—will never get committee reports nor reach the floor. Percentages of

Table 6.3 Bills introduced and rate of approval, 1991–2012

	Executive bills	All other bills
LV	84	176
1991–1994	(98%)	(22%)
LVI	56	194
1994–1997	(99%)	(15%)
LVII	32	640
1997–2000	(78%)	(25%)
LVIII	59	1,238
2000–2003	(86%)	(25%)
LIX	49	2,784
2003–2006	(63%)	(14%)
LX	41	2,737
2006–2009	(90%)	(12%)
LXI	32	3,324
2009–2012	(84%)	(12%)

Note: Rate of approval (which is shown in parentheses) refers to the number of approved bills in relation to the number of bills presented by each initiator.
Sources: Casar (2000, 2008); Nacif (2006); <http://www.diputados.gob.mx>.

approval can be misleading for the number of bills introduced in the House rose from 308 in the LII legislature (1982–5) to 3,356 in the LXI legislature (2009–12), an increase of 990 percent! Nonetheless, it must be noted that the absolute number of approved bills since the 1980s has almost doubled. They grew from 166 in 1982–5 to 431 in 2009–12, an increase of 159 percent.

What do these numbers say about the attention given to legislators or state congresses' bills versus presidential sponsored bills? At first sight one might conclude that the executive has a far more successful rate of approval and thus is more in control of the agenda. Nonetheless, if one takes into account that (a) the proportion of executive bills in relation to all bills presented has greatly diminished (from 32 percent in 1991–4 to 1 percent in 2009–12) and the average rate of approval has somewhat diminished (12 percent), and that (b) the number of legislator-sponsored bills has soared (67 percent in 1991–4 to 99 percent in 2009–12) and their rate of approval has diminished (from 22 percent in 1991–4 to 12 percent in 2009–12), it turns out that far more attention is paid to legislator-sponsored bills.

In other words, the loss of a congressional majority has led the president to initiate fewer bills. But not only is the president initiating fewer bills. Of those presented, a smaller proportion is being approved than in the past. It is also the case that legislators are concentrating on their own agenda, producing and passing more of their own bills than before. Paradoxically, because of the steep increase in the number of bills initiated by members of Congress, the approval rate of congressional bills has plummeted.

Although the approval rate for executive bills has diminished, it is still high for minority governments. The average rate of approval for the fifteen previous years (1982–97) during which Mexico had a unified government and the PRI was firmly in control of the legislative agenda was 97 percent. In contrast, the average for the fifteen years of minority governments is 80 percent. These numbers defy the notion that minority presidents in Mexico have faced a systematic opposition to their initiatives or that they have been unable to successfully negotiate their legislative agenda and is consistent with Alemán and Tsebelis' expectation in the introductory chapter. In fact, compared to other Latin American countries Mexico is well above the sample average of 65 percent (Saiegh 2010). Moreover, floor-voting analysis indicates that most of them are passed with broad coalitions that include the three largest parties.

The approval rate alone is, however, not enough to determine whether the executive has been successful in pushing through its legislative agenda. Some bills have to be sent and approved by law (all budget bills), and others lack importance if judged by their relevance to the president's agenda (e.g., digitalization of the *Diario Oficial de la Federación*, or changes in the National Lottery law). Most importantly: (a) presidents often do not send bills which they suspect will be rejected (Calderón's telecommunications reform); (b) they sometimes present bills that are then not forcefully pursued (Fox's political reform or Calderón's fiscal reform); and (c) some presidential bills are heavily amended (Fox's indigenous rights law and Calderón's antitrust law and oil reform).

To fully understand the success of the executive's agenda, it is important to examine those initiatives that were actively part of the president's addresses and/or those mentioned in the front page of one of the main newspapers during the first year of a presidential administration, that is to say, a subset of major bills. Focusing on this subset, a somewhat different picture emerges.

During his administration, Zedillo faced two very different power positions: in his first three years he enjoyed a majority in both chambers, and in the last three he lost the majority in the lower house. This fact had consequences: the number of presidential bills presented dropped from fifty-six to thirty-two and the approval rate from 99 percent to 78 percent. During the first part of his term, most of his major bills received approval from Congress: the important judicial reform that reorganized and empowered the Supreme Court; the privatization of railroads; the increase in the VAT from 10 percent to 15 percent together with other important tax reforms; the electoral reform; and the law to appease the Chiapas conflict (Ley para el Diálogo, la Conciliación y la Paz Digna en Chiapas) among others.

Once he lost the majority in the Lower House, three of his major bills were blocked. These were a labor reform bill and an amendment to the central bank law in order to transfer exchange rate policy rights to the Banco de México. The third was a proposal to allow private investors in some areas of energy and oil production, generation, and distribution which was defeated at the floor with the opposition acting as unified bloc.

Fox faced a minority government during his whole presidential term. His party came second in both chambers of Congress. In the first half of his administration, he introduced fifty-nine bills in the Chamber of Deputies out of which fifty-one were passed (86 percent). His power position in Congress was even weaker in the last three years for his party lost over fifty seats in the Lower House, which resulted in the approval of only thirty-one out of forty-nine (63 percent) of his bills. However, apart from the three budget bills, Congress approved only two of his major proposals: the Public Access to Information proposal that was reported to the floor as a joint initiative of several parties, and the Seguro Popular that reformed the health law and created a universal healthcare system. Both of these passed without major amendments. Fox was unable to get approval for three major bills: energy and labor reforms similar to those proposed by Zedillo; an important fiscal reform that included removing VAT exemptions from food and medicines; and granting taxing prerogatives to state and municipal governments.

Finally, Calderón, who was in a better position than his predecessor, introduced seventy-three bills during his entire presidency, out of which sixty-four were passed (88 percent).[24] He succeeded, at least partially, in pushing a security and justice reform, strengthening the Public Access to Information Law, the PEMEX reform and some fiscal amendments which included rising one percentage point to the VAT, a gradual increase to tobacco tax until it reaches 160 percent, a 5 percent increase in soda taxes, an increase of 5.5 percent to fuel prices, and the creation of the IETU (a kind of flat income tax). Most important, in conjunction with other parties' initiatives, Calderón was able to pass the pensions law for the State Workers Social Security System (ISSSTE) and a very important Human Rights Reform.

All of these were severely revised. In fact, two of his most important bills were heavily amended. The PEMEX reform lost most of its initial purpose of making the state oil company a more productive and competitive one. The same can be said of the package of bills regarding security and justice, which was "trimmed" and thus somewhat inhibited the full operation of his anti-crime strategy. Likewise, his tax reform was downsized to the point that it yielded 1 percent of GDP, instead of the 2.5 percent projected. In addition, four of his major bills were defeated: an in-depth fiscal reform, a labor law, the unification of local police into thirty-two state police corps, and the national security law.

If the success rate of all presidential initiatives is combined, the notion that they are approved by smaller majorities than bills initiated by members of Congress holds only to a certain point. An analysis of roll call votes for all bills shows that the average win/lose ratio of votes is lower by a difference, on average, of sixteen votes. Sixteen votes may seem like a lot, but they amount to only 3 percent of all possible votes on the floor. While non-executive-sponsored initiatives have been approved by an average of 314 votes, executive ones have passed with an average of 298 votes. This information, broken down by legislative periods, is shown in Table 6.4.

Regarding passage time there is a difference of more than one hundred days between executive initiated constitutional reform bills and those introduced by legislators, for the whole set of bills enacted during the fifteen-year period (Figure 6.3).

Finally, minority presidents are expected to make a more extensive use of vetoes in attention of opposition parties rallying together in order to push through initiatives that may run counter to presidential wishes. In the case of Mexico there is no record of presidents vetoing pieces of legislation between 1969 and 2000 when alternation occurred (Magar and Weldon 2001).[25] Consistent with Alemán and Tsebelis' hypotheses presented in the introductory chapter, from 2000 on presidents have used their veto power

Table 6.4 Majorities in roll call votes for presidential and legislator sponsored bills,* 1997–2009

Session	Average number of positive votes in support of executive bills	Average number of positive votes in support of legislator sponsored bills	Difference
LVII	241	272	31
LVIII	364	363	-1
LIX	318	324	6
LX	287	303	16
LXI	281	310	29

* Nays include abstentions.
Source: <http://www.diputados.gob.mx>.

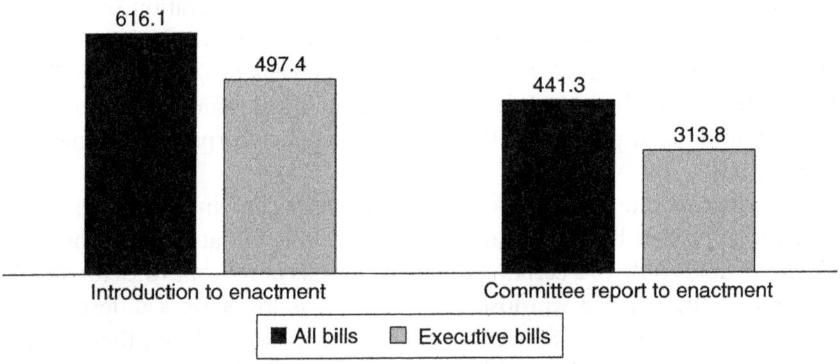

Figure 6.3 Passage time for constitutional reforms, 1997–2012 (days)
* Until February 2012.
Source: Casar and Marván (2014).

on twenty-five occasions. Table 6.5 shows the number of vetoes per legislative period and whether these observations were accepted or remain pending.

The topics of vetoes are varied—they range from budgetary issues to the criminal code or telecommunications—and the success rate has been practically absolute since none have been overridden. Although only thirteen vetoes were upheld and the ensuing laws included the amendatory observations made by the executive, the other twelve are pending so that the status quo has been maintained.

Table 6.5 Executive vetoes, 1997–2012

	# Vetoes	Observations accepted	Pending	Overridden
LVII (1997–2000)	0	–	–	–
LVIII (2000–2003)	4	3	1	0
LIX (2003–2006)	5	3	2	0
LX (2006–2009)	10	6	4	0
LXI (2009–2012)	6	1	5	0
TOTAL	25	13	12	0

Source: Sistema de Información Legislativa, <http://sil.gobernacion.gob.mx>.

COALITION BUILDING

Finally, we turn to coalition building. We do so from two angles: the incentives that minority presidents have to form coalition governments, and the actual formation of parliamentary coalitions.

The formation of coalition governments in presidential systems is optional. Nonetheless, if one assumes that the success of the executive's agenda needs support from the legislative branch of power, it should be reasonable to expect presidents in a minority situation to form a coalition government. However, one of three things may occur: a president may not be willing to relinquish a share of his cabinet in return for legislative support; the president may not find a party ready to enter a coalition government; or, as Cheibub et al. (2004: 575) argue, "when the formateur party is close in policy space to some other party (or parties) with which together it holds a majority, then it has no incentives to offer portfolios to other parties." In any case, as these same authors show, minority presidents need not fall into impasse or indicate a failure of governance.

In Mexico, contrary to what happens in many other Latin American countries where governmental coalitions have been formed,[26] presidents have opted for negotiations on a case-to-case basis and, judging by the presidents' legislative performance, there is no way of concluding that minority governments in Mexico have resulted in legislative stalemates, let alone paralysis.[27]

Although no coalitions based on cabinet and parliamentary program sharing can be found in Mexico, some congressional behavior patterns can be traced. These patterns reinforce the thesis that opposition parties in Congress have not systematically opposed presidential bills. This is true in spite of the fact that if the opposition had chosen to act in a unified manner it could have prevented passage of presidential initiatives. Moreover, the analysis of the roll call votes for the entire record of bills introduced between 1997 and 2012 shows that most are passed with widespread coalitions that include the three major parties and that parties are highly cohesive and disciplined.

In every single legislature since 1997, regardless of bill origin, distribution of power, or ideological position, most voting coalitions have included the three major parties. On average, 80 percent of floor voting coalitions in the Lower House has included the majority of legislators from PRI, PAN, and PRD together with some representatives of the smaller parties, with the exception of the 1997–2000 legislature, when this alliance was less common (46 percent). This is also true—although with a lower incidence—for executive-sponsored bills (60 percent).

Of the five legislative periods under minority government, the one under President Zedillo records the highest percentage of coalitions of the whole opposition against the presidential party (14 percent). Some of them prospered, but none regarding major bills.[28] While opposition parties coalesced to push through some constitutional reforms, for the most part they did not have enough votes to impose their preference over the president's party. Such was the case of the proposed amendment to grant power of initiative to the Supreme Court. Nonetheless, it is still true that during the entire legislature, the most frequent coalition was that of all parties (42 percent), followed by that of PRI–PAN (16 percent), which were ideologically closer in economic policy issues (e.g., the creation of IPAB, budget bills). Moreover, the PRD was left out of the winning coalition on 30 percent of the votes.

This pattern repeated itself during the first half of the Fox administration (2000–3): after the coalition of all parties (76 percent), the second most frequent coalition always included PRI–PAN and excluded the PRD (11 percent). However, in sharp contrast to Zedillo, the president's party seldom faced the joint resistance of all parties (2 percent). Once more, during Fox's second legislature (2003–6), the coalition of all parties was the most frequent (69 percent), and the second was PAN–PRI (12 percent) followed by that which excluded only the president's party (6 percent).

During Calderón's first legislature (2006–9), the coalition of all parties happened 68 percent of the time, while the second most frequent was that which included PAN–PRI (17 percent). Opposition parties allied against the president's party in only 1 percent of all floor votes. Finally, in the 61st legislature, Calderón's second, the same congressional behavior was revealed: 59 percent of coalitions included all parties and 12.6 percent involved PAN–PRI. Bloc opposition against the president's party accounted solely for 2 percent of all roll call votes. Figure 6.4 shows the proportion of roll call votes in which a particular party was excluded from the winning coalition.

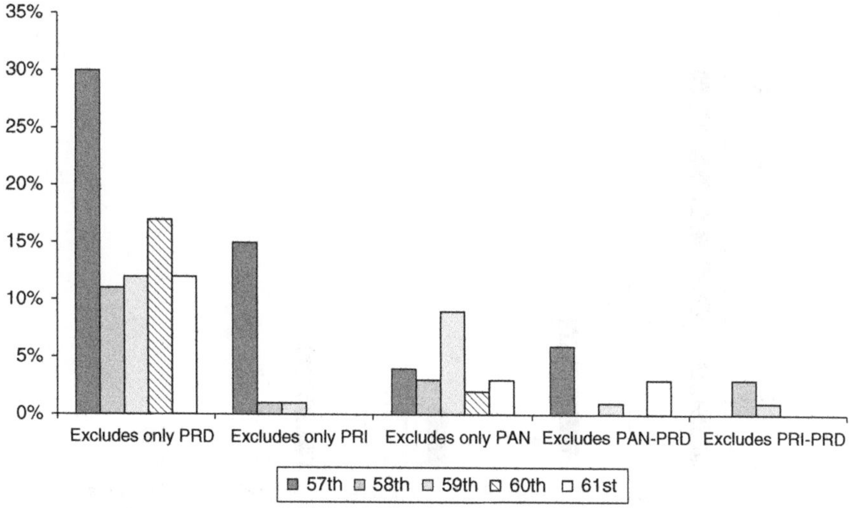

Figure 6.4 Legislative coalitions, roll call votes, Chamber of Deputies, 1997–2011
Source: Own elaboration with data from <http://www.diputados.gob.mx>.

A similar behavior emerges for executive-sponsored bills. This is the case for all five minority governments, except that of Zedillo, in which the most frequent coalition was not that of all parties, but that of PRI–PAN. It also holds that in all five legislatures the PRD (the main party on the left) is the party most often excluded from winning coalitions: on average, it was excluded 19 percent of the time during Fox's administration and 31 percent of the time during Calderón's term. The high level of exclusion of the PRD can be explained by the fact that its former presidential candidate (López Obrador) never accepted his defeat in the 2006 presidential election and openly asked his party not to join the PAN in any initiative. Figure 6.5 shows the proportion of roll call votes on executive bills in which a particular party is excluded from the winning coalition.

The overall picture that emerges from all these data is one in which the PRI has become essential in building winning coalitions. This has mainly been due to its median position in the ideological spectrum together with its advantageous situation in terms of the size of its parliamentary group. The PRI passed from being excluded from winning coalitions 15 percent of the time when it held the executive during Zedillo's administration, to being part of all winning coalitions in the second legislature during Calderon's administration despite being out of government. Thus, consistent with the ideas in the introduction of this book, when the major parties are divided the most common alliance is between the president's party and the PRI, the median party in Mexico's Congress.

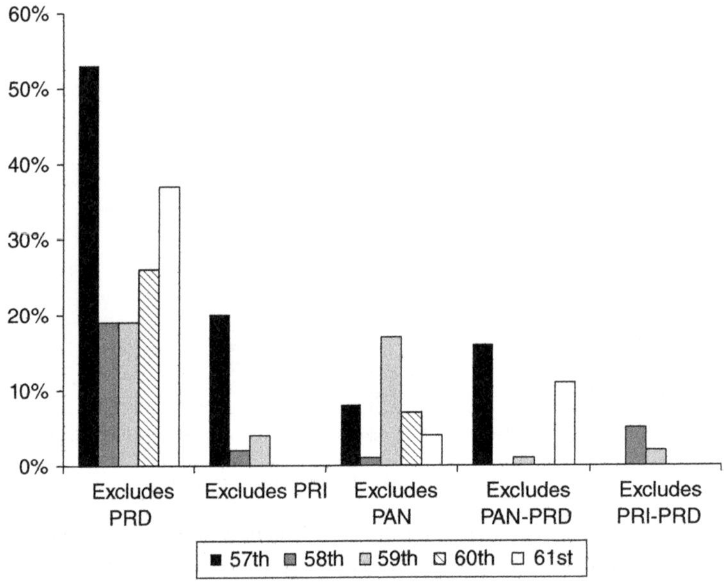

Figure 6.5 Legislative coalitions, roll call votes on executive bills, Chamber of Deputies, 1997–2011

Source: Own elaboration with data from <http://www.diputados.gob.mx>.

The PAN has a similar record to that of the PRI. If the PRI has an average participation rate of 95 percent in winning coalitions, the PAN has one of 89 percent. The difference is essentially explained by two legislatures. The first is Fox's second legislature (2003–9), when the president's party was excluded 17 percent of the time from the winning coalition because the opposition formed a successful front to block a series of fiscal measures initiated by the executive.[29] The second is Calderón's second legislature (2009–12), in which the president's party was excluded in 14.5 percent of the winning coalitions, mainly in those formed to pass the so-called political reform, which included a presidential bill, but also initiatives from all parties.

All in all, it can safely be concluded that PAN (the governing party except in the LVII legislature) and PRI (the median party) have been the two parties responsible for the passage of most initiatives and that no claim of paralysis can be sustained either for constitutional reforms that require two-thirds of legislators or for ordinary laws that require a simple majority of present members in any one session. Furthermore, it is interesting to note that during the fifteen-year period of minority governments, the subset of approved constitutional reforms—regardless of origin—has increased.[30]

Finally, data on coalition building show that "small" parties, which have had a 7 percent average share of seats in the Lower House, have seldom been crucial for the formation of a majority in Congress or for defining the passage or obstruction of a bill. An exception is that of the last legislature (2009–12), where the informal parliamentary coalition of the PRI and the PVEM in the Lower Chamber constituted a bare majority of 51.6 percent of seats. Nonetheless, only on two occasions has any one small party (PVEM, LXI legislature, 2009–12) been crucial for the approval of a piece of legislation.

The other behavioral pattern that emerges from roll call votes is that of a high degree of discipline: PRI and PAN with a Rice index of 95, and PRD with an index of 91.[31] Discipline can be explained by the substantial influence that political parties exert over the career patterns of individual legislators and by the concentration of resources controlled by the leaders of parliamentary factions. In fact, there are two electoral rules that run counter to the independence of political careers: nonconsecutive re-election and the need of a party label in order to run for office.

High levels of discipline such as those found in Mexican parliamentary groups constrain presidential strategies in forming majorities to push through their bills. Party discipline makes it very difficult to win over individual legislators' support, forcing the president to negotiate either with the party leader or the head of a parliamentary faction to reach the needed legislative majorities.

CONCLUDING REMARKS

In the absence of a majority situation the Mexican president has few institutional resources to help or ease attention and approval of his preferred legislation. Nonetheless, there is scant evidence to support the general view that, during the fifteen years of minority governments, presidents have faced an entrenched and systematic obstruction to their legislative proposals. Most probably this has been due to the fact that during these fifteen years presidents have not faced an organized majority opposition. That is, they have dealt with a plurality-led Congress (see Calvo and Sagarzazu, this volume).

Yet, the conclusion that presidents have not faced entrenched opposition to their legislative proposals has to be qualified by two facts: on the one hand, presidential initiatives are now more heavily amended as a result of compromise about policies, and on the other hand, some major bills prompted by the president were not able to pass during the years of minority governments analyzed in this chapter. It must be noted that when the sixth minority government was elected (2012) the three major parties agreed to the *Pacto por Mexico*. This pact paved the way for the approval of several important pieces of legislation that included the long postponed energy, antitrust, telecommunications, fiscal, and education reforms among others.

Whether substantial amendments or the obstruction of some major bills are due to the existence of minority governments is highly debatable. Many of the so-called structural reforms that did not pass in the period 1997–2012 did not pass either when the PRI had the overwhelming majority in both chambers of Congress.[32] What is true is that a greater number of legislator bills get committee reports and reach the floor compared to executive proposals. Nowadays legislator-sponsored bills contribute more to the total change in legislation than those of the executive.

Minority presidents in Mexico have not turned to the option of attempting coalition governments based on a shared cabinet and program as a way of gaining political and legislative support.[33] Instead, they have chosen to form oversized or ad hoc coalitions, and resort to vetoes in order to stop unwanted legislation. These options have worked out relatively well. Although not used in excess, vetoes have been successful as a means to stop unwanted legislation, as well as to introduce some final presidential amendments in the form of observations. Presidents have been less successful, however, in avoiding substantial adjustments to their proposed legislation.

Coalitions around executive-sponsored initiatives have regularly gathered the support of all or at least the three main parties with congressional representation and there is no evidence that presidential bills have been approved by smaller majorities (lower win/lose ratio) than bills initiated by other actors. Data endorse the thesis that parliamentary groups are highly disciplined for the reasons explained earlier. Although discipline can be a double-edged trait, it can be argued that in Mexico it has turned out to be positive for the fate of presidential initiatives.

The passage of substantial constitutional and legal reforms during the current plurality-led Congress (2012–15) has somewhat dispelled the notion that minority governments are doomed to failure. Nonetheless, there are still voices—especially from the PRI—that reveal a strong preference for electoral rules that are more likely to yield majority governments. The PRI is putting forward an initiative to diminish the number of legislators in both houses and changing the ratio between relative majority (RM) and proportional representation (PR) seats in favor of the former. The present ratio is 60 percent RM against 40 percent PR. The PRI is suggesting 75 percent RM and 25 percent PR for the Lower House and the elimination of the thirty-two PR seats in the Senate. In contrast, the PRD wishes to install a pure proportional system. Opposition parties are still insisting on further diminishing the powers of the presidency and of rebalancing the equilibrium of powers in favor of Congress.

In the end, the recently approved political and electoral reforms left unchanged the number and proportion of majority seats in Congress and did not manage to introduce the presidential second-ballot that was favored by the PAN and the PRD. Nonetheless, they introduced important changes that may prove consequential to executive–legislative relations, to the power of parties over its legislators, and to the workings of the political system as a whole. Re-election and the admittance of independent or nonpartisan candidacies are expected to somewhat reduce the power of party elites. The reforms also introduced the rights of citizen-sponsored bills and a sort of referendum called *consulta popular* on certain legislative and policy matters. The right to call for a referendum is shared by the executive, Congress, and the citizenry. Congress was strengthened in its appointment powers and executive prerogatives were reduced either through the sharing of powers until now reserved to the executive or by extracting from its sphere of competence whole areas of public policy like regulation of markets and telecommunications. All in all, Mexico went from having established the Central Bank as an autonomous institution in 1993 to having twelve autonomous bodies in 2014 that range from the National Electoral Institute to the Federal Telecommunications Institute and the Attorney General's Office. The functions performed by these bodies were until very recently part of the executive. How far the recently introduced changes will impact executive–legislative relations and alter the conclusions reached in this chapter remains to be seen.[34]

NOTES

1. For an historical and analytical explanation of the foundations of unitary governments and the de facto presidential powers see Casar (1997) and Weldon (1997)
2. During the Salinas administration (1988–94) changes began to erode the centrality of the presidency. This may be best exemplified by Salinas' government decision to postpone his major reforms until the second part of his term due to the bare majority his party had in Congress when he assumed the presidency. It was in that period (1988–91) when the need to forge alliances within Congress first appeared. It was also then that Congress passed a bill establishing at 60 percent the maximum number of legislators of one party in Congress and thus prevented the possibility of any one single party to reform the constitution on its own.

3. These included not only legislators but also party leaders, governors, justices, and members of the autonomous bodies that were created during the 1990s (Banco de México, Comisión Nacional de los Derechos Humanos, Auditoría Superior de la Federación).
4. The most obvious flaw became evident in 1997 when legislators became aware that the Ley Orgánica del Congreso stated that the governing body of the Chamber of Deputies was to be headed by the parliamentary group that held the absolute majority. Since no party held such majority, nobody knew how to proceed or how to install the opening session of Congress on September 1. Crisis followed and the opposition parties rallied together in order to impose a congressional agreement that the PRI had to accept.
5. The democratic transition in Mexico took place through electoral reforms that ended with the monopoly of the president's party and re-established the principles of division of powers and checks and balances.
6. It was only until 2012 that urgency motions to the executive were granted. Beginning each legislative period the president may introduce two initiatives and tag them as urgent. Each chamber has thirty days to produce a committee report and vote it on the floor. The constitution says nothing about how to proceed in case Congress fails to do so.
7. As of 2012 the constitution was amended to admit citizen-sponsored bills. The percentage of registered voters needed to present a bill before Congress amounts to 0.13 percent (roughly 106,000 citizens).
8. The constitutional reform that admits consecutive re-election, and that will be put in practice in 2015 for the first time, was constrained by establishing that the incumbent must run as a candidate of the same party that brought him/her to power the first time. It was also limited to two periods in the Lower House and one in the Senate.
9. Until 2011 the president had also a de facto pocket veto for although the executive was forced by the constitution to promulgate a bill in case it was not observed, there were no sanctions provided in case he did not. Thanks to a recent reform, if the president makes no observations to a bill within thirty days and does not publish the law in question within the next ten days, the president of the chamber in which the bill originated can promulgate it.
10. It must be noted that legislators often bend these rules through a very common practice called "parliamentary agreements."
11. The JUCOPO has the prerogative to request that a committee report be referred to the floor, waiving the regular legislative procedures.
12. In the Senate, the president of the Mesa Directiva may force a bill out of committee if twenty days have passed since reception of the bill. The committee has to come up with a report in no longer than ten days. If it fails to do so, the bill initiators may ask to switch committees.
13. The absence of limits is well established by the number of bills that have not received consideration, which in the Lower House alone reaches over 3,000.

14. For an empirical study of the budgetary power of parliamentary faction leaders see Casar (2011).
15. A case in point is the recent political reform bill that was agreed upon and approved by all parliamentary groups in the Senate under the leadership of the PRI and then blocked in the Lower House by the PRI parliamentary faction.
16. The exception being the second part of Zedillo's presidential term when he maintained the majority in the Senate (elected in 1994).
17. The G4 (a temporary alliance of all opposition parties) was formed during the first experience of minority government in order to force the PRI to negotiate positions within the governing bodies and committees in Congress as well as in some minor pieces of legislation.
18. In the 58th legislature, there were two other parties represented: the PSN, which had three seats and was considered center-left, and the PAS, which had two seats and was right-wing. In the 60th legislature, there were two more parties: the PASDC, which had four seats and was left-wing, and the PANAL, which had nine deputies and was center-left. In the 61st legislature, there was one other party, the PANAL, with nine seats. While parties are ordered according to their ideological leaning, the distribution of seats shown by the gray squares does not indicate that there is a normal distribution of preferences within each party.
19. The only exception is that of the budget bill, which according to the constitution must be approved by November 15 of each year. However, Mexico is one of the few countries lacking a provision in case this time limit is not observed.
20. It is mandatory for presidents to send Congress a written *informe de gobierno* each year on September 1 (Article 69). Although their physical presence was never compulsory, it was customary for the president to attend the opening session until 2006, when legislators from the three left parties prevented President Fox from entering Congress as a protest against what they regarded as a fraudulent election of his successor.
21. For an extended review of how the committee leadership posts are allocated see Aparicio and Langston (2009).
22. The set of major bills were collected through the statements or legislative proposals mentioned on the front page of *Reforma* newspaper at some point during the first year of each presidential term.
23. These include initiatives sponsored by state congresses that were also controlled by the president's party.
24. During the first legislature, he introduced forty-one out of which thirty-seven passed (90 percent); in his second legislature he introduced thirty-two out of which twenty-seven passed (84 percent).
25. Surprisingly, there was a relatively frequent use of vetoes (especially on pension and budget issues) between 1937 and 1969 when strong presidentialism was already in place (Magar and Weldon 2001). The authors explore some hypotheses but recognize that it is very difficult to explain vetoes with orthodox models given unified government and a high degree of discipline. Equally surprising is the sudden end to vetoes in the next three decades.

26. According to Cheibub et al. (2004), some kind of coalition existed in fifty-two (53.6 percent) out of ninety-seven minority situations in presidential systems.
27. Cheibub et al. (2004: 580) conclude that "the connection between coalitions and legislative success is at best dubious" and that "presidential democracies are equally vulnerable whether or not the government is a coalition."
28. It is important to note that opposition parties in the Senate were successful in blocking Zedillo's energy reform because his party did not hold the two-thirds majority needed for constitutional amendments. This reform did not reach the Chamber of Deputies, where, most surely, it would not have prospered either.
29. In one-third of these, the PAN walked out of the floor in an unsuccessful attempt to break the session quorum.
30. Further evidence of this can be drawn from the sixth minority government in Mexican history (2012–15). During the first two years of this government, Congress approved seventeen constitutional reforms, most of them by consensus of the three major parties. The two exceptions were the fiscal reform passed by a PRI–PRD coalition and the energy reform passed by the PRI–PAN coalition. It remains true that the center party is best positioned but also that the most frequent coalition is that of the three parties.
31. For an in-depth study of party cohesion and discipline during the first twelve years of minority governments see Casar (2008).
32. For a discussion of the power of de facto powers in shaping legislation and public policy after democratic transitions see Acemoglu and Robinson (2006). The authors make a distinction between de jure and de facto political power. The former is that which comes from political institutions. In contrast, de facto political power comes from the ability of one group or groups to overwhelm elected authorities through means and resources—force, wealth, corruption, mobilization—which allow them to choose or impose whatever policy is in their best interest at any certain point.
33. The 2014 political reform introduced a peculiar constitutional reform which states that if a minority government chooses to form a coalition government, a legislative program as well as all members of cabinet except for the heads of the ministries of Defense and Navy must be approved by two-thirds of the Senate.
34. The author benefited from the invaluable assistance of Dolores Bernal in gathering and processing data as well as commenting on this chapter.

7

Strong Presidents, Weak Parties, and Agenda Setting

Lawmaking in Democratic Peru

Aldo F. Ponce

In this chapter, I examine the distribution of legislative agenda setting power in Peru. I identify not only the institutions and political actors altering the distribution of legislative agenda setting power in Peru, but also the effects of their influence over the lawmaking process and the laws enacted. To achieve these goals, the analysis focuses on the effects produced by the interaction between institutions regulating agenda control and the positions of legislative actors.

The contribution of this study to the field of legislative studies is twofold. First, it provides insight into evaluating agenda control in a context of a weak and non-programmatic party system. The Peruvian party system has been repeatedly characterized as non-ideological (Rosas 2005; Coppedge 1998), weakly institutionalized (Mainwaring and Scully 1995; Payne et al. 2002; Alemán et al. 2011), highly fragmented, and volatile (Roberts and Wibbels 1999; Jones 2005; Ponce 2012). The country provides an ideal setting to examine the approval of major bills, as well as other bills, in the presence of a non-programmatic party system.

Second, the Peruvian case enables us to examine agenda control and lawmaking in a political context that combines a powerful president without a legislative majority and a congress that can override executive vetoes and decrees using majority vote. The Peruvian executive office has been classified as one of the most powerful among the Latin American executives (Corrales 2010; McClintock 1996; Palmer 1996; Shugart and Haggard 2001; Wise 2003; Santiso and García Belgrano 2004). Peruvian presidents have the right to enact some policies through legislative and urgent decrees, which allows them to change the status quo into a new policy that remains valid unless a majority of legislators overrides it. As I discuss in what follows, legislative deadlock does not prompt the president to legislate through decrees.

In this study, I find that initiatives from minority presidents enjoyed a rather high rate of approval compared to other Latin American presidents examined in this volume. This approval level extends to both major and minor bills. Perhaps surprisingly, most major bills originate with members of Congress, not the president. Within Congress, the party considered to hold the centrist position seems to have an advantage over their competitors in terms of bill approvals. Furthermore, the use of legislative decrees, which is positively correlated with approval rate of bills, appears to complement the legislative strategies of presidents.

The rest of this chapter is divided into five sections. The first section describes agenda setting institutions in Peru. It addresses agenda setting powers of the most relevant political actors in Peruvian politics: the president and the legislative groups (*grupos parlamentarios*). The second section discusses the main features of the Peruvian party system. The next section discusses the main hypotheses of the study, which focus on the legislative success of presidents, the advantage of the party occupying the centrist ideological position, and the use of legislative decrees. The fourth section presents descriptive statistics and outlines models used to explain the likelihood of bill approval. The last section provides conclusions and offers suggestions for future research.

AGENDA SETTING INSTITUTIONS IN PERU

In Peru, most bills are proposed by legislators or the president. But according to the constitution, five other actors can propose bill initiatives: regional governments, municipalities, professional associations, organized citizens, and autonomous institutions (e.g., Supreme Court, Central Bank, Peruvian Ombudsman, Regulator of Banks and Insurance Companies, National Electoral Court, National Office of Electoral Processes, judicial courts, Constitutional Tribunal, Office of the Comptroller General of the Republic, National Register of Identity and Civil Status).[1] These outside actors actually submit relatively few bill initiatives to Congress (3.9 percent of those proposed between 2001 and 2011). Members of Congress submit most initiatives (87.5 percent of all bills introduced between 2001 and 2011), but they are forbidden from initiating bills that demand new public expenditures. Legislators can only change the allocation of the available funds across budget headings.

Once the initiative is submitted to Congress for consideration, the Oficial Mayor of Congress sends the proposal to one or more committees, which must evaluate the initiative within 30 days.[2] When a bill is assigned to more than one committee, the committees can decide jointly on the convenience of the proposal.[3] The committee report (*dictamen*) must be approved by a majority of committee members. A simple majority vote can force a bill out of committee, and party leaders representing a majority of legislators can even skip the committee stage altogether and move bills directly to the floor of Congress.

The right to amend or obstruct bill initiatives belongs to both the president and legislators. After a bill is passed, the Constitutional Tribunal can veto it if it finds it unconstitutional. The rest of this section focuses on the most active agenda setters and those with powers to alter the content of initiatives: the president and members of Congress.

The President

The president is a powerful actor in Peruvian politics. The 1993 constitution established several advantageous prerogatives for the executive position. The president has exclusive rights over budgetary and tax policy, the ability to introduce amendments to vetoed bills, and the right to issue law-like decrees on economic-related policy. The president can also initiate ordinary bills pertaining to different policy areas, put forth constitutional amendments, and propose referenda. Moreover, the president has the authority to join some treaties, form the cabinet, dissolve Congress (if Congress twice denounces the Council of Ministers), regulate tariffs, make military appointments, and declare either a state of emergency or a state of siege.[4]

The Peruvian president holds monopoly power to propose the national budget and tax bills. The president is the only actor allowed to initiate bills on the following policy jurisdictions: territorial boundaries; international treaties; entry of foreign troops into Peruvian territory; declarations of war; peace signing; and extensions to either a state of emergency or state of siege (Article 76 of the 1993 constitution).[5]

The president also has the right to request expedited consideration of presidential initiatives in Congress. However, such presidential urgencies do not impose a deadline on Congress. Instead, they become priorities in the internal calendar of the committee where the bill is assigned. As Forno (2012) shows, most recent presidential initiatives have carried this type of request: 76.6 percent between 2001 and 2006, and 90.3 percent between 2006 and 2010. However, the percentage of the president's initiatives resolved within the first thirty days after being submitted to Congress has declined over time, from 28.9 percent between 2001 and 2006 to 20.0 percent between 2006 and 2010 (Forno 2012).

Furthermore, the 1993 constitution endows the president with the right to veto or amend an initiative previously approved by Congress. The president can veto a bill partially or totally. The president can then send back the bill with amendments within fifteen days after receiving the bill from Congress (Tsebelis and Alemán 2005). Congress needs the support of over 50 percent of legislators to override the president's veto or to accept (or override) the president's amendatory remarks. If such a majority cannot emerge, the status quo prevails (Castillo 1997). If legislators alter the content of the initiative (after submission of the amendatory remarks by the president), the president can amend the bill again. Thus, the president makes the last amendment.

As stated previously, presidents also have the authority to advance their agendas through the enactment of decrees. The 1993 constitution introduced two types of decrees: congressionally delegated decree authority—called "legislative decrees" in Peru—and constitutional decree authority—called unilateral "urgent decrees" in Peru (Articles 104 and 118 of the 1993 constitution).[6] Congress can delegate to the executive office the authority to issue legislative decrees in specific policy areas during a limited period of time (Article 104 of the 1993 constitution; Schmidt 1998). This delegation does not include the right to modify the constitution, to ratify or alter the national budget, or to approve international treaties (Schmidt 1998).[7] Once the president enacts the legislative decrees, they are referred to the Constitution and Rules Committee of Congress.

The president can also enact urgent decrees concerning economic and financial matters in extraordinary situations or crises (Article 118 of the 1993 constitution).[8] The urgent decrees are enacted with the authority of law and, unlike legislative decrees, they do not need congressional authorization. The decrees may modify current laws except for laws that refer to the protection of civil rights or taxation (Article 74 of the 1993 constitution). The constitution does not clearly define the characteristics of these extraordinary situations, and as a result presidents have used this authority for situations that can be considered non-urgent and for administrative issues that were not obviously characterized as primarily economic and financial matters (Blume 2011; Landa and León 2003).

Congress can modify or dismiss these decrees by majority vote. Within twenty-four hours after a decree is issued, the president must formally inform Congress about its content (Article 118 of the constitution; Articles 90 and 91 of the Reglamento del Congreso). Then, the Constitution Committee of Congress must study the decree and can recommend its dismissal to the plenary group. If the plenary membership accepts this recommendation of the Constitution Committee, the decree is nullified. If Congress does not take action, the decree is (implicitly) validated. The decrees remain law until another law

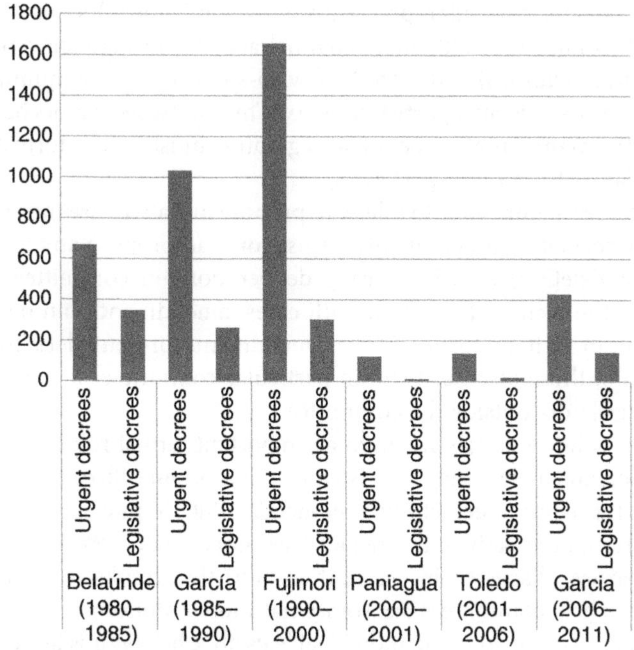

Figure 7.1 Number of legislative and urgent decrees

Source: Ministry of Justice and Human Rights; author's elaboration.

modifies or revokes them. Figure 7.1 shows the number of delegated decrees (called legislative decrees in Peru) and urgent decrees enacted since 1980.[9]

Congress

The internal rules of procedure of the Peruvian Congress tend to centralize authority. The steering committee in charge of the day's agenda in Congress is composed of the chamber's directorate (Mesa Directiva) and representatives of the different party blocs (*grupos parlamentarios*). The chamber's directorate is elected by the plenary membership under majority run-off rule (Mesa Directiva). The voting weight that each party delegate holds in the steering committee is related to their seat-share. Committee assignments and the allocation of plenary time are also affected by the seat-share of parties. Committee assignments are negotiated between the president of the chamber and the partisan blocs, and must be approved by the plenary group.

Parties possess particular prerogatives over bill introduction. Legislators who want to introduce bills must channel actions through their party blocs (*grupos parlamentarios*) and recruit a few co-sponsors.[10] The minimum number of legislators to form a party bloc is six. Thus, those legislators belonging to parties with a representation below six legislators must seek to form a new bloc with legislators from other parties.[11]

The rules legislators have to follow to propose initiatives are more restrictive than those regulating amendments. Legislators can propose any modification (change or deletion) to a bill during deliberations in committee or during debates on the plenary floor.[12] In both cases, amendments can be presented verbally or in written form. Unlike amendments presented to the plenary membership, those discussed within particular committees are rarely known to most legislators outside the committee.

In short, political parties are given an important formal role in the initiation of legislation and assignment of legislators to important offices inside Congress, including the committee setting the agenda. But despite having significant agenda setting prerogatives, in practice legislators suffer from the weakness of political parties (discussed in the next section) that results in an unassertive leadership. Thus, committees are somewhat more autonomous than expected given formal rules. In addition, individual legislative behavior is less constrained by party leadership than in most other Latin American countries.

In sum, despite Congress' ability to override vetoes and decrees with a majority vote, and to amend most bills, the executive still holds formal institutional advantages to make the first and last moves when proposing policy changes. This power should help the advancement of the president's agenda. This chapter examines the extent to which this occurs. The following section describes the legislative parties in Congress and their policy positions. This is relevant to understand the political context in which legislative actors compete and set the agenda.

PERUVIAN PARTIES AND THEIR POLICY POSITIONS IN CONGRESS

The Peruvian party system has been consistently described as weakly institutionalized (Mainwaring and Scully 1995; Payne et al. 2002), and legislators and legislative parties have been typically categorized as non-ideological and non-programmatic (Rosas 2005; Coppedge 1998; Alemán et al. 2011). The Peruvian party system consistently appears at the bottom of all classifications of party system institutionalization in Latin America (Mainwaring and Scully 1995; Payne et al. 2002; Jones 2007). In systems with these descriptions, parties experience high levels of electoral volatility (Roberts and Wibbels 1999; Jones 2005, 2007), and consequently they are short-lived. They rarely develop roots in society (Mainwaring and Torcal 2006). As a result, the appeal of parties is likely to be based on candidates' characteristics or clientelist proposals (Mainwaring 1998; Mainwaring and Zoco 2007; Rosas 2005). Voters under these circumstances rarely identify the programmatic characteristics of competing parties (Mainwaring and Scully 1995; Mainwaring and Torcal 2006; Jones 2007; Rosas 2005).

The composition of the Peruvian party system has changed substantially since the 1980 transition to democracy. The country has experienced very high levels of electoral and seat volatility. As a consequence, seat-shares in Congress have fluctuated considerably, including those of the two traditional parties in Peru—the former leftist Alianza Popular Revolucionaria Americana (APRA, founded in 1924) and the former rightist Acción Popular (AP, founded in 1956). Table 7.1 shows electoral changes since 1980. As the table suggests, electoral volatility has been strikingly high. For instance, several parties disappeared from the legislative scene, and others emerged in the form of personalist parties (e.g., Cambio 90 of Alberto Fujimori or Frente Independiente Moralizador of Fernando Olivera). APRA held a majority of seats in the period 1985–90, and Cambio 90 in the period 1995–2000. Since 2000, no single party has been able to win a majority of seats.

During the period of 2001–6, Alemán et al. (2011) found Peruvian parties to be comparatively less unified than those of other presidential democracies, but the absolute values of unity suggest that some parties and their leaders still are relevant actors, influencing the voting behavior of legislators.[13] The authors show that the government–opposition divide constitutes the main legislative conflict in the Peruvian Congress. As expected, ideological differences play a secondary role. Although mapping suggests that ideological differences across parties and regional characteristics help explain positions along an ideological spectrum, these differences are much less relevant to explaining voting behavior than the government–opposition dichotomy.

While Unión por el Perú (leftist party with support in the southern region) and Unidad Nacional (conservative party with support in the capital) occupy opposite and extreme positions along an ideological spectrum, Perú Posible (moderate party led by former president Alejandro Toledo) is located at the center of the distribution. APRA's position is relatively close to that of Perú Posible, but still skewed to the left (Alemán et al. 2011). The survey of legislators conducted by PELA (Proyecto de Élites Parlamentarias de América Latina) for the 2000s confirms that legislators from Perú Posible locate

Table 7.1 Share of seats in Congress

Political parties/period	1980–5	1985–90	1990–2	1995–2000	2000–1	2001–6	2006–11	2011–16
Partido Aprista Peruano	32.2	59.4	29.4	6.7	5	23.3	30	3.1
Izquierda Unida	~	26.7	8.9	1.7	~	~	~	~
Convergencia Democrática	~	6.7	~	~	~	~	~	~
Acción Popular	54.4	6.1	~	3.3	2.5	2.5	~	~
Frente Democrático	~	~	34.4	~	~	~	~	~
Cambio 90	~	~	18.3	~	~	~	~	~
Izquierda Socialista	~	~	2.22	~	~	~	~	~
Frente Nacional de Trabajadores y Campesinos	1.1	~	1.7	0.8	~	~	~	~
Partido Popular Cristiano	5.6	~	~	2.5	~	~	~	~
Frente Independiente Moralizador	~	~	3.9	5	7.5	9.2	~	~
Partido Revolucionario de los Trabajadores	1.7	~	~	~	~	~	~	~
Unidad Democrática Popular	1.1	~	~	~	~	~	~	~
Unidad de Izquierda Revolucionaria	1.7	~	~	~	~	~	~	~
Unidad de Izquierda	1.1	~	~	~	~	~	~	~
Partido Comunista Peruano	0.6	~	~	~	~	~	~	~
Partido Campesino Revolucionario	0.6	~	~	~	~	~	~	~
Movimiento Regionalista Loretano	~	~	0.6	~	~	~	~	~
Frente Tacneñista	~	~	0.6	~	~	~	~	~
Acuerdo Popular	~	~	0.6	~	~	~	~	~
Cambio 90–Nueva Mayoría	~	~	~	55.8	~	2.5	~	~
Convergencia Democrática-País Posible	~	~	~	4.2	~	~	~	~
Frente Obrero, Campesino, Estudiantil y Popular	0.5	~	~	~	~	~	~	~
Izquierda Nacionalista	~	1.1	~	~	~	~	~	~

Frente Popular Agrícola del Perú	~	~	~	0.8	1.7	~	~	~
Movimiento Independiente Agrario	~	~	~	0.8	~	~	~	~
Unión por el Perú	~	~	~	14.2	2.5	5	37.5	~
Renovación Nacional	~	~	~	2.5	~	~	~	~
Movimiento Cívico Nacional Obras	~	~	~	1.7	~	~	~	~
Perú 2000	~	~	~	~	43.3	~	~	~
Perú Posible	~	~	~	~	24.2	37.5	1.7	16.2
Partido Democrático Somos Perú	~	~	~	~	6.7	3.3	~	~
Solidaridad Nacional	~	~	~	~	4.2	~	~	6.9
Avancemos	~	~	~	~	2.5	~	~	~
Unidad Nacional	~	~	~	~	~	14.2	14.2	~
Solución Popular	~	~	~	~	~	0.8	~	~
Todos por la Victoria	~	~	~	~	~	0.8	~	~
Renacimiento Andino	~	~	~	~	~	0.8	~	~
Alianza por el Futuro	~	~	~	~	~	~	10.8	~
Frente de Centro	~	~	~	~	~	~	4.2	~
Restauración Nacional	~	~	~	~	~	~	1.7	~
Gana Perú	~	~	~	~	~	~	~	36.2
Fuerza 2011	~	~	~	~	~	~	~	28.5
Alianza por el Gran Cambio	~	~	~	~	~	~	~	9.2

Source: Jurado Nacional de Elecciones; author's elaboration.

themselves at the center of the distribution (its median legislator is also the median legislator of the chamber) and the other parties surround Perú Posible's centrist position (see appendix Figure 7.A1).[14]

With regard to the position of presidents, majoritarian electoral rules have contributed to the centrist position adopted by Peruvian presidents, especially after the end of the Fujimorato period (1990–2001). Their positions have been relatively close to the median legislative position of the chamber at the time, and these moderate positions have provided Peruvian presidents with an additional advantage to successfully pass their bills.

In sum, voters do not easily identify the ideological orientation of parties, but congressional votes and interviews with legislators reflect some party differences. For the most part, the political context is characterized by centrist presidents with strong prerogatives and a volatile fragmented party system. The following section develops the theoretical argument of this chapter.

EXAMINING LEGISLATIVE SUCCESS AND DECREES

Given a series of institutional prerogatives—to be the first mover on tax-and-spend policies, to serve as repository of greater policy expertise, to be able to replace legislators' work with legislative and urgent decrees, and to have greater financial resources to negotiate with other political forces in Congress (e.g., patronage, fiscal redistribution)—along with the centrist position of minority presidents and the weakness of Peruvian political parties, I would expect executive bills (including major bills) to have a relatively high rate of approval. Therefore, my first hypothesis of this study is as follows:

> ***H1.*** *Minority presidents in this favorable context should be relatively successful at getting their bills approved by Congress. This approval rate of the executive bills should be higher than the approval rate of bills initiated by members of Congress.*

The relative ideological policy positions of legislative parties might matter when explaining bill approval. Considering the volatile nature of the Peruvian party system, its non-programmatic tendencies, and the weak ideological differences across parties, I would expect that legislative parties occupying the center should be in a more advantageous position to see their bills enacted into law. Given the blurred ideological differences across parties, I can at the very least test whether or not the party placed at the centrist position of the Peruvian ideological dimension gains some advantage over its competitors. This hypothesis is consistent with the expectation of Alemán and Tsebelis, as described in the introductory chapter, regarding the advantageous position of centrist actors for passing bills. Considering these arguments, I frame the following second hypothesis:

> *H2. Bills introduced by the party positioned in the center should have a higher probability of passing than bills introduced by other parties.*

Two main approaches seek to explain the use of decrees by presidents. The first, called "unilateral theory," states that presidents employ decrees to advance their policies when they find strong opposition from congress (Gleiber and Shull 1992; Krause and Cohen 1997; Mayer 1999; Cox and Morgenstern 2002). For the Latin American case, Cox and Morgenstern (2002) argue that politically weak presidents use decrees more often when they face increasing difficulties in enacting laws through the ordinary conduits in congress. Under this view, the expected relationship between the use of decrees and the ability to pass executive initiatives in congress is negative. The initial portion of the third hypothesis (H3A) is based on the arguments of this approach:

> *H3A. The use of legislative decrees should be negatively correlated with approval rates of presidential bills.*

The second approach, called "delegation theory," predicts that legislators delegate the authority to enact decrees to the president, or acquiesce to its usage, in order to obtain several types of benefits (Epstein and O'Halloran 1999; Kiewiet and McCubbins 1991; McCubbins et al. 1987, 1989). Pereira et al. (2005: 181) summarize these potential benefits as follows: "information, flexibility in time budgeting, absence of responsibility for public policy, resolution of complex bargaining problems, and other positive returns to the legislature." Regarding these benefits, Carey and Shugart (1998) contend that legislators tend to see the extensive use of decrees as favorable to either speed up the legislative process or avoid making decisions on unpopular or controversial initiatives. Carey and Shugart also contend that the lack of policy expertise and information (compared to the executive position) pushes legislators to delegate legislative prerogatives to presidents. Reich (2002) argues that legislators prefer transferring these legislative prerogatives to the executive branch to reduce legislator transaction costs (for electorally unworthy initiatives) and concentrate their efforts on electorally more rewarding initiatives. Thus, according to this perspective decree usage does not reflect deadlock between both branches, but a collaborative context that provides mutual benefits. The last hypothesis (H3B) is based on this alternative perspective:

> ***H3B.*** *The use of legislative decrees should be positively correlated with approval rates of presidential bills.*

The following section develops the empirical analysis centered on testing the four hypotheses of this study.

EMPIRICAL ANALYSIS AND RESULTS

My data include all bills presented in Congress during the presidencies of Alejandro Toledo (from Perú Posible) and Alan García (from APRA). Figure 7.2 shows the number of all bills introduced by type of actor (legislators or the president).[15] As the figure indicates, legislators' initiatives outnumbered those of presidents.

Although legislators' total initiative production during the period surpassed that of the president, the rate of approval of presidential initiatives was greater. Figure 7.3 shows the approval rate of bills initiated by the president and members of Congress between 2001 and 2011. The high level of success for executive bills provides a first glimpse of presidential influence compared to congressional lawmaking.

The president's advantage extends to major bills. Major bills are coded as those appearing in the main pages of the *El Comercio* newspaper between 2001 and 2011.[16] Figure 7.4 shows the number of major bills both introduced by the

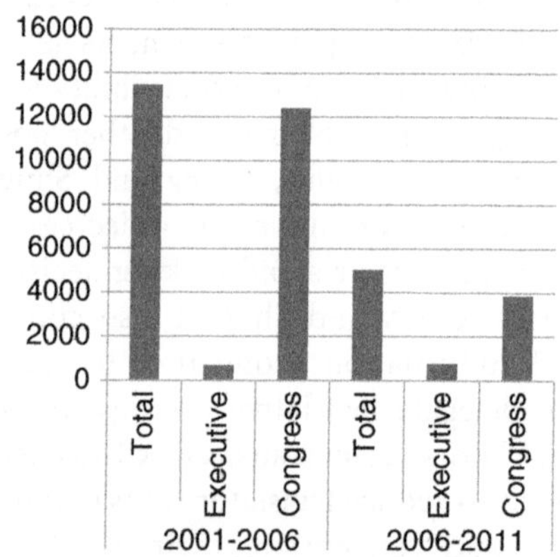

Figure 7.2 Number of all bills introduced, 2001–2011
Source: Peruvian Congress; author's elaboration.

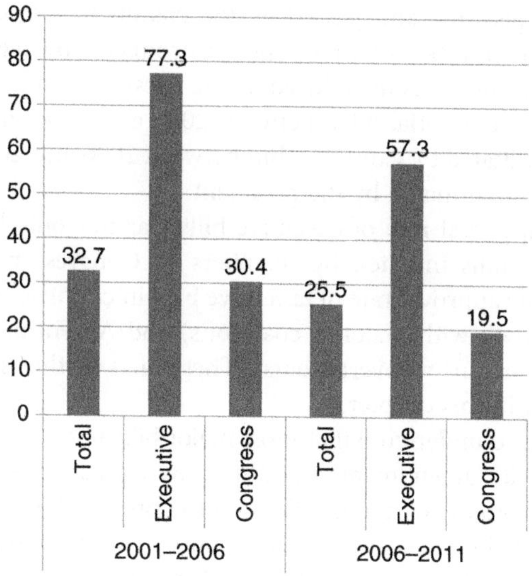

Figure 7.3 Percentage of bills approved, 2001–2011
Source: Peruvian Congress; author's elaboration.

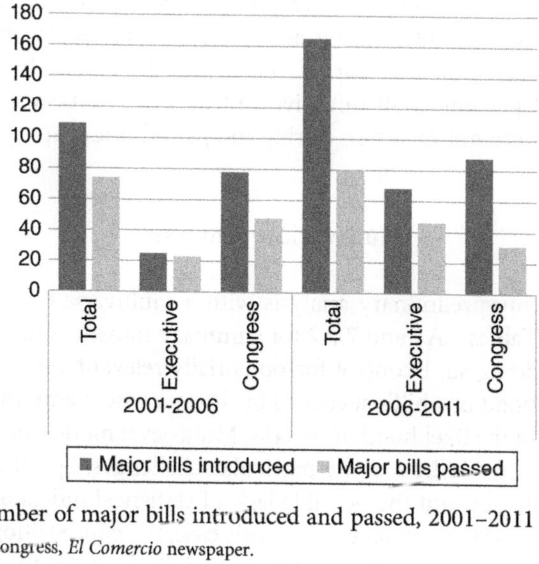

Figure 7.4 Number of major bills introduced and passed, 2001–2011
Source: Peruvian Congress, *El Comercio* newspaper.

president and legislators and passed by the chamber. Although during the study period the number of major bills introduced by legislators always surpassed that of initiatives introduced by the president, the rates of approval were higher for presidential bills. Between 2001 and 2006, most major bills approved were initiated by Congress, but between 2006 and 2011, most major bills approved were initiated by the president.

Overall, the approval rate of executive bills was not only higher than the approval rate of bills initiated by members of Congress but also high in comparison to the approval rate of executive bills in countries such as Colombia and Brazil (both with majority coalitions) and Argentina (with plurality and single-party majority governments). These facts further support the first hypothesis given in this chapter.

It is important to underscore that most major bills initiated by the president were approved with amendments introduced by legislators. During the study period, about two-thirds of major bills from the president were approved with amendments introduced outside the committee. The proportion of all major bills approved that had amendments was 69 percent.[17] I also find a positive association between the likelihood of amendment and the likelihood of approval of major bills. Most amended bills passed (75 percent for all major bills).

Amendments, allowed under Peruvian open rules, should tend to make bills more acceptable to the median voter of the chamber. This acceptability increases their chances of approval. Amendments frequently add particularistic benefits to bills that might also enhance chances of success. But legislators are not the only ones introducing amendments. Presidents often introduce amendatory observations or partial vetoes to bills passed by the Peruvian Congress (9.94 percent of all initiatives introduced). Total vetoes that reject the entire bill were not common during the period under study.

Multivariate Analysis

I complement my preliminary analysis with a multivariate empirical model (see appendix Tables 7.A1 and 7.A2 for summary statistics and definitions for variables). By doing so, I control for potentially relevant variables that could affect the likelihood of a bill's success. For this purpose, I employ a multi-level model to explain the likelihood of success. Multi-level models provide valuable statistical tools that address some particular challenges. Specifically, scholars have to take into account the possible lack of statistical independence among observations across contextual units; in this case, the composition of Congress based on electoral results (Raudenbusch and Bryk 2002; Steenbergen and Jones 2002). Failure to cluster this type of data may result in underestimated standard errors and ultimately lead to mistakes in estimation of inference analysis (Barcikowski 1981; Blair et al. 1983; Steenbergen and Jones 2002). A multi-level model is conservative, as estimated standard errors increase to account for lack of statistical independence among observations across contextual units. I employ random effects at each level of analysis. Since there are two different congresses, there are two dissimilar congressional internal compositions (different legislators and differences in parties' share of seats) and dynamics affecting (differently) the approval of bills. Consequently, I group bills according to the congress that processed the initiatives. In other words, while the bill initiatives constitute the first level of analysis, the two congresses compose the second level of analysis.

As the dependent variable, I employ a dichotomous variable. This variable captures whether or not the bill initiative was approved (taking the value of 1 if the bill initiative was approved, and 0 otherwise). In order to test the first two hypotheses, I include four key independent variables. First, I evaluate the scope of presidential influence within the chamber with a dummy variable that identified bills proposed by the president. I also interact this variable with the covariate indicating whether or not the bill was a major proposal. This interaction tests if the chance of passage for presidential bills changed when the saliency of the bill increased.

In examining the second hypothesis, I include a categorical variable identifying those bills proposed by the political party located at the center of the ideological distribution. Given the weak differences in terms of ideology across the other parties it seems reasonable to follow a conservative strategy, as the distance to the median position of the chamber was relatively similar for most parties (according to the data reported by PELA).[18] As discussed earlier, the available evidence suggests that Perú Posible occupies the centrist position. Hence, this fourth independent variable equals 1 when the bill was proposed by legislators from Perú Posible, and 0 otherwise.

As control variables, I include three dummy variables. The first two indicate whether the bill was referred to the Economy or Budget committees. Given the president's formal authority over economic legislation, these variables evaluate whether the likelihood of approval differed in these committees.[19] The third variable captures whether the president gained extra advantage during the first year in office (often called a honeymoon period).

I show the results of the first multi-level logistic regression in Table 7.2, displaying eight different specifications. The first four specifications employ all bills introduced between 2001 and 2011. While two of them do not include the control variables, the other two incorporate them as robustness check. The fifth and sixth employ only bills proposed by legislators, and the seventh and eighth employ only bills introduced by the president. Likewise, the fifth and

Table 7.2 Multi-level logistic regressions of success

	All bills				Only legislators' bills		Only presidents' bills	
Variables	Model 1	Model 2	Model 3	Model 4	Model 5	Model 6	Model 7	Model 8
Major bills	0.99**	0.96**	1.10**	1.07**	1.15**	1.10**	0.47	0.52
	(0.17)	(0.17)	(0.19)	(0.19)	(0.20)	(0.20)	(0.39)	(0.39)
Bill proposed by the president	2.04** (0.08)	2.00** (0.08)	2.06** (0.08)	2.02** (0.08)				
Major bills × bill proposed by the president			−0.71 (0.42)	−0.69 (0.43)				
Perú Posible's position	0.25** (0.04)	0.24** (0.04)	0.25** (0.04)	0.24** (0.04)	0.25** (0.04)	0.24** (0.04)		
Control variables								
Economy		0.48**		0.48**		0.54**		−0.23
		(0.04)		(0.04)		(0.04)		(0.19)
Budget		0.42**		0.41**		0.45**		0.43*
		(0.08)		(0.08)		(0.09)		(0.20)
Honeymoon								0.34 (0.18)
Constant	−0.39	−0.52	−0.39	−0.52	−0.39	−0.53	1.60**	1.47**
	(0.37)	(0.38)	(0.38)	(0.38)	(0.38)	(0.38)	(0.29)	(0.28)
Number of observations	15,425	15,425	15,425	15,425	13,761	13,761	1,180	1,180
AIC	18,727	18,575	18,727	18,575	17,042	16,869	1,097	1,092
BIC	18,766	18,629	18,772	18,636	17,072	16,914	1,112	1,123

* significant at 0.05; ** significant at 0.01.

seventh specifications do not take into account the control variables. The fifth and sixth specifications strategically employ only legislators' bills to test whether the previous results regarding advantages of the centrist party held, as I exclude bills proposed by other non-legislative actors. In addition, I use only presidential bills to examine both whether the advantage of being president when passing major bills remained relatively similar to that of passing minor bills, and whether or not the honeymoon period affected the findings.

Overall, the results lend support to the first hypothesis. The presidential bill initiatives were more likely to pass than other initiatives. Greater saliency favored the likelihood of approval. However, the coefficient of the interaction between the covariates identifying presidential initiatives and major initiatives does not reach statistical significance. The seventh and eighth specifications' results show that when only presidential bills are taken into account, the variable *major bills* is not statistically significant. Major executive bills were not approved at a higher rate than other bills when they were initiated by the president. Major bills initiated by legislators, however, were approved at a higher rate than other bills they initiated.

I also find that bills introduced by legislators from the chamber's centrist party, Perú Posible, were significantly more likely to pass than bills introduced by legislators belonging to other parties. This suggests that there are advantages to being in the center and lends support to the second hypothesis.[20] This finding also holds when only bills proposed by legislators are taken into account. Regarding control variables, bills referred to the Budget committee were more likely to pass regardless of who initiated them, while bills referred to the Economy committee were more likely to pass if they were introduced by legislators. Finally, the honeymoon period variable was statistically significant but only at the 10 percent level. The Peruvian president seemed to gain some additional advantage at the beginning of the term.

Even when the results related to the first two hypotheses (executive power and the centrist advantage) appear to be statistically significant, their marginal impacts on the likelihood of approval might not be meaningful. In order to discard this possibility, I also report predicted probabilities of approval. Table 7.3 displays these predicted probabilities, which were calculated based on the second regression displayed in Table 7.2 (a specification including the control variables). As shown, variations in my key independent variables produce a relevant impact in the probability of bill approval. The effects of being a major bill or being initiated by the president are especially pronounced.

Table 7.3 Predicted probabilities

Variables	Values of the independent variables	Predicted probabilities
Major bills	Major bills = 0	0.46
	Major bills = 1	0.69
Bill proposed by the president	Bill proposed by the president = 0	0.42
	Bill proposed by the president = 1	0.84
Perú Posible's position	Perú Posible's position = 0	0.44
	Perú Posible's position = 1	0.51

Legislative Decrees and Presidential Rates of Success in Congress

For testing the third hypothesis, I evaluate the relationship between the number of legislative decrees and the rate of success of presidential bills in Congress. The data show that the president's rate of legislative success in Congress and the number of legislative decrees were positively correlated (0.10) and that the overall rate of legislative success was very high. Both of these findings are inconsistent with the implications of unilateral theory.

Additional evidence also contradicts predictions of unilateral theory in the Peruvian case. For example, Alberto Fujimori (1990–2001) used these prerogatives aggressively during a period in which he enjoyed control of Congress through a comfortable majority. Another illustrative example concerns the administration of Alan García (2006–11). During García's years, the percentage of presidential initiatives that were approved by Congress was approximately 12 percentage points higher than that of the previous administration of Alejandro Toledo (2001–6). Nevertheless, García used decrees more frequently than his predecessor Toledo (Blume 2011).

Finally, I employ a Poisson regression using uninformative priors and a data augmentation approach (data-augmented Gibbs sampler).[21] The use of the classical frequentist approach is questionable for small sample sizes. In the frequentist approach using maximum likelihood, inferences are based on the asymptotic theory. The normal asymptotic approximation has been found to produce significant bias for small samples (Griffiths et al. 1987; Zellner and Rossi 1984; Albert and Chib 1993). In order to avoid the lack of accuracy of the frequentist approach for estimation in small samples, I employ a Poisson model.

As other studies have done (Pereira et al. 2005, 2008), I use the number of legislative decrees per year as the dependent variable and employ the rate of success of the president in Congress as the independent variable. This independent variable captures whether decree usage decreases with greater legislative success. I display the model's results in Figure 7.5.

The Bayesian model reports the posterior distribution for the explanatory variable. In this case, the estimator for the variable indicating the marginal impact of changes in the success of the president in Congress over the number of decrees per year took the values of 1.84 and 1.94 based on the quintiles at the 2.5 percent and 97.5 percent levels of the posterior distribution. In addition, the mean of the posterior distribution (1.89) is also positive. In sum, the estimation confirms the existence of a positive relationship between the rate of success of the president in Congress and the use of legislative decrees. The results lend greater support to the "delegation" theory than to the

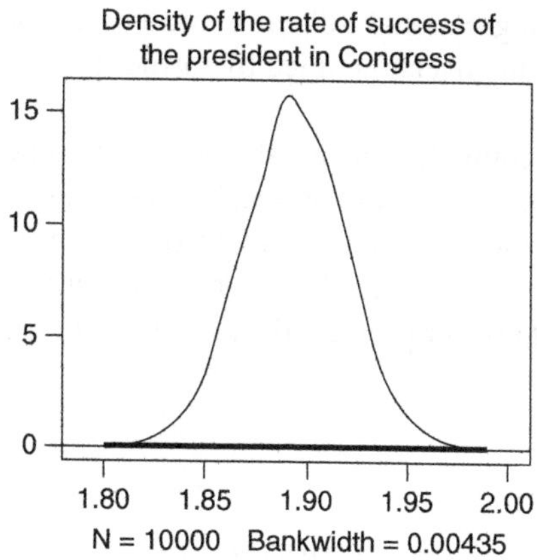

Figure 7.5 Posterior distributions of the rate of success

"unilateral" theory. Therefore, I find more evidence to support the validity of hypothesis H3B over hypothesis H3A.[22]

CONCLUSIONS

Results from this study on lawmaking in Peru offer important lessons. First, the analysis confirms the conventional view that the president is a relevant actor in the lawmaking process in Peru. The president has exclusive powers to be the first mover on policies related to economic and budgetary matters, and can initiate bills in almost all policy areas. Furthermore, the president has the ability to introduce the last amendment. In sum, the president possesses advantages that help in getting initiatives approved by Congress. The Peruvian president's ability to turn bills into laws is rather high in comparison to other Latin American presidents holding congressional majorities. Presidents also frequently enact legislative decrees. The analysis reveals a positive association between the use of legislative decrees and the legislative success of the president.

Perhaps as important as the finding of presidential power is the finding of congressional influence on lawmaking. Contradicting conventional views that legislators play a minor role in lawmaking, this study has underscored the importance of their participation. The data presented in this chapter show that legislators initiate most bills and have a share in law production similar to executive power. Moreover, legislators initiate an important share of major bills and go on to amend most major bills initiated by the president. As Levitt

(2012) points out, congressional influence and power was enhanced after the fall of the authoritarian government led by former president Alberto Fujimori (1990–2001).

In this particular context, both legislative paralysis between the executive and congressional players and any political crises as a consequence of the lack of majority of the president have been avoided. Legislative productivity seems relatively unaffected by the lack of a majority government. Arguments that claim the necessity of greater presidential powers do not seem applicable to the Peruvian case.

APPENDIX

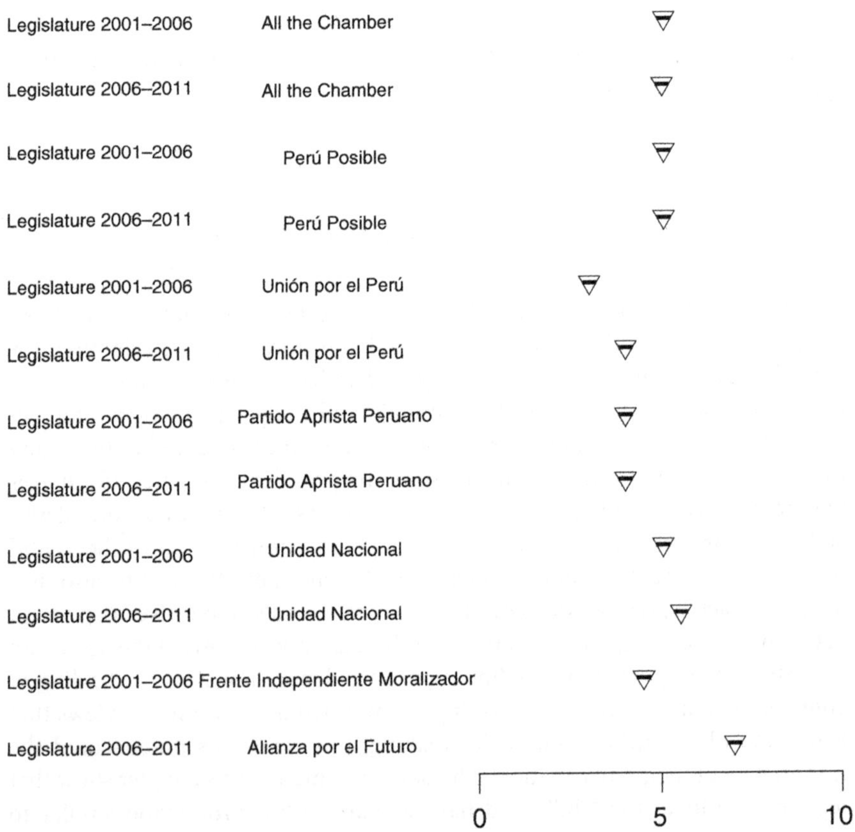

Figure 7.A1 Positions of the median legislators by party

Source: *Proyecto de Encuestas de Legisladores de América Latina*; author's elaboration.

Table 7.A1 Summary statistics

Variable	Mean	Standard deviation	Minimum	Maximum
Dependent variables				
Success	0.37	0.48	0.00	1.00
Number of legislative decrees	14.33	25.86	0.00	105.00
Independent variables				
Major bills	0.01	0.12	0.00	1.00
Bill proposed by the president	0.08	0.27	0.00	1.00
Perú Posible's position	0.22	0.42	0.00	1.00
Economy	0.21	0.40	0.00	1.00
Budget	0.06	0.23	0.00	1.00
Honeymoon	0.22	0.41	0.00	1.00
Rate of success of the president in Congress	0.81	0.07	0.71	0.95

Table 7.A2 Definitions for variables used in analysis

Variables	Definitions	Sources
Dependent variable		
Success	A dichotomous variable taking the value of 1 if the law was approved, and 0 otherwise.	Peruvian Congress. Retrieved from <http://www.congreso.gob.pe>.
Number of legislative decrees	A count variable describing the number of legislative decrees used during a given year.	Ministry of Justice and Human Rights. Retrieved from <http://spij.minjus.gob.pe>.
Independent variable		
Major bills	A dichotomous variable taking the value of 1 if the law proposed is a major bill, and 0 otherwise.	*El Comercio* newspaper. Retrieved from <http://www.elcomercio.pe>.
Bill proposed by the president	A dichotomous variable taking the value of 1 if the bill initiative was submitted by the president, and 0 otherwise.	Peruvian Congress. Retrieved from <http://www.congreso.gob.pe>.
Perú Posible's position	A dichotomous variable taking the value of 1 if the bill initiative was proposed by Perú Posible, and 0 otherwise.	Peruvian Congress. Retrieved from <http://www.congreso.gob.pe>.
Economy	A dichotomous variable taking the value of 1 if the law initiative was processed by the Committee of Economy, and 0 otherwise.	Peruvian Congress. Retrieved from <http://www.congreso.gob.pe>.

(*continued*)

Table 7.A2 Continued

Variables	Definitions	Sources
Budget	A dichotomous variable taking the value of 1 if the law initiative was processed by the Committee of Budget, and 0 otherwise.	Peruvian Congress. Retrieved from <http://www.congreso.gob.pe>.
Honeymoon	A dichotomous variable taking the value of 1 if the law initiative was proposed during the first year of the executive in power, and 0 otherwise.	Constructed by author.
Rate of success of the president in Congress	Percentage of seats held by the president's party in Congress (divided by 100).	Peruvian Congress. Retrieved from <http://www.congreso.gob.pe>.

NOTES

1. Article 107 of the 1993 constitution. Bill initiatives presented by citizens must be signed by at least 0.3 percent of the electoral population. The initiatives to reform the constitution require either the support of two-thirds of legislators or more than half of them plus a referendum to be approved. Only the president, legislators, and citizens can submit this type of initiative. Autonomous institutions, regional governments, municipalities, and professional associations must submit additional documents together with the initiative. These include an analysis of the motives of the bill initiative, a cost–benefit analysis of the proposed policy changes, and an evaluation on the impact for the environment (if necessary).
2. Committees can ask the chamber's leadership for extensions to this deadline.
3. If different committees make divergent decisions (contradictory *dictamenes*), the committee chosen in the first place to evaluate the initiative prevails.
4. The executive (with the approval of Congress) can suspend several citizen rights during no more than sixty days (forty-five days for state of siege or sixty days for state of emergency). In state of siege, more citizen rights can be suspended. The president must specify which rights are suspended (Article 76 of the 1993 constitution).
5. The president's bills must be introduced with the explicit endorsement of the president of the Council of Ministers.
6. The president needs the approval of the Council of Ministers to enact these decrees.
7. See Articles 101, 104, and 106 of the 1993 constitution.
8. See case 0008-2003-AI/TC of the Constitutional Tribunal.
9. The constitution also specifies that the Constitutional Tribunal could declare unconstitutional the urgent and legislative decrees enacted by the president and, consequently, nullify them.

10. The spokesperson of the legislative bloc (also called Directivo-Portavoz in the congressional rules) must sign the initiative. In addition, these blocs provide some technical support for elaborating the initiatives to their legislators (Sala et al. 2009).
11. The legislators through these party blocs have exclusive prerogatives to initiate bills in two jurisdictions: amnesty laws and the modification of the regulations of Congress.
12. If legislators introduce the amendment during the debate in the plenary, the president of the committee in charge of preparing the *dictamen* should provide an opinion on the convenience of the amendment.
13. APRA was the party that reached the highest scores of unity. This party has been characterized as the best organized and longest-lived in Peruvian politics (Angell 1980; Graham 1990; Roberts 2006; Dietz and Myers 2007).
14. In this survey, legislators place themselves on the left-right scale (10 points).
15. Legislative resolutions are excluded from this count.
16. These pages correspond to the first two pages of the Politics and Economy sections of this newspaper. This newspaper has been traditionally the most salient in Peruvian history.
17. The count of these amendments includes only those made outside the committees. If we included those proposed inside the committees, these figures could be even greater. I also find that most major bills introduced were amended (56 percent of all major bills).
18. See Figure 7.A1 in the appendix for a summary on these statistics.
19. For further details on the description and statistics of the variables used in the analyses, consult Tables 7.A1 and 7.A2 in the appendix. It is important to note that only 21.31 percent of presidential initiatives are sent to the Budget committee, and only 17.94 percent of them to the Economy committee. In other words, most presidential initiatives are not sent to these two committees.
20. I notice that this advantage attributed to Perú Posible, which occupies the centrist position, persists even when the voting behavior of its legislators produced the lowest scores of legislative unity between 2001 and 2006 (Alemán et al. 2011). I also point run other specifications to test the effect of the differences in policy positions on which laws are approved. First, I measure the ideological distance between the median legislator of the chamber and the median legislators of the party proposing the initiative. When two parties were co-sponsoring the initiative, I employ an average. Although this variable presents the expected sign (negative), it does not reach acceptable levels of statistical significance. Second, I include several dummy variables for each party that sponsored the initiative. Most of these variables do not seem to matter. These findings of this chapter support my expectations regarding the effect of the ideological positions: ideology matters but the lack of clear ideological differences among Peruvian parties weakens the scope of this effect. Such limitation will not be present in other Latin American countries where the party systems are relatively more programmatic and institutionalized and where citizens can more successfully identify ideological differences across parties. Finally, I run all

specifications employing a simple logistic regression. The results from these regressions are similar in the level of statistical significance to those reported by the multilevel models. Overall, the empirical analysis indicates that the reported results are robust across all specifications.

21. I run this model using the R package MCMCpack to produce the data-augmented Gibbs sampler for this estimation (Martin et al. 2009). The Gibbs sampler rests on the idea that the joint probability densities can be completely characterized by their component conditional densities. Therefore, rather than sampling from the high-dimensional density (p(β/data)), the Gibbs technique samples from the lower-dimensional *conditional* densities that put them together to define the joint density.
22. Schmidt (1998) also finds greater delegation to the Peruvian executive under a Congress lacking a majority before the enactment of the 1993 constitution.

8

Agenda Setting and Lawmaking in Uruguay

Daniel Chasquetti

In Uruguay, the allocation of legislative agenda power between the branches of government is the result of a series of institutional choices made by political parties more than fifty years ago. The first two Uruguayan constitutions (1830 and 1918) established a pure presidential system whereby Congress voted laws and the executive branch enacted or vetoed them. In 1934 a reform led to the gradual introduction of parliamentary dispositions that gave Congress greater political control over the administration. While this change gave the president exclusive powers to initiate legislation in some areas, it also included complex procedures to censor ministers that could perfectly well have led to the dissolution of the assembly and the fall of the head of government. The approval of these constitutional amendments marked a historic point of minimum separation between the executive and legislative powers (Chasquetti 2003).

A constitutional reform approved in 1952 initiated an inverse process in which institutional designs tended towards an increased separation of powers and reinforced the legislative authority of the executive. This scenario was accentuated with the constitutional reform of 1967, which established a distribution of power among the branches that was markedly favorable to the presidency. This reform granted to the executive exclusive powers to initiate legislation in three new areas, namely retirement and pensions, tax exemptions, and the fixing of wages and prices (Sanguinetti and Pacheco Seré 1970: 90–6). Other changes incorporated various principles that were originally included in the 1934 reform but had failed to produce substantive effects. Since then, the Uruguayan executive has had considerable formal authority over the legislative agenda, which has enabled it to regulate the flow of proposals and achieve favorable political results.

Uruguay's presidential system, however, is not organized around a single dominant actor; Congress continues to play a key role. The executive can hardly ignore congressional views, since the legislative arena is controlled by strong parties. Consequently, Uruguayan presidents seeking to pass their legislative programs work to build stable congressional majorities. This system, characterized by a president who is institutionally powerful but politically weak in his relationship with legislative parties, compels permanent negotiation between the branches of government. The Uruguayan president is an important player in the legislative process as a result of his formal prerogatives over the agenda, but also crucial to his performance is his ability to build favorable legislative majorities.

In this chapter we analyze the distribution of agenda power in the legislative process in Uruguay. In analytical terms, control of the legislative agenda responds to a set of institutional rules that allocate precise prerogatives and to the positions of relevant political actors. Here we examine the legislative authority of the executive as well as the allocation of agenda setting power within Congress. The results confirm the importance of institutional powers in giving the executive a prominent role in the lawmaking process; however, they also underline how Uruguayan presidents have been constrained by the need to negotiate with legislative actors that do not necessarily hold the same preferences and are not necessarily in the opposition. The analysis shows that legislators amend a large proportion of government bills and that this is usually a response to the need to establish agreements within Congress. While executives use their prerogatives, such as vetoes, to try to mitigate the impact of some of these amendments, Congress is still able to influence the direction of policy change. The empirical analysis focuses on bills from the period 1995–2010, a smaller set of major bills, and the issuance of presidential vetoes.

The rest of this chapter is divided into four parts. In the first we describe the most important institutions and identify the actors with authority over the legislative agenda. In the second we analyze the ideological positioning of the main legislative actors since the recovery of democracy in 1985. In the third we examine empirically how major bills are processed and for this purpose we test a series of hypotheses about the role played by political actors and the influence of institutional rules. And lastly, in the fourth part, we draw some brief conclusions about legislative agenda control in Uruguay.

AGENDA SETTING INSTITUTIONS IN URUGUAY

The Uruguayan political system is built around two types of structures that, to a large extent, determine the orientation of the political game. First, there are institutional arrangements that structure the relations between the branches of government. Second, there are electoral rules that influence the number and behavior of actors that participate in the decision-making process. The institutional actors with veto powers are the president and the two legislative chambers. The Uruguayan president also has some relevant authority over the initiation and scheduling of legislative proposals. In addition, the president can make changes (*observaciones*) to bills that have been passed by Congress, which can then be overridden by a super-majority. Under certain conditions, the institutional dispositions for direct democracy also favor the emergence of other additional veto players. Direct democracy mechanisms include referenda against laws that have been passed and plebiscites to introduce changes to the constitution.

According to Cox and McCubbins (1993), agenda setting power is the power given to an organ in the legislature to determine which proposed bills shall be considered and which ones shall not, and under what procedures they will be analyzed. In all legislative assemblies the power to set the agenda is geared towards optimizing the legislators' time, to averting delaying practices (such as the *filibuster* tactic) and to resolving the problem of a build-up of bills before the chambers (*bottlenecks*). When a majority acts as a cartel, it implies that it has control of the chamber's agenda so as to achieve its legislative goals. In Uruguay, the actors with agenda setting power are the executive, the presidents of the Asamblea General and the two chambers, and, under certain conditions, the chairs of the permanent committees. In the next sub-sections we expand on the most relevant presidential prerogatives and the distribution of agenda setting power within Congress.

Presidential Prerogatives

The Uruguayan constitution gives the executive certain prerogatives that favor its involvement in the lawmaking process. First, the executive not only has total and partial veto power, but also the power to introduce a last series of amendments (observations) to the partially vetoed bills just passed by Congress (Alemán and Tsebelis 2005). These actions can only be overridden by a majority of three-fifths in each chamber within thirty days after they are issued. If Congress fails to act, then the objections or amendments to the vetoed bill are considered accepted. Until the constitutional reform of 1996, presidential vetoes could be overturned by a majority of three-fifths in the Asamblea General (the two chambers together)[1] within a period of forty-five days. This change made it more costly to reverse presidential decisions since it required consideration in each chamber and reduced the allotted time to respond. As we show in the empirical section, the president's willingness to use the veto increases at the end of the term and when his legislative support in Congress weakens.

Second, the constitution specifies a series of strategic policy areas where the executive has exclusive legislative initiative, such as budgetary and tax policy, retirement and pension regimes, the creation of jobs in the public service, and the fixing of certain prices in the economy. These dispositions amount to severe restrictions for legislators and transform the president into a gatekeeper in the process of passing new policies in these areas. Areas of initiative exclusively reserved for the executive work against the emergence of a majority with an alternative legislative program.

Restrictions of this type go back to the constitutional reform of 1934,[2] but the present scheme was formally consecrated in the 1967 reform. The related constitutional amendment had far-reaching political consequences as regards the kind of legislation enacted by Congress (Chasquetti 2014). For example, in the two decades before 1967, 62 percent of total laws approved by Congress involved public spending, but in the last twenty years (1990–2010) this proportion has been only 16 percent of them. In addition, Congress has passed more laws that ratify international agreements (from 3 percent to 19 percent, perhaps as a result of the globalization process), laws of an administrative kind (from 16 percent to 41 percent), and a whole series of laws that reform regulations, create sector policies, and regulate markets (from 10 percent to 17 percent).[3] When the monopoly on the initiative in public spending passed to the executive, legislators reoriented their activities to other policy areas.[4]

Third, the Uruguayan president is also empowered to declare bills urgent, which imposes a deadline on Congress. If an urgent bill is not addressed by the plenary within the stipulated time (maximum 100 days), it becomes law automatically.[5] Uruguayan presidents, unlike their Chilean counterparts, have seldom used this mechanism. Obstacles and blockages from their own supporters seem to have discouraged their use. Since this prerogative was instituted in the constitution in 1967, only fourteen urgent bills have been sent to Congress of which only eight became law. The remaining six were reclassified as non-urgent and were buried in the congressional committees.

Fourth, the president has an agent inside the congress in the form of the vice president (VP). Indeed, the VP of the Republic is at the same time the president of the Asamblea General and the president of the Senate. He is the individual responsible for coordinating the interaction between the executive and members of Congress, and for this reason he normally takes part in both cabinet meetings and meetings of legislative party leaders.

During electoral campaigns candidates for the presidency choose running mates who are loyal, so the VP usually works in line with the president's goals.[6] In Congress, the VP tends to be a proactive actor, strengthening the agenda setting power of the government. As the main leader of the legislative majority, the VP monitors the passage of the government's legislative program, negotiating with the other party leaders and determining which government bills should be prioritized by the chambers.

Lastly, the executive has certain additional prerogatives that can be helpful, albeit indirectly, to influence the legislative agenda. For example, the president has the power to designate and dismiss his ministers and vice-ministers, and to nominate aspirants for high positions in public administration management.[7] These powers are useful when it comes to negotiating legislative agreements with other parties or with factions within the government's party. As some authors have shown, presidents in Uruguay have used these prerogatives frequently and have set up coalition cabinets that guarantee efficient legislative cartels in Congress (Chasquetti 1999; Chasquetti and Moraes 2000; Altman 2002).

Agenda Control in Congress

There are three kinds of offices that have agenda setting power in the Uruguayan Congress: the presidency of the Asamblea General, the presidencies of the two chambers, and the chairmanships of the permanent committees. However, the existence of a unified majority is a prerequisite for these offices to be able to deploy their full institutional power over the agenda. When there is no such congressional majority, these positions lose substantial power vis-à-vis the leaders of the parties. In those instances, government parties must negotiate the schedule of the plenary with opposition ones, thereby shifting power from the elected authorities and committees to the leadership of the parties.

As noted before, the VP of the Republic plays an important role in the legislative process as an agent of the executive. It is important to note that the presidencies of the Asamblea General and the Senate are the only two positions in the legislative structure whose occupant does not change during the mandate. As president of the Asamblea General, the VP receives government bills and distributes them for study and approval between the chambers. As president of the Senate, he sets the order of business inside the chamber and assigns bills to committees.[8] He also plays a crucial role in the design and composition of the system of standing committees, as will be explained in the following section. The degree of power exercised by this office, however, rests on the existence of a legislative majority for the government.[9]

The position of Speaker of the House of Representatives is less important than that of president of the Senate because each year this office is occupied by a different deputy. The *pro tempore* nature of this position weakens the influence of its occupant. Otherwise, the Speaker's functions are very similar to those of the president of the Senate (e.g., he can set the schedule of the plenary and allocate bills to the committees). The distribution of this post is typically decided in negotiations between party leaders. Since the restoration of democracy in 1985, the position of Speaker has rotated among parties (five occupants per term). In seven of the twenty-eight years since 1985, this position went to an opposition deputy, and in three instances (1986, 1988, and 2003) this situation coincided with the lack of a legislative majority in favor of the executive.[10] However, this norm does not seem to have undermined much of the power of the majority party or coalition over the flow of legislation.

The presidents of the chambers share their institutional authority with the leaders of the political parties, which in turn control the behavior of individual legislators. For this reason, the presidents of the chambers meet frequently with party leaders to exchange information and discuss the congressional agenda. These meetings are informal but important to the organization of the legislative process. Weekly meetings involving party coordinators help to define the specific policy issues that will become part of the agenda. The coordinators, who act as delegates of the party leaders, advance the factions and parties' preferences as regards the agenda, and monitor committee work. During plenary meetings, the usual procedure is for an officer of the chamber to read the content of the day's agenda and for the membership to approve it.

Finally, the chairmen of the standing committees can also influence the agenda. These positions rotate among different members, and the occupants have little time to garner much individual power. But when there is a congressional majority in control of the chamber, committee chairmen have greater leeway to accelerate or delay the analysis and voting of the bills they have been assigned to examine. The lack of a congressional majority shifts decision-making power to the party leaders, who have to negotiate the agenda and the overall flow of bills.

The system of committees of each chamber tends to be a mirror image of the executive cabinet, facilitating congressional oversight. Each chamber has sixteen committees with precisely defined jurisdictions, and a majority vote is needed to allocate a bill to multiple committees. In certain cases, special committees can be set up to analyze specific matters on the country's political agenda (poverty, indebtedness, the situation of young people or of women, etc.) or to study a major government bill.[11] In such situations, it is common for the majority party to appoint loyalist legislators as committee chairmen, and secure a majority of the membership. After the president of the chamber assigns a bill to a committee, legislators may call for the decision to be reconsidered and the bill to be sent to a different committee, but because there is no overlapping in the system of permanent committees, this does not happen very often. In the last two legislative periods, only 6 percent of committee allocations were reconsidered by the chambers.[12]

In the Uruguayan Congress, plenary debate must always be preceded by a committee report.[13] A super-majority (two-thirds of the members) can force a bill out of committee and place it immediately on the floor without a report, and a simple majority vote can schedule any bill for the next session. But getting a majority to vote to circumvent a committee is costly and requires winning the support of several party leaders. It is not the ordinary process.

A recent study of decisions adopted by the standing committees of both chambers with regard to executive initiatives sent in the period 2000–8 shows that some 20 percent were blocked at the committee stage (i.e., they were not dealt with or were voted down), 22 percent were passed but with amendments, and 58 percent were passed with no changes. The study illustrates not only that the committee's power to block legislation is not minor but also that it is associated with the government's popularity, the proximity of the next election, and the ability of the president's supporters to control the offices with agenda power (Chasquetti 2011a).[14] Thus, congressional committees matter and, when there is a majority in control of the chamber, their chairmen play a non-trivial role influencing the flow of legislation.

Once the committee reports the bill to the plenary, it opens the gates to the possibility of amendments. Both chambers of the Uruguayan Congress operate under an open-rule system (any legislator can submit amendments). The evidence shows that legislators attempt to amend bills both in the standing committees and in the plenary sessions. Usually, the key behind a successful amendment is the support of the leadership of the majority. Amendments are less likely to be introduced during the plenary debate than during the committee stage. Only one in fifty executive-initiated laws passed during the period 2000–8 received amendments during the floor debate.[15]

To sum up, in the Uruguayan Congress, the offices with agenda setting power include the presidencies of the two chambers and the chairmanships of the standing committees. It is an established norm that the presidents of the chamber meet the coordinators of the legislative parties to craft the congressional agenda. Whether some agenda power is decentralized to committees or remains centralized with the leaders of the legislative parties depends on whether the government has a legislative majority. When the government lacks a majority, authority reverts to the leadership of the parties who must bargain over the agenda.

Direct Democracy Mechanisms

In Uruguay there are various institutional direct democracy mechanisms. The most important of these are the referenda challenging laws and those implementing a constitutional reform. Referenda aimed at overturning a law must be requested by 25 percent of the citizens of the country (typically through a signed petition). In the case of constitutional reforms, the signatures of 10 percent of citizens suffice to call for a referendum.

In the last twenty-five years, both of these mechanisms have been employed frequently with the aim of overturning changes promoted by the government of the day, and to preserve a constitutionally favorable status quo for some group in society.[16] It has been argued that referenda activate (non-institutional) veto players who usually act in alliance with opposition parties and/or social organizations of various kinds (Altman 2002, 2010). For example, in December 2001 Congress passed Law 17,443, which authorized the state-owned telecommunications enterprise ANTEL to sell shares to private investors. In the early months of the following year, a coalition made up of the opposition party, Frente Amplio, and the public sector unions began a successful campaign to collect signatures for a referendum to reject this law. In May 2002 the executive responded, overturning the prior policy in the hope that by doing so he would deny the opposition a victory in the referendum. A new bill was passed into law (number 17,524) in August 2002.

In his book on direct democracy, Altman (2010: 184) asks the former Uruguayan presidents Lacalle, Sanguinetti, and Batlle whether when initiating bills they took into account the fact that direct democracy mechanisms might be brought into play. Their responses left no room for doubt: all three admitted considering the possibility that their initiatives might be overturned by the use of these mechanisms.[17]

PARTISAN POSITIONS AND PRESIDENTIAL SUPPORT

Uruguay had a two-party system until 1971, when the leftist alliance Frente Amplio made its first appearance. Before that election, the two traditional parties were the National Party and the Colorado Party. In the 1989 elections, a smaller fourth party also came into the picture. Thus, during the last decades the party system has evolved into a moderate multi-party system. Table 8.1

Table 8.1 Fragmentation of the party system in Congress (effective number of parties)

	1985–90	1990–5	1995–2000	2000–5	2005–10	2010–15	Average
Senate	2.7	3.2	3.2	3.3	2.3	2.4	2.9
Deputies	2.9	2.8	3.3	3.1	2.4	2.7	2.9

Source: Author's elaboration based on Electoral Court data.

shows party fragmentation in the Uruguayan Congress since the return to democracy in 1985 until 2015.

When Uruguay had a two-party system, parties had a catchall format with internal factions on the right, center, and left of the political spectrum. The victory of one or other faction in elections determined the positioning of the party. Thus, until the 1960s the Partido Colorado was center-left and the National Party (Partido Nacional) was center-right. In the years leading to the coup d'état of 1973 these parties inverted their ideological positions (Pérez et al. 1987). After the entrance and growth of the Frente Amplio on the left of the ideological spectrum, there was a reconfiguration of positions and the original parties both shifted to the right (González 1993; Altman 2002). Since then, the party system has tended to polarize at election time, with two markedly different coalitions.

The Uruguayan electoral rules tend to foster a moderate degree of fragmentation in the party system, and also promote parties structured as coalitions of factions. The rule for electing members of Congress is closed-list proportional representation, with the allocation of seats based on percentages of the national total.[18] At election time, voters select a presidential candidate and jointly choose a list of legislators, with lists organized by the party factions.

Party factions play an essential role in Uruguayan politics, particularly in terms of executive–legislative relations. In all parties, factions are highly institutionalized. The parties have directing bodies that include the leaders of factions, but these bodies are not able to impose discipline on the organization as a whole. There are no established party chiefs but within each party, there are faction leaders who usually develop their careers in the Senate. These leaders have the ability to control the behavior of legislators from their faction, a power born from their ability to select and order the candidates in the closed and locked list (Morgenstern 2001; Moraes 2008). Faction leaders also influence their members' committee assignments and the distribution of other positions of authority within Congress (Chasquetti 2014).[19] Both powers (to

Table 8.2 Party factions in the Senate (effective number of factions)

	1985–90	1990–5	1995–2000	2000–5	2005–10	2010–15	Average
Colorado Party	1.5	2.0	1.2	2.0	1.8	1.9	1.7
National Party	1.2	1.9	2.4	1.8	2.5	2.0	2.0
Frente Amplio	2.6	2.3	3.5	5.3	4.6	3.8	3.7

Source: Author's elaboration based on Buquet et al. (1998) and Electoral Court data.

select candidates and allocate positions with power and prestige) ensure that faction leaders have the ability to reward or punish legislators for what they do in their daily work in Congress. Thus, we could say that faction leaders within each party have the power to control the legislative careers of legislators (Altman and Chasquetti 2005).

In the last ten years, the Frente Amplio and the National Party leaders have introduced internal rules to reinforce internal unity in Congress. For instance, the *declaration of a matter of policy* by the party, used occasionally, makes it incumbent upon all members to adhere to the party line on some specific matter or bill. However, it is usually the case that factions define their positions in advance and reserve the right to dissent from the final resolution. Factions are the agents that discipline party members and the basis of party cohesion in the decision-making process. Table 8.2 shows the profile of factions in the Senate. It can be seen that the levels of factionalism in the Colorado and National Parties have remained stable over the last twenty-five years. As the Frente Amplio has gained more seats in Congress, more factions have emerged. At one point there were 5.3 factions in the Frente Amplio (for the 2009 elections there were 3.8).

In the last twenty-five years of democracy the presidents of Uruguay have governed with different kinds of cabinets: (a) single-party majority cabinets, between 2005 and 2010 (President Vázquez); (b) majority-coalition cabinets, in 1990–1, 1995–2000, and 2000–2 (Presidents Lacalle, Sanguinetti, and Batlle); (c) single-party minority cabinets, in 1985–90 and 2002–5 (Presidents Sanguinetti and Batlle); and (d) minority-coalition cabinet in 1991–5 (President Lacalle). Table 8.3 shows the type of government formed in Uruguay between 1985 and 2010, the share of seats for the president's party, and the share of seats for the cabinet coalition (when one was formed).

Most studies of discipline in the Uruguayan Congress show that the parties usually vote in a cohesive way (Buquet et al. 1998; Lanzaro et al. 2000; Koolhas 2004). The most disciplined party in the last fifteen years has been the Frente Amplio. It only showed some internal divisions in the 44th legislature

Table 8.3 Government type and lower-chamber seats, 1985–2010

Legislature	Cabinet	Period	Cabinet	Presidential party	Presidential coalition
42nd	Sanguinetti	1985–90	Minority party	41%	–
43rd	Lacalle I	1990–2	Majority coalition	39%	64%
	Lacalle II	1992–3	Minority coalition	39%	46%
	Lacalle III	1993–5	Minority coalition	27%	34%
44th	Sanguinetti	1995–2000	Majority coalition	33%	63%
45th	Batlle I	2000–2	Majority coalition	33%	55%
	Batlle II	2002–5	Minority party	33%	–
46th	Vázquez	2005–10	Majority party	53%	–

Source: Author's elaboration based on Chasquetti (1999).

(1995–2000), when there were rifts involving the Asamblea Uruguay faction (led by former Finance Minister Danilo Astori) and the Movimiento de Participación Popular faction (led by former guerrillas, the Tupamaros). Since coming to power in 2005, the Frente Amplio has shown perfect unity. The Colorado Party and the National Party also tend to exhibit high levels of unity, although relevant internal differences emerged during the 43rd legislature (1990–5), when the Colorados were in opposition and the Nationalists in government. Koolhas (2004) examines unity in the Senate floor during periods controlled by government coalitions (1990–2, 1995–2000, and 2000–2), and found that in 90.1 percent of cases (fifty out of fifty-five votes) coalitions maintained perfect discipline.

The survey data available for Uruguayan legislators show that the ideological gap between the executive and the median in Congress has fluctuated slightly, while the gap between the president and the median member of his legislative contingent has usually been narrow.[20] This is shown in Figure 8.1. It shows that until 2010, the president was typically located between the median of the chamber and the median of the majority.

In short, Uruguayan presidents have considerable institutional powers and frequently enjoy strong legislative support. This combination has been useful to pass major bills in Congress, as we will show in what follows. Parties tend to act in a unified fashion, and the available measurements show that the ideological position of the president is very close to the position of the median member of the legislative majority, which should have facilitated consensus between the government and its legislative contingent.

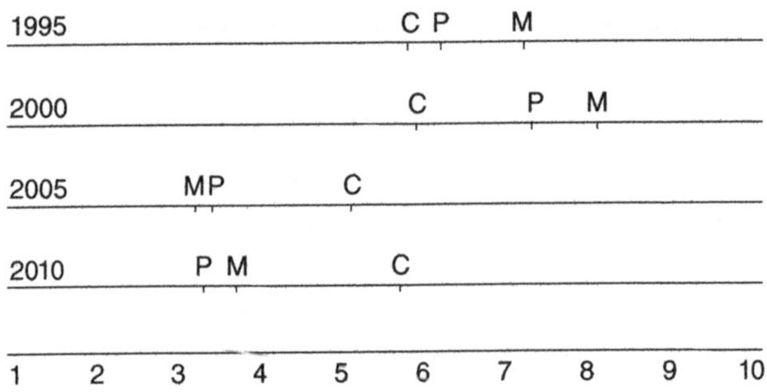

Figure 8.1 Positions of the president, the median legislator, and the median legislator of the majority

P = President; C = Median member of the chamber; M = Median member of the majority

Notes: The chart shows the position of three main actors of legislative process for the last four legislatures in the left–right dimension. In the first two cases, the presidents built coalitional cabinets with majority support in Congress; and in the last two, the presidents led party cabinets with majority support too. C always appears in the center of the scale; P is located to the left or right according to its ideological preference; and M is *always* in a position very close to P. For this reason, the key for the presidential successful in the Uruguayan legislative process involves proposing bills at points close to its legislative majority.

Source: Proyecto de Élites Parlamentarias de América Latina (PELA).

LAWMAKING IN URUGUAY

In this section we will examine empirically some of the main consequences of this institutional structure, given the positions of the main actors. The first part examines bill-to-law data to assess the share of laws initiated by the executive, the initiation and success rates of each actor, the length of time different laws spend in Congress, and how these characteristics fare when we focus on major bills. Given the importance of the president's formal powers (discussed in the first section of this chapter), the resources and technical expertise of the executive, and the closeness between the president and the median member of the governing coalition or party (discussed in the second section of this chapter), we expect presidents to initiate and get approved more major bills than members of Congress. We also expect approval to be faster in the case of major executive bills.

The second part focuses on amendments. We expect legislators to alternate their efforts between their individual goals and the collective ones associated with their parties. Since the government's agenda is a priority, particularly after an election, it could be argued that the core role of members in the lawmaking process is to amend executive initiatives rather than to initiate their own bills. If the Uruguayan Congress is a reactive legislature, as Cox and Morgenstern (2002) and Saiegh (2010) suggest, its main activity should be to pass, amend, or block government initiatives. Chasquetti (2011b) shows that the ratio of amendments to executive proposals is usually low. Moreover, the institutionally powerful Uruguayan president usually enjoys the support of disciplined parties and coalitions that are ideologically congruent. Thus, we expect most major executive bills to become law without being amended.

Lastly we examine the issuance of vetoes. As noted in the first section of this chapter, vetoes represent one of the key mechanisms used by Uruguayan presidents to influence lawmaking outcomes. Executive support and congruence with the legislature should be reflected in the issuance of vetoes, as argued by Alemán and Tsebelis in the introductory chapter. Thus, we expect the number of presidential vetoes to be associated with the president's legislative support. In addition, given that presidents tend to lose support (even among their own legislative contingent) at the end of their term, we also expect that the electoral cycle should impact the issuance of vetoes.

Bill Initiation and Legislative Success

Uruguayan presidents are the authors of around two-thirds of laws. Table 8.4 shows legislative production during the last three legislative periods (1995–2010). The first pair of columns indicates the number of bills and laws that the government and congressmen introduced in each period. The fifth column shows the total laws passed per term; and the last two show the ratio of executive-initiated laws to total laws (share of laws) and the ratio of executive bills to executive-initiated laws (executive's box score). As Saiegh (2011: 63–5) explains, these two measures are frequently used for analyzing

Table 8.4 Legislative production and success rate in Uruguay, 1995–2010

	Executive bills	Executive laws	Members bills	Members laws	Total laws	Share of laws	Executive's box score	Members' box score
1995–2000	505	348	791	191	539	65%	69%	24%
2000–5	583	399	1088	228	627	64%	68%	21%
2005–10	700	544	870	283	827	66%	78%	33%
Total	1788	1291	2749	702	1993	65%	72%	26%

Source: Author's elaboration with information from the Data Bank of the Instituto de Ciencia Política, FCS de la UdelaR.

the legislative production and refer to different issues. The *share of laws* indicates the grade of dominance executive in the legislative process, and the *executive's box score* shows the executive's success in the total approval of laws. In Uruguay, the president initiates, on average, 65 percent of the bills that become law. The executive's share of laws is slightly higher than that of the Italian executive (63.5 percent) and somewhat lower than that achieved by the Turkish government (69.9 percent), both considered by Saiegh (2011: 63) as "somewhat dominant executives."

Uruguayan presidents also have a relatively high rate of bill approval. The box score of the president is three times larger than the one for members of Congress. While about 72 percent of bills introduced by the government become law, 26 percent of members' bills reach the same outcome. Uruguayan executives appear to have a remarkable legislative record (rates are similar to those of the Italian and Paraguayan governments), while as elsewhere, bills introduced by the legislators encounter greater obstacles on the path to approval by both chambers.

However, we must not overlook the fact that the Uruguayan legislator's box score is higher than those of several other countries. Indeed, one in four bills introduced by the members of Congress becomes law before the legislative period is over. This success rate is higher than that of legislators in many other countries, such as Argentina, Canada, Chile, or Spain. Therefore, while it is true that the president is the most prominent actor in the legislative process, legislators appear to be rather successful lawmakers after all: 26 percent of their bills become law.

The data also show that a non-trivial portion of the executive's legislative agenda dies in Congress (28 percent of presidential bills). This figure underlines how the passage of particular pieces of the president's legislative program is not an assured outcome, even when the president has a majority. In the next section, we examine the passage of major laws and the amendments introduced by the legislators.

The empirical evidence discussed so far is based on aggregated data where each bill has the same value regardless of its scope or political importance. Some qualitative analyses of the passage of legislation have attempted to evaluate the relevance of different bills (Taylor and Díaz 1999; Amorim and Santos 2003). For example, Lanzaro et al. (2000) classified laws passed by the Uruguayan Congress between 1985 and 1999 based on five indicators (scope of the law, characteristics of its passage, public opinion repercussions, purpose origin, and vote in the chamber) to try to determine their level of importance. This study highlighted the decisive influence of the electoral cycle. It showed that Congress tends to pass a large number of major bills at the start of a president's mandate but fewer as time goes by.

In this study we identified as major bills those that were included as front-page news by a national newspaper (i.e., as in the other chapters in this book). More specifically, the set of major bills was collected in the following manner: any legislative proposal mentioned on the front page of the Uruguayan newspaper *El País* at some point during the first year of an administration was considered a major bill and included in the dataset. There are three periods, each associated with the first year of the democratic administrations that governed Uruguay: Sanguinetti (from 3/1995 to 3/1996), Batlle (from 3/2000 to 3/2001), and Vázquez (from 3/2005 to 3/2006).

We found a total of 119 major legislative proposals mentioned on the front page over the three periods. This includes executive initiatives as well as congressional initiatives. Of these proposals, sixty-four were actually introduced as bills in Congress. Some of these proposals were bills first introduced during the first year in office, some were bills that had been debated for some time, and others were introduced later in the president's administration. Of these major bills, thirty-four were initiated by the president and his ministers, and thirty were initiated by members of Congress.

Success rates show striking disparities between the two branches. Presidents were able to approve 94 percent of their major bills (thirty-two laws) while legislators passed 20 percent (six laws). Thus, the success rate for major bills initiated by legislators is slightly lower than their overall bill success rate, while the success rate for major bills initiated by the executive is significantly higher than its overall bill success rate. In Figure 8.2, which shows success rates for major bills, we can see that Presidents Batlle (2000–1) and Vázquez (2005–6) achieved a perfect score (100 percent success rate), while President Sanguinetti (1995–6) managed to get an 85 percent success rate (eleven laws out of thirteen bills).

Major presidential bills are passed sooner than those introduced by members of Congress, and sooner than other executive bills. Table 8.5 shows the average number of days it took for these major bills to become law as well as the average for all bills approved.[21] President Batlle, with an average of 111 days, had the fastest record; next was Vázquez with an average of 173 days; and last was Sanguinetti with an average of 340 days. Table 8.5 compares major bills to those initiated in the first year of each period. It can be seen that in the three cases, major bills were passed faster than other bills. Similarly, major laws initiated by congressmen passed faster than other non-major laws.

We should note that urgency procedures available to legislators in the regulation of the chambers were occasionally used to speed up the passage of bills.[22] The main goal for using the urgent procedures appears to have been preventing the bill from being blocked by a standing committee. Out of the thirty-five major bills introduced by the executive, five had an exceptional

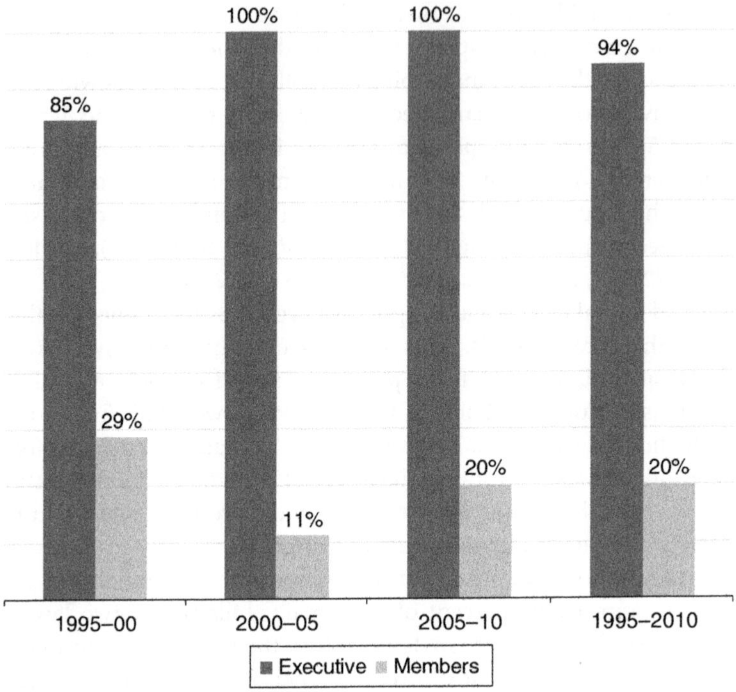

Figure 8.2 Success rates of major bills
Source: Author's elaboration.

Table 8.5 Time until passage of laws by initiator (days)*

	Executive		Legislative	
Presidents	Major laws	All laws	Major laws	All laws
Sanguinetti (1995–6)	340	477	418	728
Number of laws	(12)	(82)	(3)	(67)
Batlle (2000–1)	111	416	886	610
Number of laws	(6)	(145)	(2)	(83)
Vázquez (2005–6)	173	343	207	575
Number of laws	(15)	(140)	(1)	(102)

* Number of laws between brackets
Source: Author's elaboration based on information from the Banco de Datos Legislativos del Instituto de Ciencia Política de la FCS-UdelaR.

treatment voted by a majority of the members. Thus, while for most legislation the normal legislative procedures are used to pass the executive's legislative program, in a non-trivial number of cases (around 14 percent of major bills), congressional urgency procedures are used to push executive proposals to the plenary floor.

The Amendment Process

The executive has a high success rate and initiates most major bills, but this does not imply that legislators play a passive role in terms of lawmaking. To more fully evaluate the influence of legislators we must also extend our inquiry to the amendment process. When we examine in detail the thirty-four major bills initiated by the executive we find that the vast majority (70 percent) passed with substantive congressional amendments. This is consistent with the expectation of Alemán and Tsebelis, noted in the introductory chapter, regarding the passage of major bills. Two of the major bills did not pass the committee stage of the second chamber, ten were passed into law with no amendments, and twenty-three were amended (twenty-two in the corresponding committees of the first chamber and one in the second chamber's committee) before becoming law. In all cases the modifications were made in committee and never on the plenary floor.[23]

Interestingly, bills introduced by President Vazquez, who governed with a party cabinet and was supported by a disciplined majority in Congress, received the highest proportion of amendments (86 percent), followed by the bills introduced by presidents who built majority coalition cabinets, Batlle (66 percent) and Sanguinetti (55 percent). This information appears in Table 8.6.

The proportion of major bills that are amended is far higher than the proportion of other laws that are amended. When these data are compared to that for all bills presented by Chasquetti (2011b), the numbers are 70 percent against 22 percent (see Table 8.7). In the same way, the percentage of bills that pass the committee stage without amendments is much lower in the case of major bills (24 percent against 58 percent).

These findings regarding congressional amendments are important not only because they illuminate a hitherto unstudied area of executive–legislative relations, but also because they refute the conventional wisdom on presidential dominance. The findings can be interpreted as supporting the portrayal of Uruguayan legislators as members of a reactive legislature, where bills proposed by the government are regularly amended. Uruguayan legislators seem to be more active when dealing with major bills, even when the president's supporters enjoy a majority in the assigned committee.[24] The results also

Table 8.6 Amendments to and fates of major bills

	Sanguinetti (1995–2000)		Batlle (2000–5)		Vázquez (2005–10)		Total (1995–2010)	
Did not pass	2	15%	0	0%	0	0%	2	6%
Unchanged	4	30%	2	33%	2	14%	8	24%
Amended	7	55%	4	67%	13	86%	24	70%
Total	13	100%	6	100%	15	100%	34	100%

Table 8.7 Amendments to major and all bills

	Major bills*		All bills**	
Did not pass	2	6%	164	20%
Unchanged	8	24%	469	58%
Amended	24	70%	180	22%
Total	34	100%	813	100%

* Corresponding to the period 1995–2010.

** Corresponding to the period 2000–8.

Source: Author's elaboration with information from Chasquetti (2011b) and from the Banco de Datos Legislativos del Instituto de CienciaPolítica de la FCS-UdelaR.

underline that the amendment process occurs almost exclusively during the committee stage. Further examination also shows that in most instances, one or more ministers participated in some session of the committee where major bills were analyzed, amended, and voted on.

The Use of Presidential Veto Power

Next, we examine the usage of the presidential veto. The veto allows the president to exercise influence over the agenda either through the threat of usage or its effective application. In Uruguay, presidents can delete unwanted parts of bills, as well as amend aspects they dislike including the addition of modifications that would further their preferences (Alemán and Tsebelis 2005). We hypothesized that the usage of the presidential veto would be associated with the share of legislative seats belonging to government parties. Lower legislative support should tend to increase the likelihood that unwanted amendments are incorporated into successful bills, thus fostering greater executive involvement into the legislative process via the veto.[25]

During the past twenty-five years of democracy, Uruguayan presidents have been in a minority situation in three instances: 1985–90, 1992–5, and 2002–5.

It is true that in such cases, no president had to face a united opposition majority (since the legislature was divided into at least three major parties), but in all situations, the president's drive to enact his legislative program was strongly challenged by the opposition. It has been argued that presidents often had to settle with passing fewer laws and focusing their actions on the administrative area of public policy (Buquet et al. 1998). The apparent moderation of the president's expectations about possible legislative outcomes, however, did not seem to extend to legislators and their initiatives. Often, Congress passed laws that displeased the president, and the president in turn responded with vetoes. Moraes and Morgenstern (1995), for example, note that Presidents Sanguinetti (1985–90) and Lacalle (1990–5) ended their respective terms with less than majority support and issued an elevated number of partial and total vetoes (mainly to stop laws pushed by the opposition parties).

But this is not the only factor influencing the usage of the presidential veto. The literature on the Uruguayan case has underlined how the electoral cycle has a powerful effect on the strategies and behaviors of political actors. Buquet et al. (1998), for example, found that as the presidential term comes to an end, minor parties in the government coalition tend to move out of the cabinet. Chasquetti and Moraes (2000) show that as time passes, both the president and the parties begin to change their behavior. Presidents appear to have more difficulties passing major laws, and party factions redirect their efforts to positioning for the next election. As time goes by, members of Congress appear to focus more on their constituencies, which means—among other things—initiating bills popular with voters. Altman (2000) shows that the probability of a political group in an executive coalition remaining in the cabinet decreases as the presidential term elapses. Thus, presidents with or without a majority in Congress should be more likely to face hostile bills or amendments coming from Congress at the end of their term in office than at the beginning.

In the period 1985–2010, Uruguayan presidents vetoed a total of 89 laws (2.8 percent of the total passed laws) of which forty received a total veto and forty-nine a partial veto (including those with observations). Twenty-five percent of vetoed bills were initiated by the executive, and about 40 percent were initiated by legislators from the president's party (alone or with legislators from other parties). This illustrates how even legislators who support the government sometimes promote initiatives that do not match with the interests of the president, and how the president has in the veto the tool to fight them off.

To analyze statistically how the presidents use the veto power, we have divided the mandate in ten semesters and counted the number of laws that were vetoed in each period. Thus, we have obtained a dependent variable composed of fifty observations, each one with a specific number of vetoed laws.

To explain the number of vetoes we focus on three independent variables. The first one is the *share of seats* that the president's coalition controls in the lower house.[26] We expect a negative association between the size of the government's legislative contingent and the issuance of vetoes. The second variable is the *time remaining* until the next election. Again we expect a negative association: the farther away the next election, the fewer the vetoes. When the veto is sent to Congress in the first semester, the variable assumes the value 9; when it is sent in the second, it assumes the value 8; and so on until the last semester of the term. Finally, we add a third independent variable to capture the impact of the president's popularity. Here we control for the possibility that public support helps presidents assert their authority over Congress, making vetoes less likely. We use survey data measuring public approval of presidential performance in charge.[27] We expect a negative association with the dependent variable: more popular presidents should issue fewer vetoes.

Table 8.8 shows the results of a negative binomial regression. The three independent variables' coefficients show a negative sign, which is in agreement with our expectations. Two of the three independent variables have statistically significant coefficients: *share of seats* and *remaining time.*

These results verify our hypotheses about the use of veto power by presidents and confirm the deductions from Uruguay-centered literature. In the period 1985–2010, 69 percent of vetoes were applied by minority presidents, and 67 percent were sent in the last two years of the mandates (see appendix Table 8. A1). In short, these findings show that veto power is an important presidential tool to influence the legislative agenda. In Uruguay, presidents are less likely to use the veto during their first years in office or when they have a larger legislative contingent. Under less favorable political contexts—declining legislative support and the coming of an electoral contest—vetoes are more common.

It is also relevant to underline the importance of the amendments (observations) that the president can introduce to vetoed bills. As we explained in the

Table 8.8 The president's veto, negative binomial regression

	Coef.	Std. Error	z	P>|z|
Share of seats	–0.0307	0.014	–2.17	0.030
Remaining time	–0.182	0.054	–3.36	0.001
Popularity	–0.004	0.010	–0.38	0.705
Constant	2.739	1.300	5.26	0.000

Dependent variable: number of vetoed laws
No. obs.: 50
Pseudo R-squared = 0.1484
Likelihood-ratio test of alpha = 0 chibar2 (01) = 3.32. Prob > chibar2 = 0.034

Table 8.9 Partially vetoed laws with amendments

Total laws	26	100%
Initiated by executive	9	35%
Initiated by members	17	65%
Presidents have majority support	8	31%
Presidents lack majority support	18	69%
First three years of term	5	19%
Last two years of term	21	81%

first section, the Uruguayan presidents have the power to modify the bills passed by Congress with partial vetoes. Furthermore, when presidents send the partial veto they may also introduce changes to the legislative proposal. Evidence seems to indicate that this presidential power is used more often when (i) the bills are initiated by Congress, (ii) the executive lacks a majority support, or (iii) it is close to the end of the term.

Between 1985 and 2010, presidents partially vetoed forty-nine laws, twenty-six of which (53 percent) received amendments (observations) that were incorporated into the final text. As is shown in Table 8.9, 69 percent were submitted by minority presidents, 81 percent took place during the last two years of the president's term, and 65 percent were directed at bills initiated by congressmen.

When laws are initiated by the executive, partial vetoes typically seek to delete unwanted amendments introduced by legislators, thereby returning to the original content of the proposals. But when bills are initiated by legislators, the president's partial vetoes tend to come with amendments that introduce the government's point of view into the legislation. When presidents lack majority support in Congress, they have the opportunity to use this mechanism to introduce and pass their legislative preferences. This is consistent with the findings shown in previous sections and it demonstrates how the executive tries to set the legislative agenda, even in the worst situations.

CONCLUSION

In this chapter we examined agenda setting institutions and the lawmaking process in Uruguay. Our argument was that the executive is a crucial agenda setter, whose power is reinforced by the support of a legislative majority. A range of constitutional prerogatives, including exclusive bill initiation rights and an extensive veto, make the president a powerful actor. At least in the last four legislatures, a majority favorable to the executive has taken the control of positions with agenda power so as to regulate the flow of bills, establish legislative priorities, and block those initiatives that depart from its preferences.

This institutional configuration depends on the president and the legislative majority being ideologically close and party leaders being able to impose sufficient discipline on the members of their parties or factions. However, legislative majorities do not automatically accept everything on the president's legislative program. Our empirical study shows that legislators often amend a fair proportion of major bills, influencing the content of the policies involved. The evidence also shows that when the executive's support in Congress weakens, it tends to use vetoes more frequently. This helps the president block unwanted bills or amendments. Both of these findings are consistent with the expectations of Alemán and Tsebelis, as outlined in the introductory chapter. Vetoes are also more likely to happen when the president's mandate is close to its end, when legislators belonging to the majority tend to support initiatives that do not always coincide with the executive's interests. This kind of behavior is representative of the nature of the Uruguayan political system, where an institutionally powerful president is often politically weak, because he must negotiate permanently with strong congressional parties.

APPENDIX

Table 8.A1 Summary of vetoed laws

	Vetoed laws	
Total-vetoed laws	40	45%
Partial-vetoed law	49	55%
Total vetoed laws	89	100%
Who applied vetoes?		
	No. vetoes	
Minority presidents	61	69%
Majority presidents	28	31%
Total	89	100%
When applied vetoes?		
First 3 years of the term	29	33%
Last 2 years of the term	60	67%
Total	89	100%

NOTES

1. In Uruguay the legislative power resides in the Asamblea General, which has two chambers. This body has various powers including designating the members of the Supreme Court of Justice, the Committee of Public Accounts, the Administrative Court, the Electoral Court, promotions in the armed forces, etc. The Asamblea General also resolves legislative differences between the two chambers.
2. The first reductions in the prerogatives of Congress were established in the 1934 reform. In a situation of crisis, the members introduced a series of rules to limit the legislative initiative of Congress. First, exclusive management of financial policy was conferred to the executive and Congress was prevented from raising the amounts in the budget presented by the government. Second, the executive was given exclusive powers in the areas of initiating foreign debt and the creation of public employment. Lastly, Congress and the executive would share the initiative in the creation of taxes and tax exemption (Jiménez de Aréchaga 1947: 84–94). These dispositions did not produce the desired effect because they came into force at a time when the state structure was expanding and public spending increased to unimagined levels. In those decades legislators searched for loopholes in the constitutional order to initiate legislation that had apparently been forbidden to the Assembly (Chasquetti 2014).
3. This study is very useful for comparing changes in the pattern of legislative production. In both periods different parties alternated in government and the congressional status of the executive varied in the same way. In the first period 2,691 laws were passed and in the second 2,545 laws. These laws were classified into two main groups: those that involved public expenditure and those that did not, and each group could be further broken down into various categories. For further information see Chasquetti (2014).
4. The relation between the state and the economy was restructured in the 1980s and 1990s, and this meant that new regulations were required, new institutions were designed, and public sector policies were developed. In this scenario, the margin left open to legislators to develop constituency service was severely affected.
5. More specifically, the urgency bills have different deadlines for each stage of the legislative process. The first chamber has forty-five days and the second has thirty days. If the latter makes changes, the bill returns to the first with a new period of fifteen days. If the first chamber accepts the amendments, the Asamblea General—the joint assembly of both chambers—has ten days to resolve the conflict. If any of these deadlines are not fulfilled, the bill automatically becomes law (Article 168, paragraph 7). Congress can remove the urgent consideration nature of these bills with a vote and a majority of three-fifths in one of the chambers.
6. This has not been studied systematically in the literature. However, an analysis of various critical times in the history of Uruguay shows that the VP tends to be very loyal to the president of the Republic. Both in 1972–3, when the opposition parties called on President Juan María Bordaberry to resign, and in 2002, when some

leaders of the Colorado Party were considering asking President Jorge Batlle to resign, the VPs in each case rejected all attempts to replace the president as an ad hoc way out of the crisis.

7. For example, the constitutional procedure for designating the directors of autonomous state bodies gives the executive the initiative when it comes to nominating aspirants. The executive submits the nomination to the Senate, the Senate votes, and a special majority of three-fifths of its members is needed. Once sixty days have passed after the president's initiative, the Senate can vote for the designation with an overall majority.
8. Although the internal rules of the Senate establish a standing committee to decide on the day's agenda (*orden del día*), it does not actually work in this way since the informal meeting of the party leaders with the president of the chamber fulfills this function.
9. The internal rules of Congress require approval by a majority of members to change the plenary's agenda, so the president of the Senate can only fully exercise his power when he has majority support in the plenary.
10. This happened in 1986, 1988, 1997, 2002, 2003, 2006, and 2008. For further details see Chasquetti (2014).
11. For example, at the start of his term in office President Jorge Batlle sent two bills whose content covered a wide range of subjects and situations (so-called omnibus laws). In both instances the feeling was that the bills should be dealt with by various permanent committees that understood different aspects of these matters, and the most efficient method of resolving this in each case was to set up a special committee.
12. In the period 2000–10, out of a total of 3,244 bills, ratification of the process of some 198 was solicited. Source: Base de Datos Legislativos del Instituto de Ciencia Política de la Facultad de Ciencias Sociales de la Universidad de la República.
13. When a committee is divided in its support for a reported bill, the minority can write a second report and has the right to argue its points of view on the floor.
14. This study does not consider legislation on international politics (agreements, conventions, or treaties) since Congress has no powers to amend these and can only pass them or not pass them.
15. Of the 813 laws passed, only seventeen were amended in plenary session of the two chambers. Amendments are usually made in the standing committees. Source: Base de Datos Legislativos del Instituto de Ciencia Política de la Facultad de Ciencias Sociales de la Universidad de la República.
16. Some outstanding examples of the first type of initiatives are the 1989 attempt to annul the Expiry Law (Ley de Caducidad), the effective annulment of four articles in the Public Enterprises Law (December 1992), and the overturning of the Law of Association of ANCAP with Private Enterprises (December 2003). Examples of initiatives of the second kind are the attempt to adjust pensions by inflation in 1989, the 1994 blocking of a change linking pensions to the budget, and the failed attempt to establish a fixed percentage of public expenditure for education, also in 1994 (Altman 2010).

17. For example, Sanguinetti said, "If one did not take that into account he would be almost committing suicide. It was decisive. Especially in very substantial reforms" (Altman 2010: 184).
18. Uruguay has nineteen departments (states), two of which stand out: Montevideo, the most populated (40 percent of the country) and metropolitan district that also hosts the homonymous capital city; and Canelones, home place of 15 percent of the citizens. None of the remaining seventeen departments exceeds 5 percent of the population. While Montevideo has chosen between forty-two and forty-eight members across time, Canelones elected between eleven and fourteen. The remaining seventeen districts have elected between two and four seats.
19. At the start of the legislative period, the political parties negotiate committee membership and distribution of presidencies. This process is governed by certain basic rules that ensure power to the faction leaders. First, the positions belong to the parties; second, the positions distribution follows a proportional representation pattern; third, in the low chamber, each deputy can only be allocated in one committee, while the senators have no limits; fourth, the size of the committees must be fixed by the negotiators and can vary between three and fifteen members; fifth, in the Senate, the proposal to start the negotiation is made by its president, and in the lower chamber it is made by a special commission composed of party delegates. The most common outcome of the negotiation is that the legislative majority will control the chairmanships of the main committees and will maintain a majority of members in all committees that are connected to the government's agenda. For more details, see Chasquetti (2014).
20. On the ideological distribution scale used in surveys of public opinion and of elites the value 1 indicates far left and the value 10 indicates far right. For further information about data and methodology of the PELA (Proyecto de Élites Parlamentarias de América Latina), see the appendix.
21. The entire record of bills introduced in the period March 1995 to March 2006 was collected from congressional sources.
22. Do not confuse these procedures with the presidential power to send emergency bills to Congress.
23. Unfortunately, at the present time we lack the means to measure the content of the amendments. For this reason all amendments, whether substantial or minimal, will have the same value in this study. We know the bills were amended because the Congress Information System (Sistema de Información Parlamentaria) tells us so, based on concise committee minutes. We do not know the origins of the amendments made to the original bills as the committees do not keep a detailed record of their work. The votes recorded in minutes only give the overall outcome (for example, "passed, 5 out of 9") and almost never give each legislator's individual stance.
24. The coalition or the majority party of the president had an absolute majority in the committees that made the changes in the twenty-two amended laws. These changes required complex negotiations that extended the total processing time of each bill. The procedure in the commission has taken at least 50 percent of the time of passage by Congress in sixteen of the twenty-two laws.

25. This is consistent with Alemán and Tsebelis' expectation (see introductory chapter) regarding veto usage and the legislative support of the president. Given data limitations, we cannot discern whether this effect is driven by government status or the ideological distance between the executive and the median member of the chamber.
26. The share of seats for each party is very similar in both chambers. If we use data from the Senate, the results are the same.
27. Base de Datos Legislativos del Instituto de Ciencia Política de la Facultad de Ciencias Sociales de la Universidad de la República. Equipos Consultores y Equipos-Mori time series (1985–2010).

9

Conclusions

Eduardo Alemán and George Tsebelis

Control over the legislative agenda provides advantages that impact how bills become law and how some fail in the process. The chapters in this volume have examined those legislative rules that affect opportunities for influencing bills, discussed the positions of relevant partisan players, and investigated how they work together to affect various aspects of lawmaking. Overall, they expand our understanding of how legislatures work, confirming some aspects of the conventional wisdom while also shedding light on understudied features of legislative politics. The chapters addressed the characteristics of bill introduction and approval, the influence of the president as lawmaker, and the significance of legislative amendment activity. We do not find dominant or deadlocked presidents; instead we observe differences in the extent to which presidents succeed in enacting their programs and, perhaps more interestingly, how this is achieved.

Our concluding remarks discuss four aspects of the chapters of this volume. First, we discuss some findings that reflect why changes in the positions of major actors matter. Second, we comment on those findings that reflect on the influence of chief executives over the congressional agenda. Third, we address findings related to legislative success and productivity. Lastly, we conclude by connecting some of the relevant findings to our introductory chapter.

CHANGES IN POSITIONS

Several of the chapters have stressed the implications of losing or lacking a partisan majority in congress. The results show that within countries, increasing the number of legislative players beyond those in government increases the complexity of bargaining and makes changing the status quo more difficult. Yet, presidents have been able to navigate the lack of majority without facing the perils of deadlock. This is partly the result of both agenda setting prerogatives in the hands of the president and legislators' ability to amend presidential bills to reflect congressional preferences.

The change in government status from majority to plurality is underscored in Calvo and Sagarzazu's chapter on Argentina. The authors address how the loss of a majority in the chamber affects legislative outcomes. They note that in the Argentine Chamber of Deputies the largest party retains a significant share of important committees, even after losing a majority, which allows it to continue to exert gatekeeping power over a wide range of policies. The loss of a majority, however, has a series of consequences. Committee bargaining becomes more difficult, fewer executive bills are reported out of committee, and those bills that are reported from committee are the product of complex cross-partisan bargains which are protected by party leaders during floor debates.[1] In addition, they show that the number of amendments increases when different political parties control each chamber of the Argentine Congress.

In the introductory chapter we argued that agenda setters are more likely to get outcomes closer to their position the more centrally located they are in the policy space (keeping institutional details constant). This is consistent with Calvo and Sagarzazu's findings that (a) under majority government, the closer the Argentine president is to the median of the majority party the fewer the number of amendments introduced to his bills, and (b) after the majority becomes a plurality, moving towards the median of the chamber has the effect of reducing amendments. In the end, the success rate of bills introduced by Argentine presidents is not significantly hurt by losing a majority.[2] Plurality presidents have been able to get small parties, independents, and dissidents from the opposition to support their bills at more or less the same rate as majority presidents.

As in Argentina, when the president in Uruguay loses a partisan majority in Congress, negotiations between legislative parties become key to move bills forward. But unlike the case of Argentina, where the lack of a majority enhances the relevance of committee bargains, in Uruguay it shifts power from committee chairs to the party leadership. In the absence of a majority party, bills tend to be reported after the government's legislative faction has reached an agreement that can deliver floor passage. For the president, this means an increase in unwanted amendments passed by Congress. Chasquetti shows that the loss of congressional support increases the number of presidential vetoes. Presidents lacking a partisan majority make greater use of vetoes, including amendatory observations that allow them to fight unwanted amendments to government bills.

But the impact of losing a partisan majority is nowhere more evident than in Mexico. Casar's chapter shows drastic changes since the era of single-majority party under the PRI. The president's legislative program shrank, the success rate of presidential bills dropped, amendments to presidential bills became commonplace, and the incidence of presidential vetoes went up. Despite all of these changes, Mexican presidents have not been confronted with deadlock. Instead, Casar shows, lawmaking power has shifted from the executive to political parties, which in Congress amend most major presidential proposals and initiate most laws.

The end of majority-party dominance and alternation in the presidency worked to increase the relevance of the median party, which has become the most frequent partner on the floor of the Mexican Congress. Before 2000, a regime dimension also affected the position of parties, which worked to bring the leftist PRD and rightist PAN closer to each other. Between 2000 and 2012, the Mexican presidency was held by a minority president on the center-right, who most often allied with the centrist party. Casar shows that during this period the president's party (PAN) regularly allied with the median party (PRI) to pass most initiatives.[3]

As in Mexico, the lack of a majority party in the Peruvian Congress has worked to favor centrist parties and has not impeded the passage of most government bills. According to Ponce's chapter, the reason for this is that, since 2001, Peruvian presidents have been both centrists and in possession of substantial legislative prerogatives. Congressional amending of executive bills has also helped.

Differences between outcomes in a majority-controlled chamber and those in an evenly split chamber were underscored in Alemán and Navia's chapter on Chilean legislative politics. During the Concertación era (1990–2010), governing parties had a majority in the lower chamber but never captured full control of the upper chamber. The analysis of legislative votes shows that in the Chamber of Deputies, where agenda setting offices were in the hands of government parties, successful legislation consistently received the support of most members in the majority. Meanwhile, members of the opposition were more often on the losing side of these bills. However, when neither the opposition nor government coalitions had full agenda control, as in the Senate, cross-coalition support was more common, if not routine for those bills that ultimately passed. This seems to have favored moderate members of the governing coalition (Christian Democrats) more than their leftist allies who, like the right-wing non-elected senators, ended up on the losing side more frequently.

Compared to those in Chile, Colombian coalitions are more unstable and parties are much weaker, more volatile, and less ideological. Presidents Santos, Uribe, and Pastrana had to govern amid high party fragmentation and built majority coalitions in both chambers.[4] According to Carroll and Pachón, the government coalitions these presidents formed were unable to ensure that executive bills received floor consideration, and not always reliable in ensuring that bills opposed by the president did not reach the floor. During his second term in office, President Uribe faced a particularly low rate of legislative success. The authors link this outcome to Uribe's challenges in organizing his congressional coalition, hit hard by a criminal scandal, and to the opposition that his attempt at a third presidential term generated within his coalition. While the ability to build more stable and party-based government coalitions has grown considerably following the 2003 electoral reforms, executives continue to face considerable challenges to control the legislative agenda. According to Carroll and Pachón, the main reason for this is that congressional rules continue to empower individual legislators at the expense of parties.

Brazilian Presidents Cardoso, Da Silva, and Rouseff also formed majority coalitions (often oversized) and regularly used a battery of agenda setting tools at their disposal. The evidence presented by Hiroi and Rennó in the chapter on Brazil shows the government on the winning side in the overwhelming majority of votes. Proportionally allocated cabinets accelerate the approval of bills and a cohesive opposition appears to slow it down. The cohesion of the government coalition does not appear to have an effect on the timing of bill approval. But it is difficult to evaluate positional changes in Brazilian legislative politics. While the extent to which parties can be pinned down ideologically varies, the range of these oversized government coalitions has been large. Coalitions formed by both Da Silva and Rouseff included left-wing parties as well as right-wing parties.

PRESIDENTIAL INFLUENCE OVER THE LEGISLATIVE AGENDA

As expected, the president's involvement in the lawmaking process varies considerably across the countries analyzed. On the one hand, we have Chile and Brazil, where executives play an active role influencing the content of the congressional agenda. In Uruguay this is more evident in the Senate, given the vice president's role. Presidents in Colombia and Peru are also engaged, but to a lesser degree than in the prior countries. On the other hand, we have the presidents of Mexico and Argentina, which are less directly involved.[5] Presidents in these two countries rely more on their partisan allies in congress to move their proposed legislation to the plenary floor and to respond appropriately to the hostile amendments offered to their preferred legislation. They become involved—although comparatively less often—at the veto stage.

Presidents in Chile, Brazil, Colombia, Peru, and Uruguay use urgency motions to prioritize bills in the congressional calendar. In the case of Peru, the urgency procedure is used very frequently but it is rather toothless; in Uruguay, the urgency power included in the constitution is very robust but it is a norm to use it sparingly. In contrast, presidents in Brazil and Chile use their urgency prerogatives frequently to push bills to the floor of congress. As a result, the congressional agenda in these two countries is, to a significant extent, dictated by the priorities of the executive branch. Presidents in Colombia also use urgency procedures to accelerate the discussion of legislation, although apparently less often than in Chile and Brazil. The lack of this procedure in Argentina and Mexico limits the influence of the executive branch on the congressional schedule and prevents presidents from compelling legislators to take a stand on a particular bill.

In Brazil and Peru presidents frequently "move first" by enacting decrees to pass new policies. Their impact over the legislative agenda, however, is very different. In Brazil, decrees are provisional measures that are forced into the congressional agenda after a given deadline. Congress is compelled to address the president's decrees, and, in most occasions, it ends up turning such temporary measures into law (over three-quarters of the time).[6] At least since the early 2000s, Brazilian presidents have had a better record at getting their measures into law via decrees than via ordinary statues. But members of Congress have a chance to amend such executive decrees before converting them into permanent law, and they do it a majority of the time.[7]

The situation is very different in Peru, where executive decrees become law immediately and Congress is not compelled to take a stand. The congressional committee in charge of reviewing presidential decrees may recommend their nullification but cannot amend them.[8] The vast majority of executive decrees issued by Peruvian presidents are not overturned. Presidents are limited to issuing urgent decrees in financial and economic matters (although the interpretation of this is rather loose), but those are precisely the areas of policy where members of Congress face the greatest restrictions in terms of bill initiation. In Argentina, decrees of urgency were used regularly by presidents between 1989 and 2007. To nullify an urgent decree, which as in Peru becomes law right away, a resolution must pass both chambers of Congress. In 2010, the Argentine Supreme Court further limited the instances under which the government can claim the need to issue an urgent decree.

In the seven countries examined in this volume, it is customary for presidents to use their veto powers. As we hypothesized in the introductory chapter, presidents are more likely to use this opportunity to construct a modified version of the bill than to reject it entirely.

In the countries where presidents can introduce amendments (observations) to vetoed bills—Chile, Peru, Uruguay, and Mexico—presidents typically use this stage of the lawmaking process to propose final changes. Alemán and Navia's chapter describes how Chilean presidents use them on various occasions to modify major bills and that such amendments were accepted by the Chilean Congress the vast majority of the time. Chasquetti's chapter notes that in Uruguay minority presidents are more likely to introduce amendments to vetoed bills than majority presidents, and that they are used most often during the last two years of the president's administration. In Peru, amendatory observations are common on presidential legislation amended in Congress. Vetoes have been used more sparingly in Mexico, although more often than under one-party rule. Casar's chapter notes that in Mexico amendatory vetoes have been used more often than bloc vetoes that reject the entire bill, which is also the case in the other three countries that allow this procedure.

In the other countries—Argentina, Brazil, and Colombia—presidents can use the partial veto as a tool to delete sections of a bill. In Brazil and Colombia presidents most often prefer partial vetoes over rejecting the entire bill, and make use of them rather frequently.[9] In Argentina, vetoes are used less frequently. It is the only country of the seven studied in this volume where presidents use partial and bloc vetoes in roughly the same proportion.[10]

LAWMAKERS

In the seven countries studied in this volume most bills are introduced by members of congress and not the president. However, there is wide cross-national variation in the total number of bills introduced in each congress. For instance, in Chile the number of bills introduced each year is on average close to one per member, while in Argentina and Peru, that yearly average is greater than four per member. In Argentina, Chile, and Mexico, the number of bills initiated by members of congress has increased since the transition to democratic rule. The most striking change took place in Mexico's Congress. During the period 1991–7, the total number of bills introduced was less than one per member for the entire six-year period. In contrast, during the 2009–12 legislative period the average was close to two bills per member a year.

Most bills introduced by members of congress fail to become law. The success rate of bills initiated by legislators oscillates between a low of around 5 percent in Argentina to a high of around 27 percent in Peru.[11] Legislators' bills also have a relatively high passage rate (26 percent) in Uruguay, where legislators initiate fewer bills a year than in the prior two countries (about one-third in terms of bills per legislator). In the middle of the distribution we find Chile's Congress, where the approval rate of members' bills is around 15 percent, and Colombia's Congress, where it hovers around 17 percent. In Mexico, the sharp increase in the number of initiated bills partly explains the reduction in the passage rate of bills initiated by members of Congress since the end of one-party dominance.

Despite the apparent low levels of approval, we observe that in most chambers many (if not most) legislators come to the end of their term having authored or co-authored a bill that became law. Proposals introduced by members of congress send low-cost signals regarding their policy stances, and while most proposals die before reaching a plenary vote, they frequently become a realistic alternative to the status quo. Although many bills fail to make it out of committee, members of congress still initiate a significant share of those bills that actually become law.

In Colombia and Mexico, the vast majority of laws (two-thirds or more) originate with congress, not the president. In Peru, a majority of laws also comes from legislators' initiatives. Congress and the executive more or less split law production in Argentina and Brazil. Only in Chile and Uruguay is the share of laws originating with members of congress much lower, closer to one-third of all laws. These numbers defy the views that in Lain America executives practically monopolize the introduction of potentially successful bills and that members of congress are primarily reactive actors. However, presidential bills are fewer in quantity but have higher chance of approval than those initiated by legislators. Executive proposals also tend to be approved faster than bills initiated by members of congress; evidence of this was presented in the chapters on Brazil, Chile, and Uruguay.

Among the presidents examined in this volume, those in Chile, Mexico, and Uruguay have a comparatively high rate of legislative success.[12] Typically more than 70 percent of presidential bills became law.[13] It is also notable that since the re-establishment of democratic elections, executive-initiated bills in Chile and Uruguay have had a high rate of approval and have also made up a large majority of all laws (about two-thirds of all bills passed). In these two countries presidents play a preponderant role in lawmaking.

In contrast, presidents in Brazil and Argentina have been less successful at getting their bills enacted into law. Their passage rates fall below the median for presidential countries and are lower than those of other presidents examined in this volume.[14] The results for Brazil presented by Hiroi and Rennó contrast with earlier characterizations of Brazilian presidents as highly successful in terms of bill approval (e.g., Figueiredo and Limongi 2000). They show that the approval rate of ordinary bills introduced by Brazilian presidents has been relatively low since the late 1990s (less than 50 percent), and much lower than the approval rate of the temporary executive decrees regularly issued, which has been greater than 75 percent following the 2001 reform.[15] In Argentina, the average passage rate for executive bills has been below 60 percent, despite the recurrence of single-party governments.

In Colombia, the approval rate of executive bills has hovered around 66 percent, which is, according to Saiegh (2011), the average for coalition governments in presidential countries. The bills introduced by Peruvian executives have a similar rate of approval, but neither one of the two Peruvian presidents during the period 2001–11 had a congressional majority.

The president's legislative program typically attracts greater attention than congressional bills. In this regard, the chapters lend some support to the commonly held view that in Latin America most "major" bills are introduced by the president. When looking at the sample of bills that become front-page news, we see that in five of the seven countries examined in this volume a majority of these legislative proposals originated with the executive.[16] Why do presidents originate most major bills? This is partly the result of institutional powers, such as the exclusive right to initiate bills in some relevant policy areas. In addition, the president's staff and technical resources contribute to make presidential initiatives particularly attractive when dealing with complex policy issues, which may discourage legislators from proposing bills on similar topics and encourage amendments. Electoral campaigns in winner-take-all elections, which enhance the role of presidential candidates and their policy programs, may also contribute to the finding that most major bills are executive proposals.

Presidents play a more visible role, but legislators also originate a fair number of major bills. In places like Peru, legislators appear rather active, initiating just over half of the major bills in Ponce's sample and succeeding in their enactment close to two-thirds of the time. In Uruguay, legislators initiate a high share of major bills but are a lot less successful than presidents at turning them into law. Overall, the information presented on bill initiation illustrates legislators' proactive behavior.

Another important finding from the chapters of this volume is that most major bills initiated by the president are amended in congress before becoming law. The amendment process in Latin American legislatures has yet to be fully scrutinized. The preliminary evidence presented in this volume is consistent with prior findings from the US Congress, which show that a substantial share of the president's program is ultimately enacted with modifications introduced by members of Congress.

In Chile, major presidential bills are passed faster than others, but almost always with modifications introduced by Congress. The few that are not amended are either very short or the result of a wide consensus. In Peru, two-thirds of major bills initiated by the president and passed by Congress were amended on the plenary floor of Congress. The proportion amended in committee was likely higher. In Mexico, the end of one-party dominance resulted in a steep increase in the number of amendments presented by legislators. Nowadays major presidential bills are regularly subject to substantive modifications in the Mexican Congress. In Brazil, where presidents appear more successful at changing the status quo via temporary decrees rather than through regular statues, major presidential bills that are passed by Congress typically include substantive amendments introduced by legislators. Chasquetti finds that in Uruguay the vast majority of major bills examined (70 percent) passed with substantive congressional amendments. The proportion of major bills that are amended in the Uruguayan Congress is far higher than the proportion of other laws that are amended. The chapters on Argentina and Colombia also highlight that major presidential bills are significantly more likely to be amended than other bills.

FINAL REMARKS

The emerging literature on Latin American legislatures has brought into light the impact of a variety of institutional mechanisms that affect the bill-to-law process in presidential countries, such as amendatory and partial vetoes, executive urgencies, and decrees. It has also underlined the implications of multi-party coalitions and plurality governments in fragmented congresses, which are not common to the US context.[17] The study of legislatures in Latin America has enriched both the legislative politics literature and the study of Latin American institutions.

In the introduction of this book we argued that control of the legislative agenda depends on legislative prerogatives as well as on the positions of relevant legislative actors. We discussed differences between proposal and veto power and how some actors can influence the scheduling of bills. For each country, the chapters in this book described which offices benefit from such prerogatives and some of the main traits of the legislative parties that bargain over offices and policies. We underscored that legislative actors with significant prerogatives can be limited by the need to reach an agreement with other legislative players whose policy positions are relatively distant. Thus, institutional power can be checked by the need to build coalitions.

The chapters showed various implications of this positional constraint, such as amendments to accommodate ideologically disparate actors (e.g., Chile and Colombia), low passage rates for ordinary bills and frequent use of temporary decrees (e.g., Brazil), or more frequent use of vetoes and amendatory observations (e.g., Uruguay and Mexico). In the introduction we also argued that weak agenda setting prerogatives might be overcome by positional advantage. When lacking a majority in congress, presidents can benefit from moving to the center by, for example, reducing amendments to their bills (e.g., Argentina). As expected, the lack of a majority government also tends to favor centrist parties (e.g., Peru and Mexico).

The chapters of this book have shown not only variation in the authority of committees, but how their influence can be affected by the presence or absence of a majority. Committees' ability to act as gatekeepers or to restrict amendments varies considerably across countries. For instance, committee power in Argentina is primarily negative—to veto proposals—whereas in Chile and Brazil it is primarily positive—to propose bills and amendments. Colombia's committees, which are less numerous than in the other countries, possess some degree of both gatekeeping and proposal power, whereas in Uruguay, Mexico, and Peru, congressional committees are comparatively weaker in terms of gatekeeping and proposal power.

This book sought to examine the potential for and consequences of presidential and legislative influence in lawmaking. While numerous studies have addressed the inner workings of the US Congress and European parliamentary democracies, studies that focus on agenda setting or the internal organization of Latin American congresses remain comparatively thin. We believe this volume contributes to the understanding of how political institutions and legislative actors impact lawmaking in presidential democracies, and hope that it moves forward the study of legislative politics in Latin America.

Between them the seven country studies presented in this volume demonstrate the vitality and pivotal importance of congressional activity in the political life of these now quite well established democratic regimes. The executive dominance and top-down style of governance that characterized their periods of authoritarian rule should not lead analysts to underestimate the legislative processes that now occupy such a central place in public affairs. While the various cases display an important range of variation, it is striking how far they can all be analyzed using the tools and concepts of the established legislative studies literature. These seven include the largest and most influential democratic regimes of Latin America. However, it should be noted that not all the congresses of the region are represented here. In particular, the "refounded" constitutional regimes of Venezuela, Bolivia, and Ecuador do not display the same degree of congressional autonomy, nor do several of the smaller and more traditionally presidentialist regimes of the region. There is scope to further widen the range of comparative legislative studies in the western hemisphere, in order to establish the full "scope conditions" for the type of analysis proposed here. It is also worth noting that not all the institutional systems included in this collection are equally consolidated. Colombia is still undergoing a difficult peace process that could result in further constitutional innovations, for example, while Peru has yet to fully absorb the legacy of the Fujimori period of executive dominance, and current conflicts in Brazil suggest that there too the equilibrium between the branches of government could be further tested. More generally, Latinobarometro surveys indicate that most congresses are held in low repute at present, as are professional politicians and their parties. Their important legislative work is not always understood or respected by the general public to the extent that our case material suggests it should be. Even in the more impressively institutionalized of these newly democratized regimes there are still shadows from the past that persist, and could weaken the prestige and effectiveness of these congresses.

Notwithstanding these provisos, the main thrust of democratic development over the past couple of decades has been towards the strengthening of congressional autonomy and the maturing of sophisticated legislative procedures. This volume therefore highlights that under-appreciated aspect of Latin American democratization, and offers a framework for understanding the politics and policies in these countries.

NOTES

1. Palanza and Sin (2013) show that moving from a majority to a plurality increases the incidence of vetoes.
2. However, shifting to a plurality hurts the approval rate of the president's party (Alemán and Calvo 2010).
3. This finding is consistent with the pattern of roll rates found by Alemán (2006).
4. Pastrana lost the majority briefly in 2001.
5. Of course, they maneuver behind the scenes to get their programs enacted, particularly in Mexico.
6. See Pereira et al. (2005).
7. To roughly 56 percent of decrees according to Rodrigues Cunha (2012).
8. Since 2007, the related committee most often does not debate the decrees.
9. About 22 percent of bills passed. See Pachón and Aroca (2013) for Colombia, and Grohmann (2003) for Brazil between 1990 and 2000.
10. About 11 percent of bills passed according to Palanza and Sin (2013).
11. The passage rate of legislators' bills is very low in Brazil as well. Hiroi and Rennó, in their chapter on Brazil, do not count bills that did not come out of committee. Thus, the overall rates of approval are actually much lower than the ones they report in their chapter.

12. The average for single-party majority governments in presidential countries is around 70 percent (Saiegh 2011).
13. Within each of these countries, the share of legislative seats for government parties seems to have a positive relation with approval rates of presidential bills. For evidence on Chile see Alemán and Navia (2009).
14. See Saiegh (2011) for summary passage rates across governments and regime types.
15. See also Pereira et al. (2008).
16. Hiroi and Rennó speculate that the low number of major executive bills in their sample from Brazil is probably due to presidents advancing several salient proposals as decrees, which were not counted in their sample.
17. Studies focused on Latin American legislatures have also contributed to testing and improving theories developed primarily to explain the US case. Examples include arguments about legislators' "electoral connection," the lawmaking implications of the electoral cycle, the control of partisan cartels, and the power of committees (Alemán 2013).

References

Acemoglu, Daron and James A. Robinson. 2006. *Economic Origins of Dictatorship and Democracy*. New York: Cambridge University Press.

Albert, James and Siddartha Chib. 1993. "Bayesian Analysis of Binary and Polychotomous Response Data." *Journal of the American Statistical Association* 88(422): 669–79.

Aldrich, John H. and Richard D. McKelvey. 1977. "A Method of Scaling with Applications to the 1968 and 1972 Presidential Elections." *American Political Science Review* 71(1): 111–30.

Aldrich, John H. and David W. Rohde. 1998. "Measuring Conditional Party Government." Paper presented at the Annual Meeting of the Midwest Political Science Association, Chicago.

Aldrich, John H. and David W. Rohde. 2001. "The Logic of Conditional Party Government: Revisiting the Electoral Connection." In Lawrence Dodd and Bruce Oppenheimer, eds., *Congress Reconsidered*, 7th edn. Washington, DC: CQ Press, pp. 262–92.

Alemán, Eduardo. 2006. "Policy Gatekeepers in Latin American Legislatures." *Latin American Politics and Society* 48(3): 125–55.

Alemán, Eduardo. 2013. "Latin American Legislative Politics: A Survey of Peer-Reviewed Publications in English." *Journal of Politics in Latin America* 5(1): 15–36.

Alemán, Eduardo and Ernesto Calvo. 2010. "Unified Government, Bill Approval, and the Legislative Weight of the President." *Comparative Political Studies* 43(4): 511–34.

Alemán, Eduardo, Ernesto Calvo, Mark P. Jones, and Noah Kaplan. 2009. "Comparing Cosponsorship and Roll-Call Ideal Points." *Legislative Studies Quarterly* 34(1): 87–116.

Alemán, Eduardo and Patricio Navia. 2009. "Institutions and the Legislative Success of 'Strong' Presidents: An Analysis of Government Bills in Chile." *Journal of Legislative Studies* 15(4): 401–19.

Alemán, Eduardo and Mónica Pachón. 2008. "Las Comisiones de Conciliación en los Procesos Legislativos de Chile y Colombia." *Política y Gobierno* 15(1): 3–34.

Alemán, Eduardo, Aldo F. Ponce, and Iñaki Sagarzazu. 2011. "Legislative Parties in Volatile Non-Programmatic Party Systems: The Peruvian Case in Comparative Perspective." *Latin American Politics and Society* 53(3): 57–81.

Alemán, Eduardo and Sebastián M. Saiegh. 2007. "Legislative Preferences, Political Parties, and Coalition Unity in Chile." *Comparative Politics* 39(3): 253–72.

Alemán, Eduardo and George Tsebelis. 2005. "The Origins of Presidential Conditional Agenda-Setting Power in Latin America." *Latin American Research Review* 40(2): 3–26.

Alemán, Eduardo and George Tsebelis. 2011. "Political Parties and Government Coalitions in the Americas." *Journal of Politics in Latin America* 3(1): 3–28.

Allamand, Andrés. 1999. *La Travesía del Desierto*. Santiago, Chile: Aguilar.

Allamand, Andrés and Marcela Cubillos. 2010. *La Estrella y el Arco Iris. Cómo, Después de 20 años, fue Derrotada la Concertación*. Santiago, Chile: Aguilar.

Almeida, Acir. 2011. "Avaliação do Impacto da Emenda 32 Sobre a Edição de Medidas Provisórias." *Comunicados do IPEA* 103.

Alston, Lee J. and Bernardo Mueller. 2005. "Pork for Policy: Executive and Legislative Exchange in Brazil." *Journal of Law, Economics, and Organization* 22(1): 87–114.

Altman, David. 2000. "The Politics of Coalition Formation and Survival in Multiparty Presidential Democracies: The Case of Uruguay 1989–1999." *Party Politics* 6(3): 259–83.

Altman, David. 2002. "Cambios en las Percepciones Ideológicas de Lemas y Fracciones Políticas: un Mapa del Sistema de Partidos Uruguayo (1986–1997)." *Cuadernos del CLAEH* 85/1: 89–110.

Altman, David. 2010. *Direct Democracy Worldwide*. New York: Cambridge University Press.

Altman, David and Daniel Chasquetti. 2005. "Re-election and Political Career Paths in the Uruguayan Congress: 1985–1999." *Journal of Legislative Studies* 11(2): 235–53.

Ames, Barry. 2001. *The Deadlock of Democracy in Brazil*. Ann Arbor: University of Michigan Press.

Ames, Barry, Carlos Pereira, and Lucio Renno. 2011. "Famintos Por Pork: Uma Analise da Demanda e Oferta por Políticas Localistas e suas Implicações para a Representação Política." In Timothy Power and César Zucco, eds., *O Congresso Por Ele Mesmo: Autopercepções da Classe Política Brasileira*. Belo Horizonte, Brazil: Editora da UFMG, pp. 239–72.

Amorim Neto, Octavio. 2002. "Presidential Cabinets, Electoral Cycles, and Coalition Discipline in Brazil." In Scott Morgenstern and Benito Nacif, eds., *Legislative Politics in Latin America*. New York: Cambridge University Press, pp. 48–78.

Amorim Neto, Octavio. 2006. "The Presidential Calculus: Executive Policy Making and Cabinet Formation in the Americas." *Comparative Political Studies* 39(4): 415–40.

Amorim Neto, Octavio, Gary W. Cox, and Mathew D. McCubbins. 2003. "Agenda Power in Brazil's Câmara dos Deputados, 1989–98." *World Politics* 55(4): 550–78.

Amorim Neto, Octavio and Fabiano Santos. 2003. "O Segredo Ineficiente Revisto: o que Propõem e o que Aprovam os Deputados Brasileiros." *Dados* 46(4): 661–98.

Angell, Alan. 1980. "Peruvian Labour and the Military Government since 1968." Working Paper 3. London: Institute of Latin American Studies, University of London.

Angell, Alan. 2003. "Party Change in Chile in Comparative Perspective." *Revista de Ciencia Política* 23(2): 88–108.

Aparicio, Francisco Javier and Joy Langston. 2009. "Committee Leadership Selection without Seniority: The Mexican Case." Documento de Trabajo 217. Mexico: División de Estudios Políticos, CIDE.

Archer, Ronald and Matthew S. Shugart. 1997. "The Unrealized Potential of Presidential Dominance in Colombia." In Scott Mainwaring and Matthew S. Shugart, eds., *Presidentialism and Democracy in Latin America*. Cambridge: Cambridge University Press, pp. 110–59.

Aroca, Maria Paula and Andrés Felipe Guevara. 2013. "Las inasistencias en el Congreso: más allá de lo que dicen los medios." <http://congresovisible.org/agora/post/las-inasistencias-en-el-congreso-mas-alla-de-lo-que-dicen-los-medios/5409/>, accessed November 27, 2013.

Avellaneda, Claudia and Maria Escobar-Lemmon. 2012. "All by Myself: The Role of Personal Qualifications versus Party Affiliation in Mayoral Elections." *Latin American Politics and Society* 54(2): 109–32.

Baldez, Lisa and John M. Carey. 1999. "Presidential Agenda Control and Spending Policy: Lessons from General Pinochet's Constitution." *American Journal of Political Science* 43(1): 29–55.

Barcikowski, Robert S. 1981. "Statistical Power with Group Mean as the Unit of Analysis." *Journal of Educational Statistics* 6(3): 267–85.

Bernal, Dolores. 2009. *El gobierno dividido en México: Coaliciones ganadoras en la Cámara de Diputados*. Mexico City: ITAM.

Binder, Sarah A. 1999. "The Dynamics of Legislative Gridlock, 1947–96." *American Political Science Review* 93(3): 519–33.

Binder, Sarah A. 2003. *Stalemate: Causes and Consequences of Legislative Gridlock*. Washington, DC: Brookings Institution.

Black, Duncan. 1948. "On the Rationale of Group Decision-Making." *Journal of Political Economy* 56(1): 23–34.

Blair, R. Clifford, J. J. Higgins, Mary E. H. Topping, and Allen L. Mortimer. 1983. "An Investigation of the Robustness of the t Test to Unit of Analysis Violations." *Educational and Psychological Measurement* 43(1): 69–80.

Blume, Aldo. 2011. *Los Decretos de Urgencia de Alan García: El Abuso y la Usurpación de la Facultad Legislativa por Parte del Poder Ejecutivo. Balance Constitucional de los Decretos de Urgencia Expedidos Durante el Segundo Gobierno del Presidente Alan García Pérez*. Lima, Peru: Instituto de Defensa Legal.

Bonvecchi, Alejandro and Javier Zelaznik. 2010. "Measuring Legislative Input on Presidential Agendas (Argentina, 1999–2007)." Paper presented at the Latin American Studies Association, Toronto, Canada.

Brahm García, Enrique, Raúl Bertelsen Repetto, and Andrés Amunátegui Echeverría. 2002. *Regimen de Gobierno en Chile: ¿Presidencialismo o Parlamentarismo? 1925–1973*. Santiago: Editorial Jurídica de Chile.

Buquet, Daniel, Daniel Chasquetti, and Juan Andrés Moraes. 1998. *Fragmentación Política y Gobierno. ¿Un Enfermo Imaginario?* Montevideo, Uruguay: Instituto de Ciencia Política.

Calvo, Ernesto. 2007. "The Responsive Legislature: Public Opinion and Law Making in a Highly Disciplined Legislature." *British Journal of Political Science* 37(2): 263–80.

Calvo, Ernesto. 2014. *Legislator Success in Fragmented Congresses in Argentina: Plurality Cartels, Minority Presidents, and Lawmaking*. New York: Cambridge University Press.

Calvo, Ernesto and Iñaki Sagarzazu. 2011. "Legislator Success in Committee: Gatekeeping Authority and the Loss of Majority Control." *American Journal of Political Science* 55(1): 1–15.

Calvo, Ernesto and Andres Tow. 2009. "Cajoneando el Debate: El Papel de los Presidentes de las Comisiones en la Productividad del Congreso Argentino." *Desarrollo Económico*, 49(195): 451–77.

Cameron, Charles. 2000. *Veto Bargaining: Presidents and the Politics of Negative Power*. New York: Columbia University Press.

Cárdenas, Mauricio, Roberto Junguito, and Mónica Pachón. 2008. "Political Institutions and Policy Outcomes in Colombia: The Effects of the 1991 Constitution." In Ernesto Stein, Mariano Tommasi, and Carlos G. Scartascini, eds., *Political Institutions, Policymaking Processes, and Economic Policy in Latin America*. Cambridge, MA: Harvard University Press, pp. 199–242.

Carey, John M. 2002. "Parties, Coalitions and the Chilean Congress in the 1990s." In Scott Morgenstern and Benito Nacif, eds., *Legislative Politics in Latin America*. New York: Cambridge University Press, pp. 222–53.

Carey, John M. and Matthew S. Shugart, eds. 1998. *Executive Decree Authority*. Cambridge and New York: Cambridge University Press.

Carroll, Royce and Matthew S. Shugart. 2007. "Neo-Madisonian Theory and Latin American Institutions." In Gerardo Munck, ed., *Regimes and Democracy in Latin America: Theories and Methods*. Oxford: Oxford University Press, pp. 51–102.

Carson, Jamie L., Nathan W. Monroe, and Gregory Robinson. 2011. "Unpacking Agenda Control in Congress: Individual Roll Rates and the Republican Revolution." *Political Research Quarterly* 64(1): 17–30.

Casar, Ma. Amparo. 1997. "The Sources of Presidentialism Authority in Post-Revolutionary Mexico." PhD Dissertation, King's College, University of Cambridge.

Casar, Ma. Amparo. 2000. "Coaliciones y cohesión partidista en un Congreso sin mayoría: La Cámara de Diputados de México, 1997–1999." *Política y Gobierno* 7(1): 183–202.

Casar, Ma. Amparo. 2001. "Las Elecciones del 2 de julio y la LVIII Legislatura." In Luis Salazar, ed., *Mexico 2000: Alternancia y Transición a la Democracia*. Mexico: Cal y Arena, pp. 389–415.

Casar, Ma. Amparo. 2008. "Los Gobiernos Sin Mayoría en Mexico: 1997–2006." *Política y Gobierno* 15(2): 221–70.

Casar, Ma. Amparo. 2011. "¿Cómo y Cuánto Gasta la Cámara de Diputados?" Cuaderno de Debate 8. Mexico: CIDE.

Casar, Ma. Amparo and Ignacio Marván, eds. 2014. *Reformar sin mayorías, la dinámica del cambio constitucional en México: 1997–2012*. Mexico City: Taurus.

Castillo, Mario Freyre. 1997. *Todos los Poderes del Presidente*. Lima, Peru: Fondo Editorial de la Pontificia Universidad Católica del Perú.

Cea Egaña, José Luis. 1992. "Presidencialismo Reforzado: Críticas y Alternativas para el Caso Chileno." In Oscar Godoy, ed., *Cambio de Régimen Político*. Santiago, Chile: Ediciones Universidad Católica de Chile, pp. 102–16.

Chasquetti, Daniel. 1999. "Compartiendo el Gobierno: Multipartidismo y Coaliciones en el Uruguay (1971–1997)." *Revista Uruguaya de Ciencia Política* 10: 25–45.

Chasquetti, Daniel. 2003. "El proceso constitucional en el Uruguay del siglo XX." In Gerardo Caetano and Benjamín Nahum, eds., *El Uruguay del siglo XX*. Montevideo, Uruguay: Ediciones de la Banda Oriental—ICP, pp. 78–80.

Chasquetti, Daniel. 2011a. "El Secreto del Exito: Presidentes y Cárteles Legislativos en Uruguay (1995–2010)." *Revista Uruguaya de Ciencia Política* 20(1): 9–32.

Chasquetti, Daniel. 2011b. "El costo de Pasar: Gobiernos de Coalición y Gobiernos de Partido en el Proceso Legislativo Uruguayo." In Manuel Alcántara and Mercedes García Montero, eds., *Algo más que Presidentes: El Papel del Poder Legislativo en América Latina*. Zaragoza, Spain: Fundación Manuel Giménez Abad, pp. 537–61.

Chasquetti, Daniel. 2014. *Parlamento y Carreras Legislativas en Uruguay: Un Estudio sobre Reglas, Partidos y Legisladores en las Cámaras*. Montevideo, Uruguay: FCS-Cauce.

Chasquetti, Daniel and Juan Andrés Moraes. 2000. "Hipótesis para una Teoría del Ciclo Político Uruguayo." In Jorge Lanzaro, ed., *La Segunda Transición en Uruguay*. Montevideo, Uruguay: FCU-ICP, pp. 297–338.

Cheibub, José Antonio. 2007. *Presidentialism, Parliamentarism, and Democracy*. New York: Cambridge University Press.

Cheibub, José Antonio, Adam Przeworski, and Sebastián M. Saiegh. 2004. "Government Coalitions and Legislative Success Under Presidentialism and Parliamentarism." *British Journal of Political Science* 34(4): 565–87.

Colombia Constitutional Court website. <http://www.corteconstitucional.gov.co/relatoria>, accessed November 27, 2013.

Colomer, José María and Gabriel L. Negretto. 2005. "Can Presidentialism Work Like Parliamentarism?" *Government and Opposition* 40(1): 60–89.

Congreso Visible. 2009. "Boletin 15." *Congreso Visible*. <http://issuu.com/congresovisible/docs/congreso_visible_15_julio-diciembre_2009>, accessed December 2, 2013.

Coppedge, Michael. 1998. "The Dynamic Diversity of Latin American Party Systems." *Party Politics* 4(4): 547–68.

Corrales, Javier. 2010. "The Repeating Revolution: Chávez's New Politics and Old Economics." In Kurt Weyland, Raúl Madrid, and Wendy Hunter, eds., *Leftist Governments in Latin America: Successes and Shortcomings*. New York: Cambridge University Press, pp. 28–56.

Correa Sutil, Sofía. 2005. *Con las Riendas del Poder: La Derecha Chilena en el Siglo XX*. Santiago, Chile: Editorial Sudamericana.

Cox, Gary W. 2001. "Agenda Setting in the U.S. House: A Majority-Party Monopoly?" *Legislative Studies Quarterly* 26(2): 185–210.

Cox, Gary W., William B. Heller, and Mathew D. McCubbins. 2008. "Agenda Power in the Italian Parliament, 1988–2000." *Legislative Studies Quarterly* 33(2): 171–98.

Cox, Gary W. and Mathew D. McCubbins. 1993. *Legislative Leviathan*. Berkeley: University of California Press.

Cox, Gary W. and Mathew D. McCubbins. 2001. "The Institutional Determinants of Economic Policy." In Stephan Haggard and Mathew D. McCubbins, eds., *Presidents, Parliaments, and Policy*. New York: Cambridge University Press, pp. 21–63.

Cox, Gary W. and Mathew D. McCubbins. 2002. "Agenda Power in the House of Representatives." In David Brady and Mathew D. McCubbins, eds., *Party, Process and Political Change: New Perspectives in the History of Congress*. Stanford, CA: Stanford University Press, pp. 107–45.

Cox, Gary W. and Mathew D. McCubbins. 2005. *Setting the Agenda: Responsible Party Government in the US House of Representatives*. New York: Cambridge University Press.

Cox, Gary W., Mikitaka Masuyama, and Mathew D. McCubbins. 2000. "Agenda Power in the Japanese House of Representatives." *Japanese Journal of Political Science* 1(1): 1–22.

Cox, Gary W. and Scott Morgenstern. 2002. "Epilogue: Latin America's Reactive Assemblies and Proactive Presidents." In Scott Morgenstern and Benito Nacif, eds., *Legislative Politics in Latin America*. New York: Cambridge University Press pp. 446–68.

Cox, Gary W. and Matthew S. Shugart. 1996. "Strategic Voting under Proportional Representation." *Journal of Law, Economics and Organization* 12(2): 299–324.

Crisp, Brian and Scott Desposato. 2004. "Constituency Building in Multimember Districts: Collusion or Conflict?" *Journal of Politics* 66(1): 136–56.

Crisp, Brian and Rachell E. Ingall. 2002. "Institutional Engineering and the Nature of Representation: Mapping the Effects of Electoral Reform in Colombia." *American Journal of Political Science* 46(4): 733–48.

Crombez, Christophe. 1997. "The Co-Decision Procedure in the European Union." *Legislative Studies Quarterly* 22(1): 97–119.

Crombez, Christophe, Tim Groseclose, and Keith Krehbiel. 2006. "Gatekeeping." *Journal of Politics* 68(2): 322–34.

Denzau, Arthur T. and Robert J. Mackay. 1983. "Gatekeeping and Monopoly Power of Committees: An Analysis of Sincere and Sophisticated Behavior." *American Journal of Political Science* 27(4): 740–61.

Diermeier, Daniel and Timothy J. Feddersen. 1998. "Cohesion in Legislatures and the Vote of Confidence." *American Political Science Review* 92(3): 611–21.

Dietz, Henry and David Myers. 2007. "From Thaw to Deluge: Party System Collapse in Venezuela and Peru." *Latin American Politics and Society* 49(2): 59–86.

Dion, Douglas and John D. Huber. 1996. "Procedural Choice and the House Committee on Rules." *Journal of Politics* 58(1): 25–53.

Doering, Herbert. 1995. "Time as a Scarce Resource: Government Control of the Agenda." In Herbert Doering, ed., *Parliaments and Majority Rule in Western Europe*. New York: St. Martin's Press, pp. 223–46.

Edwards III, George C., Andrew Barrett, and Jeffrey Peake. 2007. "The Legislative Impact of Divided Government." *American Journal of Political Science* 41(2): 545–63.

Epstein, David and Sharyn O'Halloran. 1999. *Delegating Powers: A Transaction Cost Politics Approach to Policy Making under Separate Powers*. New York: Cambridge University Press.

Escandón, Marcela. 2013. "Congreso colombiano: balance del 2012 y panorama para el 2013." *Razón Pública*, April 21. <http://www.razonpublica.com/index.php/politica-y-gobierno-temas-27/3688-congreso-colombiano-balance-del-2012-y-panorama-para-el-2013.html>.

Ferreira Rubio, Delia and Mateo Goretti. 1996. "Cuando el Presidente Gobierna Solo: Menem y los Decretos de Necesidad y Urgencia hasta la Reforma Constitucional (1989–1994)." *Desarrollo Economico* 36(141): 443–74.

Figueiredo, Argelina Cheibub and Fernando Limongi. 1999. *Executivo e Legislativo na Nova Ordem Constitucional.* Rio de Janeiro, Brazil: Editora Fundação Getúlio Vargas.

Figueiredo, Argelina Cheibub and Fernando Limongi. 2000. "Presidential Power, Legislative Organization, and Party Behavior in Brazil." *Comparative Politics* 32(2): 151–70.

Finocchiaro, Charles J. and Gregg B. Johnson. 2010. "Committee Property Rights, Executive Dominance, and Political Parties in Latin American Legislatures." *Journal of Legislative Studies* 16(2): 151–75.

Finocchiaro, Charles J. and David W. Rohde. 2008. "War for the Floor: Partisan Theory and Agenda Control in the US House of Representatives." *Legislative Studies Quarterly* 33(1): 35–61.

Forno, Giovanni. 2012. "Iniciativa Legislativa del Presidente de la República: Parte II." <http://gforno.blogspot.mx/2012/01/iniciativa-legislativa-del-presidente.html>.

Fox, Douglas M. and Charles H. Clapp. 1970. "The House Rules Committee's Agenda-Setting Function, 1961–1968." *Journal of Politics* 32(2): 440–3.

Gailmard, Sean and Jeffery A. Jenkins. 2007. "Negative Agenda Control in the Senate and House: Fingerprints of Majority Party Power." *Journal of Politics* 69(3): 689–700.

Gamm, Gerald and John D. Huber. 2003. "Legislatures as Political Institutions: Beyond the Contemporary Congress." In Ira Katznelson and Helen V. Milner, eds., *Political Science: The State of the Discipline.* New York: W. W. Norton, pp. 313–41.

Gleiber, Dennis W. and Steven A. Shull. 1992. "Presidential Influence in the Policy-making Process." *Western Political Quarterly* 45(2): 441–67.

Godoy Aracaya, Óscar. 2003. "Parlamento, Presidencialismo y Democracia Protegida." *Revista de Ciencia Política* 23(2): 7–42.

González, Luis E. 1993. *Estructuras Políticas y Democracia en Uruguay.* Montevideo, Uruguay: FCU-ICP.

Graham, Carol. 1990. "Perú's APRA—Party in Power: Impossible Revolution, Relinquished Reform." *Journal of Interamerican Studies and World Affairs* 32(3): 75–115.

Griffiths, William, R. Carter Hill, and Peter Pope. 1987. "Small Sample Properties of Probit Model Estimators." *Journal of the American Statistical Association* 82: 929–37.

Grohmann, Luis Gustavo Mello. 2003. "O Veto presidencial no Brasil: 1946–1964 e 1990–2000." PhD Dissertation, Instituto Universitário de Pesquisas do Rio de Janeiro.

Gutiérrez, Francisco. 2007. *Lo que el Viento se Llevó: Los Partidos Políticos y la Democracia en Colombia, 1958–2002.* Bogotá, Colombia: Editorial Norma.

Hallerberg, Mark and Patrik Marier. 2004. "Executive Authority, the Personal Vote, and Budget Discipline in Latin American and Caribbean Countries." *American Journal of Political Science* 48(3): 571–87.

Hare, Christopher, David A. Armstrong, Ryan Bakker, Royce Carroll, and Keith T. Poole. 2015. "Using Bayesian Aldrich-McKelvey Scaling to Study Citizens' Ideological Preferences and Perceptions." *American Journal of Political Science* 59 (3): 759–74.

Heller, William B. 2001. "Making Policy Stick: Why the Government Gets What It Wants in Multiparty Parliaments." *American Journal of Political Science* 45(4): 780–98.

Hinckley, Barbara. 1970. "Congressional Leadership Selection and Support: A Comparative Analysis." *Journal of Politics* 32(2): 268–87.

Hiroi, Taeko. 2005. "Bicameral Politics: Dynamics of Lawmaking in Brazil." PhD Thesis, University of Pittsburgh.

Hiroi, Taeko. 2008a. "The Dynamics of Lawmaking in a Bicameral Legislature: The Case of Brazil." *Comparative Political Studies* 41(12): 1583–606.

Hiroi, Taeko. 2008b. "Timing and Outcome of Legislation: Brazilian Pension Reform in a Bicameral Perspective." *Journal of Legislative Studies* 14(4): 394–420.

Hiroi, Taeko. 2009. "Exchange Rate Regime, Central Bank Independence, and Political Business Cycles in Brazil." *Studies in Comparative International Development* 44(1): 1–22.

Hiroi, Taeko and Pedro Neiva. 2013. "Malapportionment and Geographical Bases of Electoral Support in the Brazilian Senate." *Journal of Politics in Latin America* 5(1): 127–50.

Hiroi, Taeko and Lucio Renno. 2014. "Dimensions of Legislative Conflict: Coalitions, Obstructionism, and Lawmaking in Multiparty Presidential Regimes." *Legislative Studies Quarterly* 39(3): 357–86.

Hix, Simon. 2002. "Parliamentary Behavior with Two Principals: Preferences, Parties, and Voting in the European Parliament." *American Journal of Political Science* 46(2): 688–98.

Hoskin, Gary and Mónica Pachón. 2011. "Colombia 2010: An Analysis of the Legislative and Presidential Elections." *Colombia Internacional* 74: 9–26.

Howell, William, Scott Adler, Charles Cameron, and Charles Riemann. 2000. "Divided Government and the Legislative Productivity of Congress, 1945–94." *Legislative Studies Quarterly* 25(2): 285–312.

Huber, John D. 1996. "The Vote of Confidence in Parliamentary Democracies." *American Political Science Review* 90(2): 269–82.

Huneeus, Carlos. 2001. *El Régimen de Pinochet*. Santiago, Chile: Sudamericana.

Inácio, Magna. 2009. "Engajemento Parlamentar no Brasil." In T. Powers and C. Zucco (eds.), *O Congresso por Ele Mesmo*. Belo Horizonte, Brazil: Editora da UFMG.

Instituto Federal Electoral. 2007. *Atlas Electoral Federal de México 1991–2006*. Mexico: Dirección Ejecutiva de Organización Electoral, Instituto Federal Electoral.

Jiménez de Aréchaga, Justino. 1947. *La Constitución Nacional, tomo VIII*. Montevideo, Uruguay: Medina.

Jones, Mark P. 2005. "The Role of Parties and Party Systems in the Policymaking Process." Paper presented at the Inter-American Development Bank Workshop on State Reform, Public Policies and Policymaking Processes, Washington, DC.

Jones, Mark P. 2007. "Political Parties and Party Systems in Latin America." Paper presented at the Symposium on Prospects for Democracy in Latin America, Department of Political Science, University of North Texas, Denton.

Jones, Mark P. and Wonjae Hwang. 2005. "Party Government in Presidential Democracies: Extending Cartel Theory Beyond the US Congress." *American Journal of Political Science* 49(2): 267–82.

Kernell, Samuel. 1986. *Going Public: New Strategies of Presidential Leadership*. Washington, DC: Congressional Quarterly Press.

Kiewiet, Roderick and Mathew McCubbins. 1991. *The Logic of Delegation*. Chicago, IL: University of Chicago Press.

Konig, Thomas and Jonathan Slapin. 2006. "From Unanimity to Consensus: An Analysis of the Negotiations at the EU's Constitutional Convention." *World Politics* 58(3): 413–45.

Koolhas, Martín. 2004. "Coaliciones de Gobierno en Uruguay, 1990-2003." Thesis, Instituto de Ciencia Política, Montevideo, Uruguay.

Kramer, Gerald. 1973. "On a Class of Equilibrium Conditions for Majority Rule." *Econometrica* 41(2): 285–97.

Krause, George A. and David Cohen. 1997. "Presidential Use of Executive Order, 1953-1994." *American Politics Quarterly* 25(4): 458–71.

Landa, César and Jorge León. 2003. *Facultades Legislativas del Poder Ejecutivo*. Lima, Peru: Congreso de la República.

Lanzaro, Jorge, Daniel Buquet, Daniel Chasquetti, and Juan Andrés Moraes. 2000. *Estudio sobre la Producción Legislativa en Uruguay, Programa de Evaluación de la Producción Legislativa en Uruguay, 1985–2000*. Montevideo, Uruguay: Poder Legislativo.

Lawrence, Eric D., Forest Maltzman, and Steven S. Smith. 2006. "Who Wins? Party Effects in Legislative Voting." *Legislative Studies Quarterly* 31(1): 33–70.

Leighton, Wayne A. and Edward J. Lopez. 2002. "Committee Assignments and the Cost of Party Loyalty." *Political Research Quarterly* 55(1): 59–90.

Levitt, Barry. 2012. *Power in the Balance: Presidents, Parties, and Legislatures in Peru and Beyond*. Notre Dame, IN: University of Notre Dame Press.

Lohmann, Susanne and Sharyn O'Halloran. 1994. "Divided Government and US Trade Policy: Theory and Evidence." *International Organization* 48(4): 595–632.

Londoño, Juan Fernando. 2008. "Bancadas e Institucionalización partidaria." In Carlos Caballero Argáez and Elisabeth Ungar, eds., *Las Bancadas en el Congreso: Ley y praxis*. Bogotá, Colombia: Ediciones Uniandes, pp. 75–95.

Londregan, John. 2000. *Legislative Institutions and Ideology in Chile*. New York: Cambridge University Press.

McCarty, Nolan M. 2000. "Presidential Pork: Executive Veto Power and Distributive Politics." *American Political Science Review* 94(1): 117–29.

McClintock, Cynthia. 1996. "La Voluntad Política Presidencial y la Ruptura Constitucional de 1992 en el Perú." In Fernando Tuesta Soldevilla, ed., *Los Enigmas del Poder: Fujimori 1990–1996*. Lima, Peru: Fundación Friedrich Ebert, pp. 53–74.

McCubbins, Mathew D. 1991. "Party Governance and US Budget Deficits: Divided Government and Fiscal Stalemate." In Alberto Alesina and Geoffrey Carliner, eds., *Politics and Economics in the Eighties*. Chicago, IL: University of Chicago Press, pp. 83–122.

McCubbins, Mathew D. 2001. "Legislative Process." In Barry Clarke and Joe Foweraker, eds., *The Encyclopedia of Democratic Thought*. New York: Routledge, pp. 403–8.

McCubbins, Mathew D., Roger Noll, and Barry R. Weingast. 1987. "Administrative Procedures as Instruments of Political Control." *Journal of Law, Economics, and Organization* 3(2): 234–77.

McCubbins, Mathew D., Roger Noll, and Barry R. Weingast. 1989. "Structure and Process, Politics, and Policy: Administrative Arrangements and Political Control of Agencies." *Virginia Law Review* 75: 431–82.

McKelvey, Richard D. 1976. "Intransitivities in Multidimensional Voting Models and Some Implications for Agenda Control." *Journal of Economic Theory* 12(3): 472–82.

Magar, Erik and Jeffrey Weldon. 2001. "The Paradox of the Veto in Mexico (1917–1997)." Paper presented at the International Congress of the Lain American Studies Association, Washington, DC.

Mainwaring, Scott. 1998. "Rethinking Party Systems Theory in the Third Wave of Democratization: The Importance of Party System Institutionalization." Working Paper 260. Notre Dame, IN: Kellogg Institute, University of Notre Dame.

Mainwaring, Scott. 1999. *Rethinking Party Systems in the Third Wave: The Case of Brazil.* Stanford, CA: Stanford University Press.

Mainwaring, Scott and Timothy Scully. 1995. "Introduction: Party Systems in Latin America." In Scott Mainwaring and Timothy Scully, eds., *Building Democratic Institutions*. Stanford, CA: Stanford University Press, pp. 1–36.

Mainwaring, Scott and Matthew S. Shugart. 1997. "Conclusion: Presidentialism and the Party System." In Scott Mainwaring and Matthew S. Shugart, eds., *Presidentialism and Democracy in Latin America.* New York: Cambridge University Press, pp. 394–439.

Mainwaring, Scott and Mariano Torcal. 2006. "Party System Institutionalization and Party System Theory after the Third Wave of Democratization." In Richard Katz and William Crotty, eds., *Handbook of Party Politics.* London: Sage, pp. 204–27.

Mainwaring, Scott and Edurne Zoco. 2007. "Political Sequences and the Stabilization of Interparty Competition: Electoral Volatility in Old and New Democracies." *Party Politics* 13(2): 155–78.

Martin, Andrew, Kevin Quinn, and Jong Hee Park. 2009. "MCMCpack: Markov Chain Monte Carlo (MCMC) Package." R Package version 0.9-6. CRAN Repository.

Mayer, Kenneth. 1999. "Executive Orders and Presidential Power." *Journal of Politics* 61(2): 445–66.

Metcalf, Lee K. 2000. "Measuring Presidential Power." *Comparative Political Studies* 33(5): 661–85.

Moraes, Juan Andrés. 2008. "Why Factions? Candidate Selection and Legislative Politics in Uruguay." In Peter Siavelis and Scott Morgestern, eds., *Pathways to Power: Political Recruitment and Candidate Selection in Latin America*. University Park: Penn State University Press, pp. 164–86.

Moraes, Juan Andrés and Scott Morgenstern. 1995. "El veto del Poder Ejecutivo en el proceso político uruguayo: 1985–1995." Documento de Trabajo 9, Instituto de

Ciencia Política, Facultad de Ciencias Sociales, Universidad de la República, Montevideo, Uruguay.

Morales, Mauricio and Patricio Navia, eds. 2010. *El Sismo Electoral de 2009: Cambio y Continuidad en las Preferencias Políticas de los Chilenos*. Santiago, Chile: Ediciones Universidad Diego Portales.

Moreno, Erika and Maria Escobar-Lemmon. 2008. "Mejor Solo Que Mal Acompañado: Political Entrepreneurs in Colombia." In Peter Siavelis and Scott Morgenstern, eds., *Pathways to Power: Political Recruitment and Candidate Selection in Latin America*. University Park: Penn State University Press, pp. 119–42.

Morgenstern, Scott. 2001. "Organized Factions and Disorganized Parties: Electoral Incentives in Uruguay." *Party Politics* 7(2): 235–56.

Mustapic, Ana María. 2002. "Oscillating Relations: Presidents and Congress in Argentina." In Scott Morgenstern and Benito Nacif, eds., *Legislative Politics in Latin America*. New York: Cambridge University Press, pp. 23–47.

Nacif, Benito. 2006. "The Fall of the Dominant Presidency: Lawmaking Under Divided Government in Mexico." Documento de Trabajo 185. Mexico: División de Estudios Políticos, CIDE.

Navia, Patricio. 2008. "Legislative Candidate Selection in Chile." In Peter Siavelis and Scott Morgenstern, eds., *Pathways to Power: Political Recruitment and Candidate Selection in Latin America*. University Park: Penn State University Press, pp. 92–118.

Negretto, Gabriel L. 2004. "Government Capacities and Policy Making by Decree in Latin America: The Cases of Brazil and Argentina." *Comparative Political Studies* 37(5): 531–62.

Negretto, Gabriel L. 2009. "Political Parties and Institutional Design: Explaining Constitutional Choice in Latin America." *British Journal of Political Science* 39(1): 117–39.

Osorio, Camila. 2010a. "Guillermo Rivera y Juan Fernando Cristo: historia de su cruzada para aprobar la ley de víctimas." <http://lasillavacia.com/historia/19190>, accessed December 2, 2013.

Osorio, Camila. 2010b. "La objeción de conciencia en la U tiene envidiosos a los demás opositores a la ley de regalías." <http://lasillavacia.com/historia/18604>, accessed November 29, 2013.

Pachón, Mónica. 2003. "Explaining the Performance of the Colombian Congress: Electoral and Legislature Rules, and Interactions with the Executive." Paper presented at the Latin American Studies Association Conference, Dallas, Texas.

Pachón, Mónica. 2009. "Colombia 2008: Éxitos, peligros y desaciertos de la Política de Seguridad Democrática en la administración Uribe." *Revista de Ciencia Política* 29(2): 327–53.

Pachón, Mónica and Maria Paula Aroca. 2013. "Presidents vs. Congress and the Constitutional Court: An Empirical Analysis of the Veto Power in Colombia, 1998– 2012." Paper presented at the Midwest Political Science Association Conference, Chicago.

Pachón, Mónica and Matthew S. Shugart. 2010. "Electoral Reform and the Mirror Image of Inter-Party and Intra-Party Competition." *Electoral Studies* 29(4): 648–60.

Palanza, Valeria and Gisela Sin. 2013. "Veto Bargaining and the Legislative Process in Multiparty Presidential Systems." *Comparative Political Studies* 47(5): 766–92.

Palmer, David Scott. 1996. "Fujipopulism and Peru's Progress." *Current History* 95(598): 70–5.

Patterson, Samuel C. 1963. "Legislative Leadership and Political Ideology." *Public Opinion Quarterly* 27(3): 399–410.

Payne, Mark, Daniel Zovatto, Fernando Carrillo Flórez, and Andrés Allamand Zavala. 2002. *Democracies in Development: Politics and Reform in Latin America.* Washington, DC: Inter-American Development Bank.

Pereira, Carlos and Bernardo Mueller. 2000. "Uma Teoria da Preponderância do Poder Executivo: O Sistema de Comissões no Legislativo Brasileiro." *Revista Brasileira de Ciências Sociais* 15(43): 45–67.

Pereira, Carlos and Bernardo Mueller. 2004a. "The Cost of Governing Strategic Behavior of the President and Legislators in Brazil's Budgetary Process." *Comparative Political Studies* 37(7): 781–815.

Pereira, Carlos and Bernardo Mueller. 2004b. "A Theory of Executive Dominance of Congressional Politics: The Committee System in the Brazilian Chamber of Deputies." *Journal of Legislative Studies* 10(1): 9–49.

Pereira, Carlos, Timothy J. Power, and Lucio Rennó. 2005. "Under What Conditions Do Presidents Resort to Decree Power? Theory and Evidence from the Brazilian Case." *Journal of Politics* 67(1): 178–200.

Pereira, Carlos, Timothy J. Power, and Lucio Rennó. 2008. "Agenda Power, Executive Decree Authority, and the Mixed Results of Reform in the Brazilian Congress." *Legislative Studies Quarterly* 33(1): 5–33.

Pereira, Carlos and Lucio Rennó. 2003. "Successful Reelection Strategies in Brazil: The Electoral Impact of Distinct Institutional Incentives." *Electoral Studies* 22(3): 425–48.

Pérez, Romeo, Gerardo Caetano, and José Rilla. 1987. "La Partidocracia Uruguaya." *Cuadernos del CLAEH* 44: 37–62.

Peterson, Mark. 1990. *Legislating Together: The White House and Capitol Hill from Eisenhower to Reagan.* Cambridge, MA: Harvard University Press.

Plott, Charles R. 1967. "A Notion of Equilibrium and its Possibility Under Majority Rule." *American Economic Review* 57(4): 787–806.

Plott, Charles R. and Michael E. Levine. 1978. "A Model of Agenda Influence on Committee Decisions." *American Economic Review* 68(1): 146–60.

Ponce, Aldo F. 2012. "Linking Citizens and Parties: How Legislatures Matter for Political Representation and Accountability." PhD Thesis, University of Houston, Texas.

Poole, Keith T. 2000. "Non-Parametric Unfolding of Binary Choice Data." *Political Analysis* 8(3): 211–37.

Poole, Keith T. 2005. *Spatial Models of Parliamentary Voting.* New York: Cambridge University Press.

Poole, Keith T., Jeffrey Lewis, James Lo, and Royce Carroll. 2009. "OC Roll Call Analysis Software." CRAN repository.

Power, Timothy J. and César Zucco Jr. 2012. "Elite Preferences in a Consolidating Democracy: The Brazilian Legislative Surveys, 1990–2009." *Latin American Politics and Society* 54(4): 1–27.

Praça, Sérgio, Andréa Freitas, and Bruno Hoepers. 2011. "Political Appointments and Coalition Management in Brazil, 2007–2010." *Journal of Politics in Latin America* 3(2): 141–72.

Prieto, Marcela. 2011. "De Uribe a Santos: La Unidad Nacional, el elemento diferenciador." Razón Pública online. <http://www.razonpublica.com/index.php/politica-y-gobierno-temas-27/2387-de-uribe-a-santos-la-unidad-nacional-el-elemento-diferenciador.html#sthash.iuCjNcny.dpuf>, accessed November 27, 2013.

Proksch, Sven-Oliver and Jonathan B. Slapin. 2011. "Parliamentary Questions and Oversight in the European Union." *European Journal of Political Research* 50(1): 53–79.

Rasch, Bjørn Erik. 2000. "Parliamentary Floor Voting Procedures and Agenda Setting in Europe." *Legislative Studies Quarterly* 25(1): 3–23.

Rasch, Bjørn Erik and George Tsebelis, eds. 2011. *The Role of Governments in Legislative Agenda Setting*. London: Routledge.

Raudenbusch, Stephen and Anthony Bryk. 2002. *Hierarchical Linear Models: Applications and Data Analysis Methods*, 2nd edn. Newbury Park, CA: Sage.

Reich, Gary. 2002. "Executive Decree Authority in Brazil: How Reactive Legislators Influence Policy." *Legislative Studies Quarterly* 27(1): 5–31.

Rennó, Lucio. 2010. "Executive–Legislative Relations in Brazil: Is 2009 the First Year of the Rest of Our Lives?" *Revista de Ciencia Política* 30: 213–30.

Ricci, Paolo and Leany Barreiro de S. Lemos. 2004. "Produção Legislativa e preferências eleitorais na Comissão de Agricultura e Política Rural da Câmara dos Deputados." *Revista Brasileira de Ciências Sociais* 19: 107–29.

Roberts, Kenneth. 2006. "Do Parties Matter? Lessons from the Peruvian Experience." In Julio Carrión, ed., *The Fujimori Legacy*. University Park: Penn State University Press.

Roberts, Kenneth and Erik Wibbels. 1999. "Party Systems and Electoral Volatility in Latin America: A Test of Economic, Institutional, and Structural Explanations." *American Political Science Review* 93(3): 575–90.

Robinson, James A. 1963. *The House Rules Committee*. Indianapolis, IN: Bobbs-Merrill.

Rodrigues Cunha, Lucas. 2012. "Tramitação e Emendamento das Medidas Provisórias: Evolução Institucional do Executivo e do Legislativo no Brasil." *Revista Jurídica da Presidêncial* 4(103): 325–55.

Rodriguez-Raga, Juan Carlos. 2002. "Cambiar Todo para que Nada Cambie." In Francisco Gutiérrez Sanín, ed., *Degradación O Cambio: Evolución Del Sistema Político Colombiano*. Bogotá, Colombia: Iepri-Norma Editors, pp. 221–60.

Rodriguez-Raga, Juan Carlos. 2011. "Strategic Prudence in the Colombian Constitutional Court, 1992–2006." PhD Thesis, University of Pittsburgh.

Roll, David. 2005. *Partidos Políticos y Congreso: Elites Políticas y Mayorías Parlamentarias en Colombia en la Década de los Noventa*. Bogotá, Colombia: Arfo Editors.

Rosas, Guillermo. 2005. "The Ideological Organization of Latin American Legislative Parties: An Empirical Analysis of Elite Policy Preferences." *Comparative Political Studies* 38(7): 824–49.

Rudalevige, Andrew. 2002. *Managing the President's Program: Presidential Leadership and Legislative Policy Formulation*. Princeton, NJ: Princeton University Press.

Saiegh, Sebastián M. 2009. "Political Prowess or Lady Luck? Evaluating Chief Executives' Legislative Success Rates." *Journal of Politics* 71(4): 1342–56.

Saiegh, Sebastián M. 2010. "Active Players or Rubber Stamps? An Evolution of the Policymaking Role of Latin American Legislatures." In Carlos Scartascini, Ernesto Stein, and Mariano Tommasi, eds., *How Democracy Works. Political Institutions, Actors and Arenas in Latin American Policy Making*. Washington, DC: Inter-American Development Bank and DRCLAS-Harvard University, pp. 47–76.

Saiegh, Sebastián M. 2011. *Ruling by Statute: How Uncertainty and Vote Buying Shape Lawmaking*. New York: Cambridge University Press.

Saiegh, Sebastián M. 2014. *Ruling by Statute: How Uncertainty and Vote Buying Shape Lawmaking*. New York: Cambridge University Press.

Sala, Mariella, Jorge Aragón, and Miguel Cruzado. 2009. "Etica Parlamentaria, Desempeño Profesional de los Congresistas y Fortalecimiento de las Bancadas." In Jorge Valladares, ed., *Estudios Sobre el Congreso Peruano: Grupos Parlamentarios, Disciplina Partidaria y Desempeño Profesional*. Lima, Peru: Fondo Editorial de la Universidad Antonio Ruiz de Montoya, pp. 123–67.

Salazar, Natalia. 2011. "Instituciones Políticas y el Proceso Presupuestal." Paper presented at the National Colombian Economic Congress, Universidad de los Andes, Bogotá, Colombia.

Sanguinetti, Julio María and Álvaro Pacheco Seré. 1970. *Ante la nueva constitución*. Montevideo, Uruguay: Editorial ARCA.

Santiso, Carlos and Arturo García Belgrano. 2004. "Legislative Budget Oversight in Presidential Systems: Governance of the Budget in Peru." Paper presented at the Regional Seminar on Fiscal Policy, Santiago, Chile.

Santos, Fabiano. 2002. "Partidos e Comissões no Presidencialismo de Coalizão." *Dados* 45(2): 237–64.

Santos, Fabiano and Acir Almeida. 2005. "Teoria Informacional e a Seleção de Relatores na Câmara dos Deputados." *Dados* 48(4): 693–735.

Santos, Fabiano and Lucio Rennó. 2004. "The Selection of Committee Leadership in the Brazilian Chamber of Deputies." *Journal of Legislative Studies* 10(1): 50–70.

Schmidt, Gregory. 1998. "Presidential Usurpation or Congressional Preference? The Evolution of Executive Decree Authority in Peru." In John Carey and Matthew S. Shugart, eds., *Executive Decree Authority*. New York: Cambridge University Press, pp. 104–41.

Schofield, Norman. 1978. "Instability of Simple Dynamic Games." *Review of Economic Studies* 45(3): 575–94.

Shepsle, Kenneth A. 1979. "Institutional Arrangements and Equilibrium in Multidimensional Voting Models." *American Journal of Political Science* 23(1): 27–59.

Shepsle, Kenneth A. and Barry R. Weingast. 1987. "The Institutional Foundations of Committee Power." *American Political Science Review* 81(1): 85–104.

Shugart, Matthew S. and John M. Carey. 1992. *Presidents and Assemblies: Constitutional Design and Electoral Dynamics*. New York: Cambridge University Press.

Shugart, Matthew S. and Stephan Haggard. 2001. "Institutions and Public Policy in Presidential Systems." In Stephan Haggard and Mathew D. McCubbins, eds., *Presidents, Parliaments, and Policy*. New York: Cambridge University Press, pp. 64–102.

Shugart, Matthew S., Erika Moreno, and Luis E. Fajardo. 2007. "Deepening Democracy by Renovating Political Practices: The Struggle for Electoral Reform in Colombia." In Christopher Welna, ed., *Peace, Democracy, and Human Rights in Colombia*. Notre Dame, IN: University of Notre Dame Press, pp. 202–66.

Siavelis, Peter. 2000. *The President and Congress in Post-Authoritarian Chile: Institutional Constraints to Democratic Consolidation*. University Park: Penn State University Press.

Silva, Rafael S. and Suely MV Araujo. 2012. "Os Agenda Holders no Congresso Nacional Brasileiro." Paper presented at the Congreso Latinoamericano de Ciencia Política Quito, Ecuador.

Sinclair, Barbara. 1983. *Majority Party Leadership in the U.S. House*. Baltimore, MD: Johns Hopkins University Press.

Sinclair, Barbara. 1986. "The Role of Committees in Agenda Setting in the U.S. Congress." *Legislative Studies Quarterly* 11(1): 35–45.

Sinclair, Barbara. 1994. "House Special Rules and the Institutional Design Controversy." *Legislative Studies Quarterly* 19(4): 477–94.

Steenbergen, Marco and Bradford Jones. 2002. "Modeling Multilevel Data Structures." *American Journal of Political Science* 46(1): 218–37.

Steiner, Gilbert Y. 1951. *The Congressional Conference Committee: Seventieth to Eightieth Congress*. Urbana: University of Illinois Press.

Stiglitz, Edward H. and Barry R. Weingast. 2010. "Agenda Control in Congress: Evidence from Cutpoint Estimates and Ideal Point Uncertainty." *Legislative Studies Quarterly* 35(2): 157–85.

Strøm, Kaare. 1998. "Parliamentary Committees in European Democracies." *Journal of Legislative Studies* 4(1): 21–59.

Taylor-Robinson, Michelle M. and Christopher Diaz. 1999. "Who Gets Legislation Passed in a Marginal Legislature and Is the Label Marginal Legislature Still Appropriate? A Study of the Honduran Congress." *Comparative Political Studies* 32(5): 589–625.

Tsebelis, George. 1990. *Nested Games: Rational Choice in Comparative Perspective*. Berkeley: University of California Press.

Tsebelis, George. 1994. "The Power of the European Parliament as a Conditional Agenda-Setter." *American Political Science Review* 88(1): 128–42.

Tsebelis, George. 1995. "Decision Making Inside the European Parliament." In Barry Eichengreen, Jeffry Frieden, and Jürgen von Hagen, eds., *Politics and Institutions in an Integrated Europe*. Berlin: Springer, pp. 42–64.

Tsebelis, George. 1999. "Veto Players and Law Production in Parliamentary Democracies: An Empirical Analysis." *American Political Science Review* 93(3): 591–608.

Tsebelis, George. 2002. *Veto Players: How Political Institutions Work.* Princeton, NJ: Princeton University Press.

Tsebelis, George and Eduardo Alemán. 2005. "Presidential Conditional Agenda Setting in Latin America." *World Politics* 57(3): 396–420.

Tsebelis, George and Eunyoung Ha. 2014. "Coalition Theory: A Veto Player's Approach." *European Political Science Review* 6(3): 331–57.

Tsebelis, George, Christian Jensen, Anastassios Kalandrakis, and Amie Kreppel. 2001. "Legislative Procedures in the EU: An Empirical Analysis." *British Journal of Political Science* 31(4): 573–99.

Tsebelis, George and Jeannette Money. 1997. *Bicameralism.* Cambridge and New York: Cambridge University Press.

Ungar, Elisabeth. 2008. "El Congreso: Un balance desalentador." *El Espectador*, December 2. <http://www.elespectador.com/columna95641-el-congreso-un-balance-desalentador>, accessed December 1, 2013.

Uprimny, Rodrigo. 2009. "Democracias, mayorías y deliberación." *El Espectador*, April 27. <http://www.elespectador.com/opinion/columnistasdelimpreso/rodrigo-uprimny/columna138169-democracia-mayorias-y-deliberacion>, accessed November 28, 2013.

Vogler, David J. 1970. "Patterns of One House Dominance in Congressional Conference Committees." *Midwest Journal of Political Science* 14(2): 303–20.

Webb Yackee, Susan. 2003. "Punctuating the Congressional Agenda: Strategic Scheduling by House and Senate Leaders." *Political Research Quarterly* 56(2): 139–49.

Weingast, Barry R. 1989. "Floor Behavior in the U.S. Congress: Committee Power under the Open Rule." *American Political Science Review* 83(3): 795–815.

Weingast, Barry R. 1992. "Fighting Fire with Fire: Amending Activity and Institutional Change in the Postreform Congress." In Roger H. Davidson, ed., *The Postreform Congress.* New York: St Martin's Press, pp. 142–68.

Weldon, Jeffrey. 1997. "The Political Sources of *Presidencialismo* in Mexico." In Scott Mainwairing and Matthew S. Shugart, eds. *Presidentialism and Democracy in Latin America.* New York: Cambridge University Press, pp. 225–58.

Wise, Carol. 2003. *Reinventing the State: Economic Strategy and Institutional Change in Peru.* Ann Arbor: University of Michigan Press.

Zellner, Arnold and Peter Rossi. 1984. "Bayesian Analysis of Dichotomous Quantal Response Models." *Journal of Econometrics* 25: 365–93.

Zucco Jr., César and Benjamin E. Lauderdale. 2011. "Distinguishing Between Influences on Brazilian Legislative Behavior." *Legislative Studies Quarterly* 36(3): 363–96.

Zucco Jr., César and Timothy Power. 2009. "Estimating Ideology of Brazilian Legislative Parties, 1990–2005." *Latin American Research Review* 44(1): 218–46.

Author Index

Tables and figures are indicated by an italic *t* or *f* following the page number.

General Index

Tables and figures are indicated by an italic *t* or *f* following the page number.

AN

INDUCTIVE AND PRACTICAL TREATISE

ON

BOOK-KEEPING

BY

SINGLE AND DOUBLE ENTRY,

DESIGNED FOR

COMMERCIAL INSTITUTES, PRIVATE STUDENTS, AND PRACTICAL ACCOUNTANTS:

CONTAINING

FOUR SETS OF BOOKS BY SINGLE ENTRY,

AND

SIX SETS BY DOUBLE ENTRY.

ALSO,

A Set of Steamboat Books;

PRACTICAL FORMS FOR KEEPING BOOKS,

CALCULATED TO SAVE LABOR IN THE VARIOUS BRANCHES OF BUSINESS;

COMMERCIAL CALCULATIONS;

A TABLE OF FOREIGN COINS AND MONEYS OF ACCOUNT, ETC.

BY

S. W. CRITTENDEN, ACCOUNTANT,

AUTHOR OF AN "INDUCTIVE AND PRACTICAL TREATISE ON BOOK-KEEPING," HIGH-SCHOOL EDITION, AND OF "AN ELEMENTARY TREATISE ON BOOK-KEEPING, FOR COMMON SCHOOLS."

PHILADELPHIA:
E. C. & J. BIDDLE, No. 6 SOUTH FIFTH STREET.
1854.

STEREOTYPED BY L. JOHNSON AND CO.
PHILADELPHIA.

Printed by T. K. & P. G. Collins.